D1001287

The Juhl Letters
to the *Charleston Courier*

A View of the South, 1865–1871

Edited by John Hammond Moore

University of Georgia Press, Athens

Library of Congress Catalog Card Number: 68–55754
International Standard Book Number: 0–8203–0248–1

The University of Georgia Press, Athens 30602

Printed in the United States of America

To
Mary Elizabeth Massey

. . . when will dawn the bright and glorious day
when heated passions of men shall subside to rest,
and all the states be enfolded in one bond of Union
knowing no North, South, East, or West
in unfriendly political array, but the flag
which protects and floats over our commerce
will truly symbolize the government
which first unfurled it to the breeze
with its e pluribus unum, *"distinct as the billows,*
yet one as the sea"?

Juhl in the *Charleston Courier*, April 30, 1866

Preface

The "stillness" following Appomattox is not as quiet as it once was. Comer Vann Woodward, John Hope Franklin, Robert H. Woody, Francis B. Simkins, Kenneth Stampp, Joel Williamson, James M. McPherson, and others have sifted and brought to light much information concerning the Reconstruction years. The great flurry of interest in the Civil War itself has raised many questions which can only be answered by delving into postwar decades. But when one turns to the former Confederacy for answers, the stillness is awesome and real. Few Southerners took the time or had the desire to comment on what was happening. There is a handful of published reminiscences, and occasional Yankees such as John William De Forest *(A Union Officer in Reconstruction)* and James Pike *(The Prostrate South)* described their experiences in Dixie.

Here in these letters published in the *Charleston Courier* is an on-the-spot account of how one very articulate Southerner viewed Reconstruction, 1865–1871. Julius J. Fleming by no means limits his observations to his native South Carolina. He traveled extensively, kept pace with events at both the state and national level, and without mincing words voiced clear and consistent opinions concerning education of the freedman, development of the South's economy, and the progress of Reconstruction itself. Fleming's writing often reflects the standard textbook picture of a defeated South licking its wounds; but sometimes it doesn't. It is when Fleming fails to conform to the currently accepted portrait of post-Civil War life that his words take on special significance. That there was chaos, anarchy, and hard times he would not deny. But at the same time, people were born, married, went to parties and tournaments, planted crops, and tried to carry on as best they could. Some, including Fleming, might at times even joke about the topsy-turvy world in which they lived. Apparently he was not alone in opinions which now seem at variance with what interpreters tell us happened during Reconstruction. For, if he had been, his letters to the *Courier* would have ceased long before 1871.

Everything that Fleming wrote for the *Courier* is not included in the pages which follow. Sometimes his letters became repetitious and trivial, and there seemed no good reason to reproduce paragraphs which contribute nothing to our understanding of local and state affairs during a troubled period or fail to reveal how a rural Southerner viewed national events during those years. Omissions within letters are indicated by ellipses. Spelling, punctuation, and abbreviations—often erratic since various typesetters put Juhl's work into print—have been standardized throughout.

My main source was obviously the *Charleston Courier*. Its pages provide not only the Juhl letters but substantial information concerning many aspects of the life of Julius J. Fleming. Sumter newspapers at the South Caroliniana Library, University of South Carolina, were also extremely helpful—the *Watchman*, *News*, and *True Southron* (a Reconstruction name for the *Watchman*). Other publications shedding light on Fleming's career include the *Chester Standard*, *Edgefield Advertiser*, *Edgefield Chronicle*, *New York World*, *Charlotte Journal*, *Atlanta Constitution*, and the *Southern Christian Advocate*. Unpublished materials consulted include United States census reports, Sumter County courthouse records, the notes of Anne King Gregorie (author of *History of Sumter County*) deposited in the archives of the South Carolina Historical Society, and the faculty minutes of the University of Georgia and the College of Charleston.

Among the individuals I am indebted to for special assistance are Mrs. William P. Baskin, Sr., of Orangeburg, South Carolina

(Fleming's granddaughter), and her son, William P. Baskin of Bishopville, South Carolina; Janie Revill, George D. Levy, and Chapman J. Milling, Jr., all of Sumter, South Carolina; Prof. Nash Boney, History Department, University of Georgia; Virginia Rugheimer, Librarian, Charleston Library Society, Mrs. Granville T. Prior, Secretary-Archivist, South Carolina Historical Society, and T. R. Waring, Editor, *Charleston News and Courier*, all of Charleston; E. L. Inabinett, Director, South Caroliniana Library, and Charles E. Lee, Director, South Carolina Archives, both of Columbia. In addition I am indebted to many librarians who have answered scores of queries. Among them are Ann Carter Long, Tusculum College; Mrs. Gertrude Morton Parsley, Tennessee State Library and Archives; Peter A. Brannon, Alabama Department of Archives and History; Mrs. Ligon Henderson, Carnegie Public Library, Rome, Georgia; Mrs. Kathryn Arnold, Chattanooga Public Library; Mrs. M. H. Mims, Edgefield County Library; Mary Vaughan Powers, College of Charleston; and Mattie Russell, Duke University. Above all, I want to express my thanks for assistance given by the staff of the Winthrop College Library, especially Annette Shinn, Reference Librarian.

Introduction

Julius J. Fleming was a shadowy figure who, except for a few brief years, left no distinct imprint on South Carolina's past. As school teacher, college president, Methodist minister, Baptist preacher, coroner, magistrate, editor, lawyer, would-be politician, and newspaper correspondent he was a multifaceted individual with a variety of roles and occupations.

The years Julius Fleming chose to illuminate are important ones. Beginning in July, 1865, over a six-year period, he contributed some two hundred letters to the *Charleston Courier*. Most of these were written from Sumter, then a county seat of about two thousand, a hundred miles north of Charleston. In his columns Fleming, using the pen name of "Juhl," discussed the weather, crops, race relations, economic conditions, the Ku Klux Klan, politics, and many seemingly inconsequential but frequently revealing details concerning day-to-day life in the wake of military defeat.

In addition to life in Sumter, Juhl tells us about visits to Columbia, Walhalla, Darlington, and other points in South Carolina, trips to New England, New York, and Florida, and an extensive tour with the Georgia Press Association in August, 1869. Since this is the same trek which catapulted a young man named Henry Woodfin Grady into the limelight, Juhl's letters as the official correspondent of the *Charleston Courier* take on special significance. Juhl was certainly paid for these contributions, but a century or so later there is, I fear, no way of knowing how much. If merely an amateur he would not have been included on the Georgia tour—and surely no one would have written so much, so consistently for nothing!

What sort of man was Julius J. Fleming? First and foremost he was an able writer, a keen observer of the world about him. In appearance he was rather tall and slim. But, more important, Juhl is an interesting personality because at first glance he seems so out-of-step with his times. He was well-educated at a time when few around him had more than rudimentary schooling. When most Southerners marched off to war, he stayed home. During the early days of Reconstruction he viewed with equal alarm the policies of the Radical-carpetbag-Negro camp and those of the disorganized, ineffectual pre-Bourbon Democrats. Fleming's disenchantment with the Democrats once they got into power led some old-timers inaccurately to write him off as a scalawag. And, as his career indicates, Julius was restless. His granddaughter, Mrs. William P. Baskin, Sr., of Orangeburg, South Carolina, a bright-eyed little lady, remembered him as "one of those people you can't read." He was changeable, moody, seemed very unhappy at times. He was, it appears, something of an enigma to his own family.

Julius J. Fleming was born in Charleston, South Carolina, December 7, 1823, the son of Margaret and John Fleming. His thirty-three-year-old father was a carpenter and, according to family tradition, came to America from Scotland. His mother was born in Charleston on February 5, 1796, daughter of Captain Richard Lewis. She was married to John Fleming on October 3, 1812. In addition to Julius, the Flemings had seven other children who grew to maturity, the most prominent being William H. Fleming (1821–1877), a distinguished figure in the annals of South Carolina Methodism.

In July of 1838 young Julius was sent to the University of Georgia. Just how much he learned at Athens is not known, but it is apparent this fifteen-year-old had a good time. In March, 1839, he and several friends were summoned before the faculty to explain the presence of a "pack of cards (playing)" in their rooms. A few weeks later Fleming was on the carpet for "gross inattention to his studies." At first the faculty considered demoting him to the Grammar School, but instead placed him on strict probation. Before a fortnight passed Fleming was in trouble again. He was accused of being disrespectful to an instructor. The faculty suggested that his father withdraw him from college; but, before the senior Fleming could act, his son—as these faculty minutes reveal—was in still more serious difficulty.

May 3rd. Wagner, Hancock & Fleming were summoned before the Faculty, in consequence of information which had been received by an officer, based upon undoubted Evidence. [These three students were all from Charleston and lived at the same rooming house in Athens.] The charges were: 1st, that they had been in the habit of frequenting a notorious dram-shop & Billiard room, in a remote part of Town, during study hours. 2nd, that they had been to the Circus contrary to expressed law & in disguise (masquerade or blacked) to avoid detection. 3rd, that they had been in the habit of leaving their rooms at night & annoying peaceful citizens by the injury of their property.

On being questioned, Fleming acknowledged readily everything alleged against him. Hancock, neither acknowledged nor denied, & Wagner denied everything. The Faculty directed the secretary to inform Wagner that he must leave college forthwith on the pain of higher punishment—& that his father be written to with a statement of the facts. In the case of Hancock & Fleming, it appeared that the latter had left town for home at his father's desire—all further proceedings in reference to him were consequently stayed. A petition was presented from Hancock—couched in very respectful & contrite terms—& throwing himself upon the clemency of the Faculty—whereupon it was resolved that George Hancock is restored to his station in the College—& relieved from the jeopardy in which he has been placed—but that he is to consider himself under the strictest probation in every respect.

Thus ends the career of Julius Fleming at the University of Georgia, although these events are not without relevance in his later life.

Apparently, and with considerable evidence to buttress his views, Papa decided young Julius should attend college closer to home and enrolled his son at the College of Charleston. Sobered by his father's presence, he applied himself to his books and graduated second in a class of thirteen in March, 1842. His salutatory oration, delivered before "a brilliant and numerous audience of both sexes" in Charleston's First Presbyterian Church, was entitled "On Genius Eclipsed." Following graduation Fleming went to Philadelphia where he spent three years in preparation for the Methodist ministry. At commencement ceremonies held in March, 1845, the College of Charleston conferred an honorary master's degree upon "Rev. J. J. Fleming."

In February, 1846, young Reverend Fleming, A.B., A.M., became president of a struggling little school in Greeneville, Tennessee. He remained there only one session; and when he resigned Greeneville (now Tusculum) College suspended operations until 1854. By August, 1847, Fleming was back in his hometown making plans for the opening of Charleston Neck High School. He would lead this four-year-old institution for the next two years. An ad in the *Charleston Courier* (December 15, 1847) described the school in this manner:

CHARLESTON NECK HIGH SCHOOL
MEETING NEAR MARY-STREET

REV. JULIUS J. FLEMING, A.M., PRINCIPAL. This institution is emphatically select in its pupils; and no greater number will be admitted, than can be faithfully instructed by the teachers engaged. Complete instruction given in every department, from the elemental branches of English, to a full preparation for any class in the South-Carolina College. Next quarter begins on the 1st Monday in January. For particulars, apply as above.

4   Although obviously busy, Fleming did not neglect his moral and

social life. He was a frequent Sunday speaker at the Orphans'
Church, actively promoted the interests of numerous temperance
groups including the Charleston Total Abstinence Society, and on April
26, 1848, took as his bride, Anna E. Mouzon, daughter of Mr. and Mrs.
L. H. Mouzon of Charleston. The ceremony was performed by his
brother, William.

As the year 1849 opened, the world must have looked bright indeed
to young Julius Fleming. He had a wife, a good job, and was gradually
becoming a person of some importance in Charleston. Then disaster
struck. His wife's death in July was followed by that of his father in
November. A few weeks later Fleming turned over the high school to
James Steedman and accepted a post as a Methodist minister ("on
trial") at Charlotte, North Carolina.

To forget his sorrow, Fleming plunged into innumerable activities. In
July, 1850, the tiny village of Charlotte was stirred by a protracted
revival—three meetings a day for over three weeks. The *Hornet's Nest*, a
local weekly, reported on July 13 that there had been some fifty conver-
sions to Methodism since Fleming appeared on the scene. Two weeks
later this same newspaper noted that, in addition to those converted, "a
large portion of the congregation are still showing a deep anxiety in
regard to the salvation of their souls."

When Methodist clergymen held their annual conference at Wades-
boro, North Carolina, in December, 1850, Fleming reported collections
of $55.75 for the year. He was then, according to the Methodist practice
of shifting their ministers from place to place, assigned to Black Swamp
Station, an outpost in the southern corner of the state. There he worked
with A. M. Creitzberg, a man who would become one of the worthies of
South Carolina Methodism—an honor denied Julius. Shortly before
the next annual session in December, 1851, Fleming married Laura
Kirk of Ridgeland, daughter of William J. Kirk of St. Peter's Parish, one
of four parishes in Beaufort District where Black Swamp was located. A
few weeks later they set up housekeeping in Spartanburg.

In 1853 the Flemings were back in Beaufort District at the Savannah River Mission where Julius worked among the slaves on rice plantations. This was an important appointment because it obviously affected Fleming's attitude toward race relations in postwar decades. In 1854 the young minister and his wife returned to the "up country" and a post at Chester, South Carolina. Late in April of that year Julius wrote proudly in the *Southern Christian Advocate* about the dedication of a new church with "spacious, glazed windows." The work of Methodism in the Chester area, he emphasized, had all too often been hindered by the lack of commodious, heated churches, something which the opposition frequently had. In November, 1854, the Flemings again moved, this time to Sumter. Although they did not realize it, this community would be their home for nearly half a century.

The year 1855 was uneventful. Julius busied himself bolstering up the work of the church, aided by his brother William who was also stationed in the Sumter area. However, on February 6, 1856, an advertisement appeared in the *Sumter Watchman* which would alter dramatically the life of Reverend J. J. Fleming.

SUMTER ACADEMY

The Trustees of this Institution have unanimously elected Rev. J. J. Fleming, A.M., Principal. The Academy is now open for the reception of pupils. Mr. FLEMING is a citizen of this place, and obtained his education in Charleston, Philadelphia, and at the Georgia University. He graduated with distinction, taking the honors of his Class, and has had, as a Teacher, considerable experience as a Principal of a High School in Charleston, and President of Green[e]ville College, Tennessee.

Complete instruction will be given in all the usual branches, and young men prepared for any class in college.

Good board at reasonable rates can be had at private homes. For terms, &c., apply to the Principal or the undersigned.

W. F. B. HAYNESWORTH,
Secretary

The local academy needed a principal, and Fleming was eminently qualified for the job. But, within a few days a ruckus of unusual proportion erupted, an upheaval which rocked the very foundations of the little community of Sumter. The new principal had enemies who claimed it improper for him to hold two positions at the same time. In their opinion it was inevitable that his work as a minister would suffer. Throughout the spring months pro-Fleming and anti-Fleming forces filled the columns of the *Watchman* with vitriolic denunciations of each other. In one issue a Fleming backer, "Fiat Justitia," flailed the words of a group of Methodist laymen as nothing but "a pieball jumble of Sophomorean balderdash!" Although Fleming had substantial support, Bishop John Early of Lynchburg, Virginia, eventually stepped into the fray and relieved him of his ministerial duties.

As this tale of rancor and bitterness unfolds, it is evident Fleming was retained in Sumter for a second year over the vehement opposition of several of the elders of his church. Part of their attack centered upon a hassle which Fleming had with a parishioner concerning attendance at a circus. Julius J. Fleming—the man who had once been expelled from the University of Georgia for destroying personal property, frequenting bars, and going to a circus in blackface—asked William K. Dixon of Bishopville to promise he would not attend a circus. Dixon refused and Fleming suspended him from the church, but subsequently had to reinstate him. This issue plus Fleming's new position as principal created circumstances which those opposed to him used to his disadvantage.

Julius continued his connections with Sumter Academy until sometime in 1858 when classes were suspended, but his ties with Methodism were damaged beyond repair. In January, 1858, he was baptized as a member of the First Baptist Church of Sumter and five months later ordained as a minister of that faith. "One of the largest audiences we have ever seen [was] in Sumter to witness the services," wrote the editor of the *Watchman*. Despite opportunities to do so, Reverend Fleming (Baptist) never officially accepted a pulpit, yet sternly maintained this new religious affiliation until his death.

Just how Fleming supported his growing family in the late 1850s is not clear. Yet the census of 1860 reveals they were living quite comfortably. Julius J. Fleming, "Clergyman, B.," had real estate valued at $9,000 and personal property worth about half that amount. He was then thirty-seven, his wife thirty. Their oldest child Sallie was seven. James Norwood (Mrs. Baskin's father) was six, and William J. K. Fleming was four. Fleming's mother, sixty-three, was also living with them.

If this man's situation on the eve of the Civil War is difficult to fathom, his course during that conflict is even more inexplicable. As a clergyman he was exempt from military service. Early in 1863 he began to assume a myriad of duties—deputy clerk of courts, magistrate, coroner, editor of weekly and semiweekly editions of the *Watchman*, secretary of the local home guard, and chairman of the area committee to facilitate the flow of supplies to Confederate depots. Somehow, all these responsibilities permitted Reverend Fleming to become Captain Fleming, possibly an honorary title earned through his organizational efforts on the home front.

In June, 1863, Editor Fleming detailed in the columns of the *Watchman* failure of his "Nassau Enterprise." He had hoped to collect cotton in the Sumter area, take it to the Bahamas, and there purchase supplies badly needed by local planters. Fleming applied first to Wilmington and then to Charleston, but there were no blockade runners available for such a venture.

It is obvious that Julius Fleming was one of those individuals one hears little about in the history of the Confederacy. He did not rush off to war; instead he remained at home, perhaps because of extenuating circumstances. Mrs. Baskin recalled that her grandfather once terrified her with a large rifle which he inferred had been used in the

Civil War, but evidently not by him. As others marched away he stepped into the breach and took over numerous duties. The multiplicity of these activities and responsibilities is underscored by this notice in the *Watchman* (January 6, 1864):

J. J. Fleming, Magistrate, Coroner, and Deputy Clerk of the Court: at the Clerk's Office, Court House Square.

Attends to the collection of claims of deceased soldiers; negro labor on the Coast; negroes lost in the public service; applications for exemptions under State or Confederate laws; petitions or memorials for discharge or furlough, in special cases, of persons already in service; and every form of deed, or other legal instrument of writing, drawn up with neatness and dispatch. Also prepares all the necessary papers for disabled soldiers, who wish appointments as Clerks, Wagon or Forage Masters, in the Quartermaster's Department.

Then, early in 1865 when it looked as if the entire staff of the *Watchman* would soon be in uniform, Editor Fleming dispatched a letter to Confederate authorities stressing the vital role of a weekly press as a medium to distribute news and military orders. The authorities agreed, and the *Watchman* continued to publish until April when Sumter was overrun by Union forces. The invaders so mangled the press and the type that the newspaper did not resume publication for several months. Thus invasion terminated Fleming's editorial responsibilities, and peace wrote an end to his home front activities. By the summer of 1865 when he began to write for the *Charleston Courier*, Fleming was still magistrate, coroner, and deputy clerk of courts. And, at the clerk's office or at his home on Washington Street, he would collect a claim, prepare a title, will, deed, or any other document "with neatness, dispatch, and legal accuracy, at the most reasonable rates." For all practical purposes, the Civil War turned a Baptist preacher into a lawyer. But of much more importance to us today, the war also transformed the Reverend Julius J. Fleming into "Juhl," the Sumter correspondent of the *Charleston Courier*. Fleming's activities and interests (1865–1871) are detailed fully in the letters which follow. As Sumter's spokesman to the outside world and, at times, as an early public relations man, he described both day-to-day existence and events which have shaped regional and national life to the present day.

The last quarter century of Julius J. Fleming's life can be summed up rather quickly. With the final *Courier* letter of August, 1871, his career as a journalist came to an end. Early in 1872 he purchased a nineteen-hundred-acre estate, Hiwassee Plantation, near Statesburg. Just what his plans were are not clear; perhaps this was merely an investment. He sold the land in four sections a year later.

In the fall of that same year (1872) the Radical-Republican state machine placed F. J. Moses, Jr., of Sumter in the governor's chair. On the local scene the Democrats met and decided it was useless to oppose the Moses slate. However, a group of Bolters (dissatisfied Republicans and hopeful Democrats) carried on a spirited statewide campaign. This faction was headed by Judge J. T. Green, candidate for attorney-general. In a nine-man race for the South Carolina House of Representatives, Fleming came in fifth. He received 1,112 votes, but trailed far behind the fourth successful aspirant who had 3,031 ballots. All of the Moses men were elected, three of them being Negro nominees.

The following year, while Moses seemed to be carrying everything before him, a meeting in Sumter erupted into a heated debate over the use of school funds. Dogberry Hurst, a trustee of the Sumter Free Schools, made a sweeping oratorical effort, promising to crush his critics when he finally released a full report. Fleming then arose and, according to the *Sumter News* (July 17, 1873), in "an earnest and forcible speech . . . labored to show the meeting that the money raised for the Free Schools had been grossly misapplied and squandered." Julius said he was certainly in favor of public education, but he believed taxes collected for this purpose were being "frittered away and stolen."

In the mid-70s Fleming increased his legal practice through formal connections with a distinguished Charleston firm, Porter and Brawley, and he also expanded the scope of his activities to include bankruptcy proceedings in federal courts. In 1876 when Wade Hampton and his Red Shirts finally redeemed the state of South Carolina from carpetbag rule, Fleming does not appear to have been active in the revived Democratic ranks. And, as the so-called Bourbons took over the reins of state and local government his law practice declined. It is apparent that his "soft" attitude towards the Negro, as well as his erratic religious, business, and professional life, made him suspect in the eyes of many Democrats.

The census of 1880 discloses that Fleming still listed his occupation as "lawyer." His household consisted of his wife, his daughter Sallie who never married, his son Willie, and a year-round Negro servant, Gabriel Wilder. Norwood Fleming, his eldest son, had recently married Harriet Miller, the daughter of a local druggist. He, his wife, and their three-month-old daughter were living with the Miller in-laws on Church Street. In this same year Fleming made his third and last ill-fated bid for political office. According to a soul-searching post-mortem appearing in the *Charleston News and Courier* (November 29, 1880), Julius said he became an "independent" candidate for solicitor of the Third Judicial District at the request of Democrats "of the straitest sect."

The Republicans, after Democrats had really placed me in the field, offered to give me a regular nomination in their Judicial Convention, but I advised against it, and they then resolved at their several County

Conventions, as I was informed, to place my name on their ticket. And, whatever others may think of it, I do not hesitate to say that *I thank them for their confidence and support. They*, at least, were true to their pledges, but what became of my whilom Democratic supporters I know not. One of two things are certain: They either went back upon their unsolicited solemn declarations and sternly avowed religious principles when they cast their ballots, or the returns of the managers, even of the admitted count, are entirely *inexplicable*, as they credit me with only the strictly Republican vote. During the entire campaign I pursued the even tenor of my way, attending no meetings of either party, and certainly never asked any man to vote for me; and when I discovered on the morning of the election what kind of machinery was relied upon to carry the Democratic ticket, I did not even attempt to vote; and hundreds of my supporters after waiting here all day failed at last to deposit their ballots, as they were counted out.

The result claims a majority of fourteen hundred twenty-four votes in favor of my opponent, with reference to which I have only this to say, that Box No. 1 in this town was thrown out *and should have been counted*, in the published opinion of Governor-elect Haygood and Attorney-General Youmans, the highest law officers in the State; and, as this box contained fourteen hundred and ninety-six votes in my favor, *the majority would be and is mine*. And this, independent of the thousands of other similar votes thrown out in this and the other counties of the Third Judicial Circuit, on the ground of irregularities, for which the Democratic managers were alone responsible, whether prearranged or not. From the general picture of fraud throughout the State, Beaufort County seems to stand out in bold relief; and the Democrats there are certainly entitled to the plume, when they say *"they have not as yet learned to make one Democratic vote count as five and five Republican votes as one"* and that they cannot be induced to degrade themselves so far as *"to steal an election."* May the day yet come when the whole State will occupy the same healthy plane!

In the early 1880s Fleming had to settle up the accounts of Fleming

& Sons, a disastrous attempt to set up a small bookshop and printing establishment in Sumter. By the mid-80s Julius abandoned law completely and returned to teaching, conducting a small preparatory school for boys at his home on Washington Street. At the same time, his wife was operating a kindergarten. Among her pupils was her granddaughter, Esther Fleming (Mrs. William P. Baskin, Sr.).

In the spring of 1892, now nearly seventy, Fleming decided to sell his home in Sumter and move to Edgefield to live with his daughter, a music teacher. There he died very suddenly four years later on March 25, 1896. The *Edgefield Chronicle* mourned him as "a courtly, polished gentleman, emphatically of the Old South Carolina school." The *Edgefield Advertiser* of April 1 featured a laudatory obituary which, while perhaps somewhat more fiction than fact, provides some additional insight into Fleming's career.

JULIUS J. FLEMING, ESQ.

In the year 1892 the subject of this notice disposed of his possessions in the town of Sumter, S.C., where he had lived for forty odd years; and, together with his wife, in June of that year removed to Edgefield to spend his remaining days with his daughter who had provided a home for her parents here.

Mr. Fleming was born in Charleston seventy-three years ago; was educated in that city and in Philadelphia and at the University of Georgia where he was graduated with distinction. His experiences in life were many and varied. He taught school for a number of years and for a time was president of a college in Green[e]ville, Tenn. In the fifties he settled in Sumter, S. C., and was there editor of the Sumter *Watchman* and Sumter *News*. About the year 1865 he was engaged on the editorial and reportial staff of the old Charleston *Courier*—and his contributions to that sterling journal of the ancient regime were always gems of clear cut thought and classic beauty. We heard a distinguished South Carolina Judge say, on one occasion, that his writings in the *Courier* were "perfect models of pure English undefiled," and that he did very much towards driving Radicalism and the vanpires [*sic*] that fed on our prostrate state from her borders. He gave the name "ring-streaked and striped" to the republican legislature that first assembled in Columbia after the reconstruction period in our history and his descriptions of the personel [*sic*] of that body was of the richest and raciest.

In the sixties he was sent by the *Courier* to Florida to write up the Land of Flowers and eighteen letters entitled "on the wing and on the wave" added much to his already high reputation as a writer. Later he was sent by the same paper with the Georgia Press Association to write up the mineral, industrial and commercial wealth of the Empire State—a work which he did so well that an ovation was tendered [him] in the city of Atlanta.

Mr. Fleming became a member of the Sumter bar in 1867, practiced in the courts of the eastern part of the State for twenty years, and his triumphs in that arena were his greatest achievements. The same Judge alluded to above told us that the Sumter courts were sometimes called "Fleming's courts because he had all the business."

And he travelled much, had met many great ones of earth, had seen and heard Calhoun and Clay and Webster; had visited at their homes Longfellow and Bryant and Holmes, and of these and many others of the dead past he had a wonderful store and fund of memories and incidents—a most delightful raconteur. But there is an end to all things! Our old friend came to Edgefield to die; he told us so, and that he was prepared [to do]. His checks on time had all been cancelled, and he was ready for the last accounting. His triumphs and his failures alike, "as prayers and deeds, pierce starward like a song, and yonder skies hold records of his toils and tears."—On Wednesday morning last at the grey dawning he died; on Thursday his remains were laid to rest in our Baptist cemetery, "where heaves the turf on many a mouldering heap." But, his spirit, ransomed, redeemed, disenthralled, is enjoying what, in mortal life, the eye of faith alone can explore.

Two weeks later the *Advertiser* published a charming little poem which Julius had composed during the Christmas season of 1894—

"Impromptu Lines Inspired by and Dedicated to Miss [Florence Adams] of Edgefield, S. C., by one of her many friends."

Norwood Fleming, Mrs. Baskin's father, died shortly after his own father's death and was buried in the same grave. Her grandmother and aunt subsequently moved to Ridgeland where Julius's widow died in 1905.

Thus ends the tale of this unusual individual who has left us a revealing portrait of a controversial era. One cannot help thinking that there must have been thousands like him during the hectic middle decades of the nineteenth century—men who do not quite fit the rigid mold which genealogist, historian, and novelist cast for them today.

THE PICTURE Juhl paints of life in South Carolina during the last six months of 1865 is that of a people picking up the pieces of an existence shattered and changed by war and defeat. Although life was far from gay, the scene was certainly not one of utter despair. True, there was too much drinking, Negro vagrancy was increasing, and an occasional racial incident occurred. In the opinion of Correspondent Fleming, South Carolina faced two vital questions: how can peace and quiet be permanently secured, and how and where will farmers find an adequate, reliable labor force? In the effort to answer the latter query, Juhl outlined the first steps which would lead to the well-known system of sharecropping.

As for Negro suffrage, he thought giving the vote to those just released from slavery sheer folly. At the same time, he was equally critical of a state legislature which enacted laws defying Congress and seemed to take little cognizance of the decision reached at Appomattox. Concerning military occupation, he had firm convictions: it was absolutely necessary for the maintenance of stability and order. Yet, despite these overpowering issues, there was time for an occasional outing to Columbia, a tournament, or a pleasant social gathering. Perhaps the word which best sums up the mood of South Carolina throughout these months is not anxiety, despair, or gloom, but simply relief. One senses in these letters a certain resignation and security. The war was over and done with.

SUMTER, S. C., July 22

A most distressing occurrence took place in an adjoining district a few nights ago. An old gentleman residing in the country who, from the circumstances, must have anticipated and prepared for a visit from robbers, hearing someone on his premises at night, hailed three times and, receiving no answer, fired his gun with fatal effect at the object of his suspicions and his fears. Advancing to ascertain the effect of his shot, with indescribable anguish he discovered the body of his son in the last agonies of death—a son who had long been a prisoner at the North and whose partial deafness prevented his hearing his father's challenge. . . . A sad warning to all; for, even in the present unsettled state of the country and notwithstanding the comparative impunity with which robberies and murders have been committed in some neighborhoods, one cannot be too cautious in the use of firearms.

In this section the seasons, with the exception of a short spell of intensely hot and dry weather early in July, have been favorable to the crops. The grain crop is generally promising, but much less has been planted than usually owing to the interruption of labor. Thousands of the colored inhabitants embraced the opportunity afforded by General [Edward E.] Potter's visit in April last to go to the coast, and the majority of these have never returned, and of those who have returned many show but little disposition to resume habits of industry and a settled life.

The Negroes are to be pitied. The new order of things has burst upon them too suddenly. They were not prepared for it. They do not understand the liberty which has been conferred upon them. A freedom which still involves the necessity of earning their bread by the sweat of their brow does not seem to them much of a boon after all. Of course, there are exceptions, but as a class they have the wildest notions, and many of them leaving their former homes are wandering over the country in a state of idleness, which must lead to want and crime. It is perfectly transparent that they must work or perish. The white man works, and so must they. Many of their former masters, accustomed heretofore to lives of elegant leisure, have cheerfully taken hold of the plough, the hoe, and the axe, and are setting their servants an example of worthy imitation. . . .

To the new system of labor, inaugurated by the government for the culture of these southern lands, there will, no doubt, be given a fair trial. The planters, generally, are adopting it, and the military supervision now established will afford ample protection against serious errors on either side. How it will work remains to be seen. The president has said that if it should be found that the two races cannot live harmoniously in the same country, then the blacks must be colonized; and perhaps this will be best for both parties, for many here believe that such is the only hope of the country and must be the final result. There are intelligent planters in the district who are now ready to welcome white immigration and to divide off a portion of their estates into small farms which emigrants can readily obtain by purchase or lease as they may prefer. The climate is healthy and, unlike the low country, is favorable to white labor.

And there need be no doubt as to the encouragement which the people here are prepared to extend to such emigrants—an encouragement which the government may safely endorse, for it would effectually and forever seal the bonds of union. For what was the life-blood of secession and the real *casus belli?* Slavery. And, slavery being now dead, we are all one again. But we are weak. Give us then the right kind of population with at least a larger portion of white labor than we now have and we are strong again. Strong to move on together with the rest of the Union in the high pathway of enterprise and toil.

The dynasty which was built up by the institution of slavery has passed away. Let no fabulous tales of cruelty to the freedman be received at the North. And, in looking at the black man, let us not withhold our sympathies from the white. Let not the fact be forgotten that through all this land the war has left its desolating marks; families robed in mourning; Davids mourning their Absaloms, and Rachels weeping for their children and refusing to be comforted because they are not, and that by one sweep the wealth of the country is taken away, and a people accustomed to wealth and ease are suddenly reduced to poverty, humiliation, and toil. Towards these people, in their quiet submission to the government, the nation may well affort to be magnanimous.

The Union troops are here. The 30th Massachusetts, Colonel [F. H.] Whittier, garrison the place. Thus far the best of order prevails in the town. The courthouse and contiguous grounds are used as barracks, offices, and camp. The health of the command is excellent. The cars are running again, and we are once more brought into communication with the outer world. Your *Courier* and northern papers of late dates are on our tables. Some of them advocate universal suffrage. They would give the untutored black man of the South the right to vote and invite him in the first hours of his deliverance to take part in the legislation of this great country. This, to say the least, is premature. Don't expect the young bird to fly when first it emerges from its shell; such an attempt would betray its folly and involve its destruction.

Give them a vote now and what would inevitably result? The rich landed proprietors employing large numbers of ignorant laborers whom they could control by a word or a barbecue, in a matter to which the Negro at present attaches no importance, would hold the elections in their own hands. The poor white man, with his single vote, would be voiceless as the grave in the counsels and legislation of the state. Have the advocates of this measure considered how potential it would make the wealthy proprietor and how much it would wrong the poor men of the South?

The *National Eagle* of July 1, published in Claremont, New Hampshire, says editorially: "It is stated, on what is assumed as good authority, that the courts of South Carolina will pronounce the Emancipation Proclamation as unconstitutional. If so, and the United States courts overrule such a decision, then the danger of a renewal of the conflicting authorities will be imminent. There can be no longer a doubt that it will require consummate statesmanship to settle permanently these discordant elements and inaugurate a purely republican form of government in the lately revolted states which the Constitution guarantees." Now this is all erroneous and we protest against it as doing the people of this state, as far as we know them, great injustice. The war is over never to be renewed. There is no danger of any future conflict or future trouble unless the blacks create it. If all the troops were withdrawn from this country and a hundred fiery orators were allowed to stump the state from the mountains to the seaboard in favor of another attempt at secession, their efforts would end in an ignominious failure. Let the nation accept this as a faithful report and do justice to our people. Our citizens have renewed their allegiance to the government, and they look to no courts, either state or federal, for the restoration of a dynasty and a system which four years of war and bloodshed extinguished forever.

JUHL

SUMTER, S. C., August 8

Is the war really over, and are we entering once more on the unruffled bosom of a peaceful tide, or are there elements of discord still abroad in the land, and is faction and the spirit which prompts to internecine strife again to prevail? Verily the minds of many are not altogether free from solicitude while pondering these questions. Not simply the question of Negro suffrage, which—it appears to us—is being prematurely thrust upon the country, but other matters awaken profound anxiety at the present juncture: certain local elections in Virginia are announced in the papers to have brought on and admitted an issue again between secession and Union candidates, resulting largely in favor of the former. Now, we do not consider that such a matter in any way endangers the Union or involves the probability of armed hostility to the government, but we do consider that it must and will go far towards continuing a military government over such election precincts and the states in which they are found. And we protest against, and most earnestly deprecate, any such issue or result in South Carolina.

We have had enough of war, enough of blood and desolation and famine and death. The effort for a separate southern government has been tried on a scale of grandeur equal to all the resources of the then wealthy and influential and proud-spirited South and has proved a failure. It has left the country exhausted and bleeding at every vein. And we now want peace, a full and perfect restoration to the Union, and deliverance from all agitation and party strife. Governor [Benjamin F.] Perry's proclamation orders an election in September for delegates to a state convention, and we hope in that election the people will assert their rights. We hope they will sternly refuse to be led by politicians of larger or smaller growth. We hope they will remember the past and nominate and elect none but trusty men— men who will inflict no fresh sorrows upon the country—men who will sustain and insist upon, in good faith, the principles to which by a solemn oath we now stand pledged, and who will, as soon as practicable, conform the state constitution to those requirements with which alone we can now hope to prosper. An opposite course will only result in defeating every hope of our civil restoration and leave us, perhaps for years, a mere military province under the shadow of a great master empire. On this question we have no fears for Sumter District. May the whole state be of the same mind.

As far as is known to the writer, everything here is moving on as quietly as could be expected. A few instances of bad conduct have indeed occurred; but the action of the military authorities has been salutary in exerting a wholesome restraint upon the lawless, and has exhibited firmness tempered with moderation and forbearance in the administration of law and preservation of order.[1] The streets of the town have been cleaned, drains opened, and the strictest police regulations maintained. All this has been and is highly necessary. And, there can be very little doubt that if the military forces were withdrawn from this country before the complete inauguration of state government, a reign of anarchy and terror would at once ensue. . . .

Among things of minor moment, we have mention that a number of new stores have been opened here, their shelves filled with everything from which we were so long cut off by the blockade, and that our streets are quite lively and exhibit a considerable share of business activity. The three g's—gold, greenbacks, and groceries—bring out the cotton and put the king once more in lively motion. By the way, although the war has damaged the old gentleman and knocked away his crown and sceptre, he seems quite respectable still, and his society is courted and his drafts honored at sight. Very little cotton has been this year planted in the district, but it appears there is enough of former crops to brighten up your old city if it is ever allowed to reach you. The break in the Northeastern Road at the Santee greatly embarrasses travel, and transportation of heavy freights seem almost impracticable. If you want Charleston and the rest of mankind to feel the rising tide, you must open up the routes of travel and make these great railway arteries complete and continuous. Can there not be found enough of labor and energy in the country to rebridge the rivers which roll between us and the sea?

JUHL

1. Several weeks later the *Sumter Watchman* (September 27, 1865) contained a small ad of special interest. Mrs. N. J. Farrell, Mrs. Elizabeth J. Criss, and Miss Adele Durban apologized for wearing small Confederate flags in their hair, emphatically denying that any insult to the authorities was intended.

SUMTER, S. C., August 10

A file of northern papers has just come to hand containing some things to amuse and some to gratify and some to annoy. Mrs. Grundy indulges her muse at the museum and in the most facetious vein describes the catastrophes by which Barnum's curiousity shop is summarily closed for the season.[2] We are not surprised to hear that while the fire raged the whale showed much sympathy for its illustrious exhibitor and actually *blubbered*, while bruin came down from an upper window *bare*-ly in time; and that, at the close of the highly exciting scene, the pitying angel dropped a tear for Barnum, which the prince of showmen, with his characteristic eye to the future, promptly *bottled*. There is also a case of "beastly" intoxication recorded in the *Troy Times*. A certain cow, it is said, drank eighteen gallons of whiskey which had been left exposed near a still and has been on a regular bender ever since, but she makes some amends for her frolic by giving two quarts of milk punch daily! All which is duly vouched for.

In the most of the northern journals it is gratifying to note a disposition to do justice to the South, and your able New York correspondent (to whom we waft, in return for his good wishes, our kindest greetings) seems confident that the majority of the people there are thus included. But there are, unfortunately, exceptions to this; as, for example, in several numbers of the *New York Evening Post* we notice with profound astonishment and regret the misrepresentations of its correspondents from the South and West. From the statements which these writers make and the spirit they manifest, one is almost forced to the conclusion that their pay is to be regulated by the number and bitterness of the libels on the South.

2. *Mrs. Grundy* was a short-lived humor weekly published in New York by Alfred Carroll, July 8–September 22, 1865. P. T. Barnum's Manhattan museum was destroyed by fire on July 13.

Fortunately for us, the whole land is now dotted with United States garrisons, officered generally by men of discernment who are able to form, from personal observation, a correct estimate of southern life as it now is. These will be able, by their letters and after their return by their personal influence, to correct the gross misstatements which are now being made to the northern public. And, may we not hope that the strong tide of negrophilism which, for so many years, has been rising and swelling until it covered the land, has reached its flood; and that, the blacks being now free, calm reflection and a knowledge of facts will soon satisfy the public mind that there are others in this sunny land who really need and better deserve the sympathies of the great heart of the nation? We do look indeed for a strong ebb tide soon to sweep away the scales which have obscured the vision of many, when the strong arms of the North will be twined around no man or race merely because of an ebony skin, but when those arms will be thrown in confiding friendship and unswerving support and affection around their white brethren of the South who have passed through the deepest humiliation and trial, but who are of one blood and one race and one country with them still.

It is wrong to suppose, as alleged by the writers for the *Post*, that there is at the South a general feeling of hostility towards the blacks. They may act in such a way as to create such a feeling, but at present it does not exist. We know that there is an earnest desire for their welfare and a sincere regret that they are not educationally and mentally prepared for the freedom so suddenly thrust upon them. As it is, liberty with them too often runs into licentiousness; and, we are certain that in the upheavings of our social fabric under the transitions of the past few months, the white race has been thus far the chief sufferer, but has nobly and without a murmur stood the shock and done its full duty kindly and faithfully to those so long accustomed to its care.

General [Quincy A.] Gillmore has recently made a tour through this section of the state, making a personal inspection of the different posts, and no doubt his visit will have a salutary effect. General [George L.] Beale's headquarters are at Darlington C.H., a beautiful village between Florence and Cheraw. It is almost buried in foliage, but the sombre shades of its venerable oaks are relieved by the flowering vine and fragrant blossom. Its refined inhabitants are regaled every afternoon with the rich music of the brigade band. Colonel Whittier commands at Sumter and is deservedly esteemed for his kind and conciliatory course. Captain Reid is the energetic and affable provost marshal and has administered the oath of allegiance to over seven hundred citizens at this point already.

The anxiety to see the *Courier* increases, judging from the fact that it is a very difficult matter for subscribers to get hold of their papers; and, when they come to hand, they bear marks of having been considerably handled. . . .

The *Great Eastern!* Presumed to be rolling on through the Atlantic with her twenty-five-thousand tons aboard. Will she come through? Will the cable break? We wait to hear.

JUHL

SUMTER, S. C., August 24

September approaches, and with it comes the elections and the convention which are to decide the status of the state. Columbia is the place appointed for the meeting of the convention. There the Convention of 1860 assembled, although it afterwards adjourned to Charleston—the convention which launched the state upon the stormy and fatal waves of revolution and war. *Then* the capital was one of the fairest cities in the South. The cleanliness and beauty of its well regulated streets, the elegance of its public and private edifices, the refinement and hospitality of its inhabitants, the sacred repose of its classic shades and the ceaseless activity communicated to business by its numerous railroads made it a place of great interest and importance—the pride of the state. *Now* we need not describe it. It has passed through the scathing fires of war, and its crumbled ruins serve to "point a moral," if not to "adorn a tale." To every member of the coming convention, its scenes of desolation—loveliness blighted and wealth destroyed and glory departed and beauty literally turned to ashes—must be suggestive of saddening thoughts and wise counsels. . . .

Governor Perry assured the president that South Carolina would be among the first to wheel into line, and at present we can discover nothing to prevent his assurance from being amply verified. And, if the state (after exhibiting a valor worthy of her antecedents) gracefully yields to the judgments of the nation and promptly conforms to the will of the government, let the nation be magnanimous towards her and betray no want of confidence in the integrity and sincerity of her people. A reconciliation should be perfect and complete and natural, or it is no reconciliation at all.

A case of miscegenation occurred in a village in the state of New York. The parties were living quietly together, having been regularly married. The young men of the place determined that it should not be tolerated and made a night attack upon the house where the couple lived. The Negro husband, or his mother, fired upon them, and one of the party, a returned soldier, was killed. An inquest followed, and the court which sat upon the case, in dismissing the prisoners charged with the killing, admonished them to leave the community; that it would be dangerous for them to remain there; and, while the law allowed a Negro to marry a white woman, yet it was a gross violation of propriety to do so, and it would not be tolerated.

Now this seems to us plain and sensible enough. But had it occurred at the South it would have been instanced by some northern journals as an illustration of southern lawlessness and violence and lynch law proclivities. It would have been quoted as an evidence of unjust hostility to the black race. But it occurred in New York state, and it meets with no rebuke. Why should it be otherwise had it occurred here? Is it not palpable that New York has established an impassable gulf between the degraded inmates of the Five Points and the graceful agile forms which night wraps in rosy slumbers in the magnificent palaces of her merchant princes? There are rainbows, it is true, even at night, but they require the lunar rays to give them being; and the darkness soon divests the sky of the beauteous hues of the prism which were painted there by the glorious light of day. Is the inference plain? God may have made of our blood all the nations of men, but society has everywhere drawn lines of distinction between classes and conditions; and these lines of distinction will exist, in defiance of all the efforts of human levelers, while rivers run and the deep blue oceans roll. They will exist at the North and our friends should not quarrel with us if they continue to exist at the South. This is all we ask—no more, no less, than our northern brethren claim for themselves. The red light of battle has passed away; and now, in the name of justice and a common civilization and common brotherhood, let peace bring healing in her wings.

The Sumter market: cotton, thirty to thirty-five in greenbacks; and groceries an advance of twenty-five to one hundred percent on Charleston prices, owing to high rates of freight, unusual delays attending the forwarding of the same, and a natural ambition on the part of the merchants to make hay while the sun shines. Larger stocks and more competition might reduce these figures.

Two hundred and fifty bales of cotton have been shipped from this depot since the road has opened, and one hundred bales are at the depot waiting cars, all for your city.

JUHL

... The new era which gives liberty to some threatens seriously to restrain the liberties of others. The hogs which from time immemorial have enjoyed the freedom of this goodly town are to be impounded by order of the post commandant, if caught running at large within the corporate limits from and after the first of September. Some years ago that august body yclept the town council published a similar order and made a desperate attempt to abate the nuisance against which the present military order is leveled. But it proved abortive; each porker had a friend and remonstrant in its owner, and their united complaints were too much for the city fathers. They had to succumb, and the streets continued to be enlivened with the presence of these comely and cleanly and modest animals. We have, however, somewhat more faith in a military mandate than in that waste of paper—an ordinance of the town; and, we strongly incline to the opinion that any hog or pig, however respectable and well behaved, which may appear in the streets of our beautiful village after the first proximo, will do so at their peril.

On Thursday of this week there was a large sale of government (condemned?) horses and equipment in this place. The horses would have made up an admirable stable for Don Quixote, from which he could at pleasure have matched his beloved and incomparable Rosinante; and, strange to say, they brought from thirty to over one hundred dollars each. The sale attracted a large crowd from the surrounding country; and, the main street of Sumter for the time furnished (to a man of lively imagination and easy faith) a bird's-eye view of the Epsom races or the great day of the Derby stakes.

The military are now engaged in taking the agricultural statistics of this and the adjoining districts—a work which must involve a great deal of trouble, but which, when ready, will constitute a fund of valuable information. ...

JUHL

SUMTER, S. C., August 29

The question of suffrage continues to occupy the attention of the country. How far, if at all, this franchise should be restricted, is ably discussed in the newspaper press and in the political conventions which are now being held in the different states. . . .

. . . At present there are but three states in the Union which give the right of suffrage to whites and blacks on equal terms. These are Maine, Vermont, and New Hampshire, and their Negro population is so small that it never can materially affect the ballot. The great state of Massachusetts, the pioneer and leader in the march of freedom and the zealous advocate of the rights of man, requires of every voter ability to read the Constitution in English and to write his name. In South Carolina men vote who can neither read nor write. Rhode Island requires a property qualification of $134 in real estate. New York, which allows a white man to vote after one year's residence, requires a black man to have resided three years in the state. And Connecticut is the only New England state which makes color a test, and it allows only such Negroes to vote as were freedmen at adoption of the state constitution in 1818. All the other states, even including Kansas, West Virginia, and Missouri, expressly exclude the Negro from the ballot box. With a few exceptions the state constitutions also exclude Indians, and in Oregon they likewise debar a Chinaman from the privilege, however long his residence or extensive his freehold.

Now, in the face of these facts, with what right, justice, or reason can it be expected that the southern state conventions, which are soon to meet, shall break down the wholesome lines of distinction which the past has drawn and which the wisdom and experience of other states have approved, and invest with this sacred and potential franchise large masses of untutored freedmen who know nothing of the genius of our constitutions, laws, and government? It would be as wise and prudent and safe and hopeful to entrust to their management the

Great Eastern in her next attempt to fish up and splice and finish paying out the submarine electric wires which are to unite two continents by sending flashes of thought in an instant of time through the realms of Behemoth from shore to shore.

The late Democratic convention in Maine affirms that the ballot is the right of every American citizen, but that each state is the judge of the restriction upon its exercise. And each state must be regulated in a great measure by the character and extent of its black population. General [Jacob D.] Cox, the Union candidate for governor of Ohio, avows his opposition to striking from the state constitution the word "white" and giving the freedmen the privilege of suffrage. He is in favor of colonizing the blacks in Florida and its contiguous territory as a dependency of the United States, and says that to tolerate the commingling of blacks and whites in this country would be to perpetuate disorder and confusion, and that the bestowal of the ballot upon the former would but make such confusion worse and confounded. This sensible view of the suffrage question, it is hoped, the wisdom of the whole country will endorse.

The drought continues with damaging effects on late crops, although there is now a very good prospect of rain. There are some places in the district where the corn crop will not average more than three bushels to the acre, and some acres will not yield even a peck. But other neighborhoods have been more fortunate and will average ten or more bushels to the acre.

The town is well regulated and continues quiet, with the exception of occasional freaks by John Barleycorn. Some of these might amuse your readers; but the recording angel of the Turks makes it a rule never to chronicle or remember what a man does when he is drunk, in a passion, or underage—an example we may safely follow.

The South is at present under military rule. United States troops garrison all the important points—a wise measure on the part of the government, as it defeats the lawless in their attempts at anarchy and

33

gives protection to all classes of citizens. The Indian troubles in the West and the control and supervision of the freedmen of the South will furnish ample employment to the army for six months to come. With reference to this latter class, there are many who believe there is trouble ahead owing to their extravagant elation of spirit and wild anticipation of future settlements. A strong hand will be required to insure peace and obedience to the laws. In some places it seems the citizens have considered the presence of troops among them as offensive. In Fayetteville, North Carolina, a well-behaved white garrison has been withdrawn, and Negro troops sent to occupy the town, owing to some improper conduct on the part of the citizens. And, the same is true of other places. Sumter and the adjacent country is fortunate in having the 30th Massachusetts Veteran Volunteers stationed here—a regiment kept well in hand by the commanding officers and exerting a happy influence in securing obedience to law and protecting all classes in the quiet enjoyment of their rights.

JUHL

SUMTER, S. C., August 31

The condition of the colored race is changing from bondage to freedom. Will this transition increase their happiness and promote their best interests for time and eternity? Will it tend to advance them in the scale of moral and religious development or leave them to sink into vagrancy, vice, and degradation? They certainly need guides and instructors; we might use a stronger word and say that, like minors, they need guardians. If left to themselves, uncontrolled, uninstructed, uncared for, we cannot indulge in a very hopeful view of their future. They will need the Sabbath School and the pulpit; for, to them in their present circumstances, more than at any former period, should the gospel be faithfully preached.

Whatever hard and bitter things may have been written against the

South for its former treatment of these people, however savagely isolated cases of cruelty may have been magnified into allegations of such acts as the general practice of the country, and however dark may have been considered the blot which slavery, under the most favorable aspects, made on the picture of southern society, as viewed from a northern viewpoint, it can never be truthfully asserted that the southern people neglected the religious instruction of the blacks while under their care. In all our churches, of every name and creed, at the regular service the galleries have been appropriated freely to the colored people, and during the day or evening of every Sabbath a special service has been held for their particular benefit. And it is a well-known fact that there was scarcely a large plantation which the missionary did not visit, catechizing the children and instructing the adults in the saving truths of Christianity. In defiance of the miasma of swamps and rice fields and heedless of the warning which Chesterfield gives:

The dews of the evening most carefully shun,
Those tears of the sky for the loss of the sun,

these devoted men were found in the heats of summer and the frost of winter, ministering to their spiritual wants. . . . [3]

According to the *Louisville Journal*, the agitation of Negro suffrage has had the most baleful effects upon the late elections in that state. In many of the southern and eastern counties where the elections would have otherwise resulted largely in favor of emancipation, the proslavery candidates triumphed, large numbers of Union voters among the poorer classes having given them their support, not from opposition to emancipation, but from the dread that the right of

3. Throughout 1853 Fleming served in the Savannah River Negro mission of the Methodist Church.

suffrage would be extended to the blacks. In this way the radicals are injuring their own cause by pushing upon the country an issue for which it is not yet prepared.

Brazil invites immigration, and there are not wanting those among us who seem inclined to cast their fortunes beneath her flag. But Brazil is at war with the neighboring states, and in this age, when the issues of battle are joined and nation rises against nation, it is impossible to foresee what will be the event. In going thither our emigrant friends who are dissatisfied with this country as it now is might be jumping from what they think a frying pan into what might prove a fire!

The merchants here complain bitterly of the delays in forwarding freight from your city. Goods shipped five weeks ago on the Northeastern Railroad have not yet come to hand. This is a long time for capital to lie dormant, and goods of a perishable nature must be ruined *in transitu*.

The rain has come at last but so long delayed that some of the rice is past redemption.

JUHL

SUMTER, S. C., September 4

Some correspondents of the northern press persist in representing our people as animated with a deadly hatred to the North—a hatred which nothing but the presence of a military force keeps in check; that southern men take the oath, but do not consider it binding and ridicule its obligations; and that there is everywhere exhibited a murderous antagonism to the blacks, which would rejoice in their absolute extinction. Drawing largely on their powers of invention and really seeing but little of the internal life of the country as they pass rapidly through it, these writers manage, nevertheless, to fill columns of New York and other mammoth sheets with letters which are about equally divided between insipid twaddle and deplorable exhibitions of mendacity and vengeful exaggeration.

With any faith in their statements, we could not be surprised that Boston merchants should memorialize the president in favor of continuing a military government over the South and should oppose our early restoration to civil rule and a place in the Union. He who slanders his neighbor shall be cut off, and an action will lie in a court of law against the offender who damages in proportion to the libel. What then should be done with those who maliciously misrepresent a whole people and who in the first hours of peace, when the good men of every section are striving to heal the wounds of the past and when the South lies at the feet of the government, impoverished, disarmed, and humbled, strive to awaken in the northern mind a feeling of distrust and hatred towards us, which, with all our faults, we have never merited? And, what a spectacle is it at such a time, when the mayor of a southern town (Fayetteville) has to contradict officially the false statements most gravely made by one of these correspondents! Would it not be well for your northern readers to consider seriously which is the most likely to be true—the representations which are made by ill-informed and imaginative writers for papers, or the statements and exhibits which are presented to the southern press and which are exposed to the critical supervision and (if incorrect) to the prompt contradiction of the military authorities?

The whole country may be congratulated upon the happy selection made by the government of General [Oliver O.] Howard as chief of the Freedmen's Bureau. There is scarcely any position which at this time is invested with higher responsibilities or more arduous duties; no position in which a blunderer could do more harm or an able, well-informed, and patriotic incumbent can accomplish more good. And, from the recent address of the chief of the bureau to an auxiliary association in Maine, it is evident that the appointment could have been given to no man better qualified to appreciate and rightly discharge its difficult and complicated duties. In that speech he explains the object of the bureau—to secure to the blacks all the benefits of a well-regulated state of freedom; to regulate labor, encourage education, and promote obedience to the laws; to prevent the freedmen from congregating in such numbers as to oversupply the demand for labor at any point, leading, as such a course would inevitably do, to idleness, vagrancy, and crime; and thinks it best for the Negro to remain on the same lands they have heretofore cultivated and where under the contract system they will be entitled to proper compensation.

He is opposed to a permanent establishment in Washington for the purposes for which the bureau labors, as "the subjects are entirely matters for state control," and thinks the whole business should be left to the states as soon as they are able and willing to undertake the work. He does not discuss the question of suffrage, but rather intimates that this likewise is a matter for each state and the future to decide. And, to show the propriety of this position, it is only necessary to remark that in Vermont there are but 80 and in New Hampshire only 190 Negro voters; while in South Carolina, if the franchise were given to the blacks, they would control the state, having a majority of two or three to one in twenty out of thirty districts.

The business of this town has very much increased, and the numerous stores appear to be doing a thriving trade. Large quantities of cotton are rolling in upon us for shipment, it being by no means an unusual sight to see a half dozen or more four-horse wagons, heavily laden with the great staple, in a single train passing through the town. The market is depressed, the best samples bring but twenty-five to twenty-six cents. Notwithstanding this, however, rogues continue to steal it, and the planters complain of the losses they have sustained from the depredations committed by Negroes (in some cases white men) from the town and elsewhere, who carry it off by one or more bales at a time. These larcenies give employment to the provost court, and some few of the lawyers take interest enough in the business to enter *con amore* into the new practice. Money seems to circulate freely, and greenbacks are held in high esteem. The number of soldiers and strangers now tarrying here or visiting the town from time to time add very much to the amount of the circulating medium among us and seem to have brought on that long desired period when

Those who have money, get still more—
While those get money, who had none before!

The election comes off today, but as there is no opposition and no excitement, the vote polled, as is usual in such cases in this country, will probably be small. The candidates are either known to have been always Union men or are reported to be entirely so now, whatever may have been their antecedents.

On Saturday afternoon last a special train from Darlington landed Generals [George C.] Meade and Gillmore at our depot, where they were received with appropriate honors by the military, and whence they proceeded, in a carriage, to a private residence. The visit was, doubtless, one of inspection, and they left the same night by special train for Columbia, where it is expected they will have an interview with Governor Perry.

The bridge over the Congaree, on the South Carolina Railroad, is up, and trains pass over. When the iron is relaid on a gap of nine miles between the river and Orangeburg, we will be blest once more with a continuous rail to your city. This ought to be completed in a few weeks, and our merchants and people will then cease to be annoyed by the inevitable Santee and its wretched flat.

There were 235 votes polled at this box today, and the impression is that Messrs. John N. Frierson and F. J. Moses [Sr.] are ahead; the third man uncertain. The country boxes will be heard from tomorrow, the votes counted, and the election declared. One thing seems certain, that this district goes the Union ticket, whatever the rest of the state may do.

JUHL

SUMTER, S. C., September 12

In the late issue of the *New Era*, an excellent weekly published in Darlington, the editor endeavors to convince the people of that quiet village that a fire engine and a good hotel are desiderata which should be speedily supplied. His argument was good and should have been convincing; how far it will accomplish his intent, deponent pretends not to say. In this notable town we have the advantage of our Darlington neighbors in both the aforesaid particulars. We have hotels; one of them has an imposing front, with majestic columns and a long range of dormitories, dining rooms, etc., extending to the rear, and is kept by a lady; the other is kept by a veteran caterer, whose long experience ought to qualify him to furnish a most appetizing cuisine. (We write not from personal test.) Both are on the west side of Main Street. And we have an engine capable of throwing a very effective stream over the highest buildings in the town; and this has been recently furbished up by the military and put in excellent order for instant use—a most timely precaution, as owing to the long drought, a fire breaking out at this time might, if not promptly arrested, prove a great calamity.

Sometime since, an outrage was committed by a freedman on the person of a married lady residing some half-mile from town. The circumstances of her recent confinement gave additional horrors to the rape. The crime was committed in the daytime, the husband was absent, no friend was near, and the villain escaped. Within a few days he has been traced, discovered, arrested, and will no doubt soon be tried, and, it is hoped, properly disposed of.

One of our most intelligent citizens, a close observer of men and things, has just returned from a northern tour, embracing a visit to the capital and metropolis of the nation. He represents New York, Philadelphia, and Washington as crowded with Southerners, and the entire North in a perfect whirl of business activity. He left things here dead; he found there a world of wondrous life and moving humanity. Even nature seemed fresher, greener, more vigorous, and beautiful. The feelings of the people, with some exceptions, were most cordial and friendly towards us, and the bonds of Union were being rapidly woven into an indestructible woof.

He had an interview with the president, and describes him by one word—"massive"; a massive forehead and broad chin, indicative of firmness, very neatly dressed, and of pleasant, agreeable manners, receiving with every manifestation of kindness numerous Southerners who were admitted to an audience at the same time with our informant. The president evinces an earnest desire to aid the South in recovering its lost position in the Union and (our informant believes) stands between us and the extreme Radical party, who would make the South a mere farm of the North and administer upon it as a derelict estate. He thinks that, previous to the Werze [Capt. Henry Wirz] trial, Jefferson Davis was in no danger of a capital conviction; but the testimony in that case is having a damaging effect upon the late leader of the South. But the impression is (and it seems but reasonable) that magnanimity and clemency towards Mr. Davis could not injure the government, while it would greatly tend towards soothing the southern people and attaching them to the Union more heartily than ever.

Many are anxious for the restoration of civil government and exhibit a feverish anxiety for the removal of the national forces from the state. The latter disposition we neither entertain nor endorse. We cannot ignore the transparent facts which stand out against it; the great numerical disparity between the white and black races in this country; the seeming inability on the part of some of the former to recognize fully and de facto the new political and social and personal rights which the revolution has conferred on the blacks; and the restless and unsettled condition of the latter and their dispositon to disorganize and upset the country if not properly restrained; and the undisputed fact that the state is disarmed and has no redundant population to spare from the pursuits of labor for the field of arms, or even for an extended police force. For these reasons, therefore, it appears to us that even after the state shall resume its executive and legislative and judicial control over its own people, the sudden withdrawal of the United States troops would be unwise and undesirable. And your readers will find this opinion, however unpalatable it may be to some, amply justified by coming events.

This country has not experienced for many years a more damaging drought than the present, for it still continues, only slightly relieved by light and very partial showers. It has been very fatal to the rice, potato, and pea crops. And in fact, gathering our information from reliable sources in all parts of the state, we hesitate not to say that the present cotton crop of South Carolina will not much, if at all, exceed five thousand bales; and there will not be enough provisions raised to supply the existing population. A very large part of our territory was ravaged by Sherman's and Potter's armies, and the planting interest almost annihilated. Many of our people have not yet recovered their horses and mules and will be visiting your city with the hope of regaining their lost property. And, in every case where such property can be identified, it is presumed and hoped, for the good of the country, that it will promptly be given up.

The resumption of the mails would be a great blessing to this country. Newspapers cannot circulate except on the lines of railway and other routes of public travel, and consequently multitudes are kept in the dark as to passing events. And yet, it is very important that the people should be kept informed, especially at this critical juncture in our history. We have daily trains on the roads. Cannot the postmaster-general be induced to bless us once more with a daily mail and gladden even the byways and hedges with the passing postboy in saddle or sulkey? Let the news fly, and give the people light!

The state convention will now occupy much of the public attention. Owing to the absence of mail facilities, we are still in ignorance of the probable character the convention as a body will assume. Of one thing we feel assured, that it will greatly disappoint a large part of the state, if it shall raise an issue on any important point with the national government. We trust it will prove, in feeling and sentiment and action, fully abreast of the times; that wisdom and harmony will prevail in all its counsels; and that it will suffer no disaster to come upon us by an insane attempt to resurrect a dead institution and galvanize a dynasty which has passed away.

Some of the planters of this district have authorized me to say that they not only invite white immigration, but are ready to furnish land on accommodating terms. Such emigrants can employ as many freedmen as they may need and doubtless do well.

There is a good opening here for a temperance lecturer. Any man of good address who is willing to pay his own expenses for the sake of opening his batteries on the demijohns, casks, and bottles which now circulate in our midst may find a platform, and perhaps an audience, by making early application. The only interruptions to the general good order which prevails in this community may be ascribed to strong drink.

JUHL

SUMTER, S. C., September 20

After such a grand and general smashup as secession produced, it will necessarily take a long time to ascertain and realize the extent of the damage. The humiliation involved in such a decisive defeat as the South experienced, in its attempt to establish an independent government, was in itself considered by many as damaging enough. But, when to this is superadded the overthrow of slavery, the institution upon which unhappily depended the productive wealth and importance of this country, the confiscation of lands, the accumulation of debt and taxes, the great and sudden changes in the status of the population, and the withering impoverishment of multitudes who were formerly strangers to poverty and want, you have a pyramid of disasters standing forth on a desert plain with no Nile to bring with its fertilizing waters fresh verdure and beauty to the landscape again.

The late struggle has unquestionably entailed upon us and our posterity a long train of evils. We are now only entering the threshold of a penal experience which will be protracted into coming years. The loss of the public records may be classed among the almost irreparable disasters. In this particular, South Carolina has greatly suffered. State records and papers of importance are gone forever. Some of the districts, Clarendon for example, have had the entire contents of their district offices destroyed. Titles, deeds, wills, judgments, decrees have disappeared in the flames of war. And how much of confusion, how much of litigation, how much of perplexing embarrassments and perhaps of injustice and fraud may not all this involve? The public documents belonging to this district were removed in time and are preserved, unless ruined by exposure and carelessness. In the confusion attending their removal, it is not unlikely that some of the papers may have been lost.

The courthouse has been for some time in the hands of the military—the courtroom (upstairs) being occupied as barracks and the lower offices by the adjutant, provost marshals, and provost judge. Colonel Whittier is, however, making arrangements to vacate the entire building and has already turned over the clerk's office to its old and time-honored use as the repository of the records and judicial transactions of the district. The civil magistrate is once more in the chair, and with certain restrictions, is allowed to resume his duties.

The town is full of life. The paymaster has recently replenished the exhausted purse of the soldier, and money circulates freely. Cotton keeps rolling in, thirty, forty, fifty bales at a time. There are weddings among the white folks and weddings among the black folks, and we hear of a grand ball soon to come off at Stateburg, the music for which is to be furnished by the brigade band from Darlington. . . .

During the days of the Confederacy we paid fabulous prices for everything. As a people we paid an immense amount of blood and treasure for the privileges of making the experiment. And, as individuals, we expended piles of Memminger scrip for the necessaries of life, and then were half starved. Think of $350 for a sack of flour and $40 for a gallon of molasses. And now we are catching a glimpse of the same snake of extortion peeping out of his hiding place and watching for a chance to afflict with his fangs an already distressed people and to poison fatally the greenback currency of Uncle Sam. Some time ago excellent beef was bought in this market at 6 cents and bacon at 12½ per pound; now beef is 12½ and bacon 35. For such a felonious attempt to carry us back into the Confederacy, while the convention is trying to establish us in the Union, these parties should be arrested and tried for treason.

In defiance of all the beneficent designs of the government, the faithful and untiring efforts of the troops and the wishes of the planters, the number of idle vagrant freedmen increases. Many of the blacks wander from place to place. They know not whither nor why, unless it is from an unfortunate fancy they have for an idle and quasi-gypsy life. This, unless corrected, must occasion much suffering and mortality among them. A Negro man who went from this place to try his fortune on the coast returned a few weeks since with malignant fever. The Negroes with whom he took up his quarters became alarmed for fear of contagion, and turned him out of doors. Last week he died in an old field in the suburbs, and his body was found among the weeds, where the rain had been beating upon it. Neither the

45

authorities nor the citizens knew of his situation until the fatal result was communicated. And many others may and must die in the same manner, unless they give up their vagrant habits and adhere to some fixed habitation and honest employment.

The first number of the *Sumter Watchman*, since the collapse of the late struggle, is issued today. The office was entered by Potter's forces in April last, one number of the *Banner of Freedom* issued, and the press broken up, and the type knocked into *pi*. Mr. [Allen A.] Gilbert has, with characteristic energy, repaired damages and takes his station again on the walls, whence he flings his banner to the breeze. His first number is a good impression and will, no doubt, be cordially greeted by the many who read the *Watchman* in happier days.

JUHL

SUMTER, S. C., September 29

The grand tournament at Stateburg yesterday was quite a success. It drew together an immense concourse of people. The day was lovely—a perfect Indian summer day in sky and atmosphere, and, as the morning advanced, the various roads converging at the place of meeting appeared crowded with a moving throng in every style of travel, horseback, muleback, two wheels and four wheels, all animated with an apparent ambition to make their roadsters and the dust fly. The readers of the *Courier* have so often had graphic pictures of the tournaments of the olden times, that it is only necessary to say that in all the details and arrangements of such friendly trials of prowess and skill, the affair of yesterday corresponded with those which so often formerly arrayed the young men of Carolina in generous emulation in the presence of beauty. After an exciting and well-sustained contest, the prizes were awarded, in the order named to Messrs. [James] Cantey of Camden; J. S. G. Richardson, Jr., and Screven Dinkins of Sumter. The usual formalities attending the election and crowning of the queens of beauty were not dispensed with. The occasion was enlivened with music by the military band [29th Maine] from Darlington, and the day closed with a grand ball at one of the elegant private residences which grace the Hills. We understand arrangements are being made to repeat the whole affair in this town a fortnight hence.

Mr. Henry Haynesworth, for many years postmaster at this office, has recently been reappointed; but he is required to take an oath that he never sympathized with the rebellion, and this he is unable to do. In fact if this formality is not pretermitted very few southern men will be able to qualify for any office in the gift of the government. In the case of our postmaster it is understood that by military advice he is to hold his office and discharge its duties without pay until Congress meets, when his fate, in common with that of many others, will be decided.

As intimated in former letters, the Negroes of the South must not be left without adequate provisions, legal and benevolent, for their instruction, moral advancement, and proper restraint. On two points they have very lax notions—the sacred obligations of the marriage relation and the sanctity of an oath. The first is calculated to make them vicious and dissolute members of society; the second makes them dangerous as witnesses in the courts, where life, character, or property may be imperiled. The Freedmen's Bureau have taken action on the subject of intermarriages and directed that henceforth they be required to procure a license, have the ceremony duly performed by an ordained minister or a lawful magistrate, and a certificate of marriage furnished to the parties, who will then be held liable for any infraction of the contract. . . .

The weather is now beautiful, but unfortunately for all of us except the doctors and druggists, there is more sickness in the community than has been known for years past at any one time.

JUHL

Sumter, S. C., October 3

Yesterday was a sales day and brought quite a crowd to town. . . . The unusual spectacle of three auction sales of furniture, in full blast at the same time on Main Street, attracted attention to the fact that some of the numerous families who, during the war, sought refuge in our midst, were making arrangements to strike their tents and return to their old and long deserted homes. . . . They go back to halls which they left with regret; halls to which they now return to be reminded by familiar scenes of many loved faces which have passed away forever. And they leave us with the auctioneer's bell and the cry, "and a half and a half—four and a half—do I hear five? Take your feet off that hair seat!—and a half. Once, twice, third and *last* time—and down it goes"—as the parting adieu.

A freedman had stolen a fine blooded mare from a gentleman of Camden. The owner of the animal tracked him to this place and was engaging parties to assist in her recovery, when the mare and her rider are seen crossing one of our thoroughfares; immediate pursuit is made and the capture effected. The hue and cry which this affair raised carried the crowd away from the auctioneer's eloquence in a rolling tide of jubilant, hot, and excited humanity.

Thirdly, as the Reverend Governor [William G.] Brownlow would say, there were certain highly respectable parties to be tried for stealing cotton. Another respectable party, the principal witness, had the parties of the first part arrested and bound over to keep the peace, under an apprehension which he believed their threats justified, that his life was in danger. This had somewhat the appearance of Scylla and Charybdis—the military custody and charges on the one hand and the inflexible arm of the civil law on the other. The trial was postponed, certainly not on account of the weather for the day was beautiful and most favorable for cotton picking, whether in court or out of it. The peace recognizance was duly entered into and it is hoped that all parties concerned will settle down to an amicable frame of mind, and the proper ownership and possession of the cotton be established and secured, which is understood to be the sole object of the prosecution.

Today the military vacated the courthouse, and the buildings with its offices will soon be arranged and set in order for the courts. That this is gratifying to the public cannot be denied.

The troops in garrison are now encamped in a beautiful grove in the immediate vicinity of the town, not far from the residence of Colonel Whittier and family, and the same military police and surveillance will doubtless be exercised within and over this corporation.

As the *Courier* is read extensively by those in high places, both in the national and state governments, and its correspondence is known to be careful as well as ample in its remarks on the times, perhaps it would be wrong to omit the assurance that the removal of the military would be a calamity to the country. This is unquestionably a fact. Officers high in rank and possessing information which does not reach the public are fully aware of it. And citizens of undoubted intelligence and nerve acknowledge their uneasiness and anxiety on the subject.

The two vital questions before our rulers and people are: what means shall be adopted to secure quiet and peace to the county and avert impending perils? And, what means will be necessary to secure such labor to the planters for another year as will be certain, reliable, safe, and productive?[4] On both these points there is a great deal of well-founded anxiety in the minds of the best informed; and evidently, if we are not already on a lee shore, we are sailing in waters where there are rocks and quicksands, which are none the less dangerous because they are concealed from view. "The prudent man foreseeth

4. Colonel Whittier's General Order No. 26, published in the *Sumter Watchman* (September 20, 1865), states that all persons had to enter into contracts with freedmen living on their plantations by October 1 or "they will be liable to have their crops confiscated for the benefit of the freedmen."

the danger and hideth himself, but the fool passeth on and is punished. . . . "

JUHL

SUMTER, S. C., October 5

A military commission has been in session here for several days past, composed of Lt. Col. F. H. Whittier, president; Capt. C. S. Burgess, Lt. J. C. Duff, and Lt. J. R. Leary, members; and Capt. E. R. Clark, judge advocate. The court has been closely engaged with the trial on Tuesday of two freedmen for an aggravated case of perjury seriously affecting the estate and reputation of a white man. And, on Wednesday came up the case of Will Jackson, a freedman, charged with rape. . . . The findings of the court will not transpire until reviewed and passed upon by the general commanding.

In Kershaw District there have been nearly three hundred [work] contracts approved up to date, signed by nearly four thousand freedmen.

In Clarendon District the following is the result of the military statistical report: number of plantations, 229; number of acres, 196,387; number in cotton, 586; in corn, 19,573; in rice, 1,793; in wheat, 587; in peas, 13,337; in potatoes, 1,797; in sorghum, 267; number of working hands, 2,562; number of nonproducers, 2,560. How are the freedmen working? Answer: good, 69; fair, 46; bad, 21. The planters have made contracts and the crops are reported good, 64; fair, 63; bad, 11. Treatment of freedmen, good, 23; fair, 7; bad, 1. This is the military report for the present year when the freedmen have every inducement to work from their interest in the crop.

It will be seen that there is very little cotton planted and the planters say that under the present system, without military enforcement, there will be still less planted next year. A prominent planter of Salem, Sumter District, who planted some forty acres of cotton this year, says his cotton has balled more heavily than usual. But, notwithstanding this, when in former years the Negroes picked 130 to 150 pounds per diem to the hand, now they scarcely reach 50 pounds each. . . .

JUHL

SUMTER, S. C., October 28

A most distressing occurrence took place in the adjacent district of Clarendon on last Thursday night, 26th inst., resulting in the death of Pvt. John Tusseder of Company K, 30th Massachusetts Veteran Volunteers. It appears that some disturbances had occurred on a plantation about ten miles from Manning among the freedmen; and, on complaint being made to the military authorities, the planter was advised to use his firearms in case his dwelling was again invaded. On the night in question a guard was sent from Manning and, on arriving at the planter's dwelling, the officer in command knocked at the door, but before any response was made, Private Tusseder pushed the door open and entered, and as he did so, received the contents of the planter's gun in his left jawbone and jugular, killing him instantly. The gun was fired evidently under the impression that the freedmen were in a state of revolt and were forcing an entrance into the house. The body of the deceased was brought to this place and will be buried with the customary military honors. The occurrence is universally regretted.

There were 273 votes polled in this district at the recent election for governor. Of this number, General [Wade] Hampton received 270 and Colonel [James L.] Orr, 3. This result may be accounted for, as in other places, by two considerations: first, General Hampton's unbounded personal popularity, and secondly, the dissent generally expressed by the people to the action of the convention caucus in forestalling the popular verdict by nominating a governor after agreeing to give the election to the people.

On the 19th inst. we not only had the eclipse in a cloudless sky, but the grandest affair in the shape of a tournament which this county has ever witnessed. Some thirty knights, in splendid attire and magnificently mounted, contended for the prize in the presence of several thousand spectators. Music and beauty's smiles graced the occasion, and fun and merriment were not wanting. At 5 P.M. General [John D.] Kennedy addressed the crowd from the courthouse steps. He is a candidate for Congress and endorses President Johnson heartily. He has a very able and formidable opponent in the Hon. C. W. Dudley of Marlboro. At night there was a grand fancy ball in the courtroom. . . .

JUHL

SUMTER, S. C., November 8

Col. C. W. Miller, a native of this district but now a resident at Marion, made a speech here on Monday last as a candidate to represent this congressional district in the next Congress. On Tuesday Hon. C. W. Dudley of Marlboro, another candidate for the same position, addressed the Sumter public. There are already four candidates in the field, and it is expected that one of them will be elected; and, if the railroads can get the successful candidate to Washington in time, it is hoped that he will be allowed to take his seat. . . .

The refugees from your city who have sojourned among us during the war are daily leaving us for Charleston. We are losing in this way, and you are gaining a number of substantial citizens; among them are the names of Dr. St. John Phillips, Capt. J. Dougherty, Messrs. Bernard and J. F. O'Neil, J. McKergan, J. F. Steinmeyer, and others.

The planters generally entertain but little faith in their ability to make a crop next year under the present system of labor. As to cotton, it is out of the question. The Negroes exhibit growing indisposition to work. What Judge [Francis H.] Wardlaw's new code will do, if the legislature adopts and the government allows it to be enforced, remains to be seen. But something must be done to enforce and secure regular, systematic, and reliable labor, or this fine country becomes a wilderness. The Negroes at present are in a very restless condition; groups of them are seen at our street corners unemployed, and the devil's workhouse (and idle mind) is in full blast.

JUHL

SUMTER, S. C., November 16

On Tuesday last, the 14th inst., a court of magistrates and freeholders was convened at this place for the trial of the case of the state *ex rel. Angus Chisolm* v. *Sophronia Brown*, tenant holding over landlord. The action was brought by the plaintiff to eject the defendant from premises now occupied by her in the town of Sumter. The court was organized (J. J. Fleming and I. N. Lenoir, magistrates presiding), a jury of twelve freeholders duly impanelled and sworn, and Col. J. D. Blanding appeared for the plaintiff and J. S. G. Richardson, Esq., for the defendant. The counsel for the plaintiff had opened the case and was proceeding to introduce evidence when the following note was handed in to the court:

I don't think Chisolm has taken the oath of allegiance. If not, he has no right to prosecute in any court in the United States.

(Signed) Whittier, Lt. Col.

Upon receipt of this note and before making the matter public, the magistrates called up the plaintiff's counsel and requested him to remove the difficulty by inviting his client to come forward and take the oath, which a magistrate is now authorized to administer. After conferring with his client, counsel addressed the court and, acknowledging that the plaintiff had not taken the oath and did not intend to take it, urged the magistrates to proceed with the trial. The court in giving its decision stated that the magistrates presiding claimed to be conscientious men, yet they had taken the oath; that the counsel representing both parties were conscientious men, yet they had taken the oath; that every freeholder on the jury was considered a conscientious man, and yet the entire jury had subscribed to the oath; the magistrates could see no reason why the plaintiff should virtually claim the sanction of the court to his avowed refusal on alleged conscientious grounds to comply with what the government required of all as a *sine qua non* to citizenship. In this decision both magistrates concurred; and they further stated that they could not regard this as a conflict between the civil and military authorities, as it was a point decided by the magistrates upon information given to them, which in their judgment disqualified the plaintiff from presenting the case. And, thereupon, they discharged the jury and ordered that the plaintiff pay the costs.

This brief report is sent to you from the fact that it involves a question which a civil court has been called upon to decide for the first time probably in this state since the war. And, whether the magistrates were right or wrong, it may be added that some of our first lawyers approve their decision, and jurors have said that if the decision had been otherwise, they would have left their seats. The court was neither interrupted nor dissolved by any order from the military commandant (as has been erroneously reported), but on the contrary has been indebted to the military authorities for the use of the provost judge's courtroom whenever requested. And, on this very occasion, that room was vacated by a court-martial in order to accommodate the civil court. . . .

JUHL

The great topic of interest now is the question of labor for another year, and to this end mass meetings have been held both of the planters and the freedmen in this and other districts. The planters have conferred together, in conjunction with the military authorities and the officers of the Freedmen's Bureau, and have agreed upon a form and the terms of contract for another year. And the freedmen have been addressed on their present condition and future prospects and especially as to their duty to themselves and to the country under the new dispensation. In Darlington, on the 18th inst., the planters adopted a form of contract which meets the approval of the bureau, and which seems to be unexceptionable, fair, and equitable to planter and laborer. And, on the day, General [W. P.] Richardson, commanding in eastern South Carolina, and the Reverend Mr. [Benjamin F.] Whittemore, the popular and able chaplain of the 30th Massachusetts, delivered addresses to the freedmen who were there assembled—addresses which were admirable in tone and spirit and precept, well timed and judicious, and which, if appreciated, must be followed by the happiest results. For the sake of the freedmen, the planters, and the country at large, we wish the same could be said of all the addresses which have been made to these people.

On Thursday there assembled in this place an immense throng of planters and freedmen. The planters assembled in the courthouse at 11 A.M. and organized with Col. John N. Frierson in the chair and Julius J. Fleming as secretary. The chairman opened the meeting with a very appropriate and eloquent address, and then successively introduced General R[ufus] Saxton, Reverend M[ansfield] French, and General Richardson who gave their views of the new system of labor, its operations on the Sea Islands and elsewhere, and predicted the happiest consequences to the planters themselves, if they would give it a fair trial and manage their laborers judiciously. Remarks were also made by Rev. H. D. Green, Judge Moses, and Col. J. D. Blanding, and a very able committee appointed to report on a form of contracts. That committee recommended the form adopted by the Darlington meeting, advising however, that in all cases where it was practicable, the system of "stated wages" be preferred to the pro rata of the crop.

When the committee retired, Hon. F. J. Moses was called for and in a brief but very handsome address thanked his constituents for the confidence with which they had continued him as their representative in the senate of the state for twenty-five years—a position which he was now obliged to vacate, owing to his elevation to the bench. His honor took occasion to impress the duty of hearty allegiance to the general government and animadverted upon the new code for the freedmen, which, he said, was an experiment to be tried, and—if it failed—it could be abrogated by another regular or called session of the legislature.[5]

Many prominent planters of Kershaw and Clarendon were present at this meeting, and among other distinguished gentlemen who seemed to take great interest in the proceedings was the Right Reverend Bishop [P. N.] Lynch.

It was estimated that there were several thousand freedmen in town. They were as a general thing a smiling face, and seemed in a state of hilarity and frolicksomeness. And, when at 2 P.M. they gathered around the liberty pole, beneath the flag which a gallant breeze unfurled in all its glory, it was a picture peculiar to the new era which has dawned upon us. They were addressed by General Saxton and the Reverend Mr. French—the speech of the former being judicious and

---

5. Fleming refers to the famous "Black Codes" passed by the 1865 session of the South Carolina legislature. His report of this meeting can be found in the *Sumter Watchman* (January 3, 1866). Fleming identifies French as an associate of the Freedmen's Bureau and states that the committee recommended hiring Negroes at stated wages of $40–$120 per annum.

appropriate, the speech of a dignified soldier and a sensible man; that of the latter, with some good things, contained expressions and sentiments calculated in no way to reflect credit on the speaker or to benefit his colored friends. At the risk of occurring Mr. French's displeasure, it may be remarked that the true friend of the black man will encourage in him no dreams which must end in disappointment, and which, while entertained, will make him dissatisfied with his present condition, and that it is in bad taste and worse policy to draw comparisons between the two races, reflecting invidiously upon the white man.

The day passed off quietly. A freedman was stabbed by a gentleman from the country, upon what provocation we have not heard—but is recovering. The party committing the assault has been bound over to answer.

On some few plantations, but very few, the freedmen have made contracts for next year. As a general thing, they appear very uncertain how to act or what to do. There is no doubt they have a lingering idea that they are yet to have land for themselves, and this may induce them to postpone any regular engagement for services, until the planters are seriously embarrassed and the prospect of the coming crop very much impaired.

Today is Christmas. It is the natal day of the Prince of Peace, and yet all the day the air has resounded with savage detonations of the villainous saltpetre crackers and squibs, and the schoolboys' cannon keep up the music; but in other respects we have quiet, thanks to the military order closing up the grog shops during the holidays.

It is understood that the district courts are not to go into operation until so ordered by the proclamation of the governor; and in the meantime the district judges draw no pay, a wise arrangement to save needless expense to the state, as it is quite likely the provost courts will retain jurisdiction in all cases of Negro litigation for some time to come.

JUHL

SUMTER, S. C., December 31

... In a previous letter, occasion was taken to refer in not very flattering terms to the speech delivered by Reverend Mansfield French to the freedmen of Sumter. It is probably due to that gentleman—it certainly is due to the public, both North and South—that something more should be said in the same connection. It appears that on the 19th of November last a meeting of the Freedmen's Aid Commission was held in the city of New York.... Then and there appeared Mr. French who created a perfect wail among the audience by representing that condition of the colored people in lower and Sea Island Carolina and Georgia as "miserable in the extreme" and their prospect for the coming winter as "mournful beyond expression." "According to the opinion of the military officers of that department and his own, after all has been done that could be by the government and the various benevolent societies, without doubt *thirty thousand must die of disease, starvation, and cold* before March next." (The italics are not ours.) This was what was said to a northern audience....

But in Sumter, to the planters and the freedmen alike, he tells no such tale of horror and woe. On the contrary he represented the condition of the Negro since emancipation as vastly improved; wherever he had been they were doing well, especially so in this state. He represented the Sea Islands as an El Dorado; said that the freedmen had their farms, their comfortable homes, their schools and churches; that they were already worth from two hundred to five thousand dollars each; and, to show the Negroes how prosperous were their brethren who were farming on their own hook, he adduced an instance in which certain freedmen had by subscription furnished a full suit of clothes to their former master who had appeared among them sadly impoverished, all tattered, ragged, and torn. Not a word about suffering or want among the freedmen did we hear from him; but very many gilded pictures were held up to view, which we thought at the time were not worth a ——— doughnut. Now how can Mr. French reconcile his statements to a northern audience with his speech to the Sumter planters and freedmen? And how can truthful, honest, and honorable officers longer allow him the sanction of their names and association?

The fact is, the Negro wants no such guide or teacher. He has indeed an ebony skin, and he needs improvement and instruction, and will in time receive both; but he is rapidly come to the conclusion that his best friends are those who have known him since childhood, who cared for and watched over him in his bondage, and will cheerfully lend him a helping hand now that he is free. The Negroes should be well cared for. It should not be forgotten that during the war when the white men were absent in the army and none but the women and children left at home, they were orderly and obedient, making the crops as usual and working cheerfully on the fortifications, and in many cases attending to their masters through the roughest campaigns with unswerving fidelity.

And, since their emancipation, considering their ignorance and the sudden change in their political status and the very many agencies brought to bear upon them, after infusing poison where they required wholesome aliment, they have behaved in a manner justifying the liveliest hopes of their future usefulness and success. And it is hoped and believed that in a very short time the mass of this population will be satisfactorily settled, either in farming for themselves (for some planters have already furnished them with land, stock, and implements to do so, for a share of what they make) or as hired laborers for the year under the contract system. And your correspondent believes that the less is done in the way of special legislation for these people, either by Congress or the state, the better it will be for them and the country. They are free, and if labor is left to regulate itself all will be well.

It is apprehended that much of the work of the late legislature will have to be undone or done over. The criminal law as amended is emphatically a bloody code. To make a larceny, where a bale of cotton or a horse is stolen, a capital felony without benefit of clergy is to insure the acquittal of everyone arraigned on such an indictment. The juries will not convict where death is the penalty for such offences. . . . Besides, there are features in both the freedman's code and the criminal law as amended calculated to draw upon us fresh and fierce broadsides from the unfriendly majority which now controls Congress. Hence, many believe that under the circumstances it would have been better to have made no such ostentatious legal and judicial distinction between the races, but to have slightly modified the common law and left that law to cover and regulate the entire population. This would have been less expensive and onerous to the people and certainly less offensive to those whose renewed antagonism it were folly to invoke.

JUHL

1866

DURING THIS YEAR Juhl was somewhat less confident about the future
of the South. He had good reason to be concerned. The system of contract labor tried for the first time on a wide scale suited no one. Negroes
often failed to understand the terms, and planters frequently broke these
agreements as soon as the heaviest work of the season was completed. In
addition crops proved to be poor. Burglaries, outrages, disorders of all
sorts became more common. The attitude of the Radicals of the North,
the meddling interference of Freedmen's Bureau agents, and the exodus
of leading citizens to other regions did little to inspire confidence.

It is in the midst of this chaos, anarchy, and starvation—apparently
some Southerners of both races actually did go hungry during 1866—
that Julius J. Fleming began to give voice to concepts which a later
generation would point to as the revolutionary ideas of a "New South."
On March 8 he chided the South for importing hay and corn from other
sections of the nation, urged local planters to abandon their one-crop
economy and become more self-sufficient. In this same letter Juhl berat-
ed northern newsmen who continued to picture the South as a land in
rebellion. As long as such reports were current it would be impossible to
attract northern capital. A few days later, turning his attention to the
Negro, Juhl pointed out that the only way to still "the voice of the
phrenzied, fanatic, and crazy Radical" was to give the freedman equal
justice and leveled a scornful finger at South Carolina legislators who
continue to pass specific and distinct laws for the black man. If the
freedman is to be given the vote, he must be educated. If Yankee school
teachers wanted to do the job, so much the better. After all, only a few
years ago leading citizens of the South were hiring northern tutors for
their own families. And, according to Juhl, "some of the most distinguished southern gentlemen" were quietly encouraging northern volunteer efforts to establish Negro schools. On September 11 Juhl had this
penetrating comment concerning the importance of this matter in
southern life:

1866   They [the Negroes] form a large and important part of the state. Are jails cheaper than school houses? Is ignorance the prolific source of crime? While learning may have been prudently debarred the slave, will it be wise to neglect and discourage this in the freedman? The subject is suggestive of much more than is here expressed and is worthy the statesman's attention. These people are our neighbors, and for years will doubtless be found in our midst; and, if we allow them to create around them[selves] a malarious and tainted atmosphere, the infection will spread to our own habitations. Hence, to improve their condition is to benefit ourselves. But, of this, more anon.

SUMTER, S. C., January 2

... A stranger who visited our town on yesterday, which happened to be the long-looked-for first of January, would have thought that our black population was most horribly demoralized. From an early hour the freedmen were seen coming in by every road from the country, some of them from great distances, until Main Street became a perfect sea of ebony faces, and the citizen who ventured abroad found great difficulty in navigating a passage. In this great gathering there was scarcely a woman or child to be seen, but it was estimated that nearly every black male adult in the district was present. As they brought nothing in to sell and exhibited no disposition to purchase, and as there was no speech to be delivered, it was somewhat difficult to imagine the cause of such an assemblage on such an exceedingly unpleasant day. Conversing with many of the more intelligent among them, it became obvious to us that the mass of the freedmen were exceedingly dissatisfied with the terms proposed to them for the present year. They alleged that the proportion (one-third) of the crop to be allotted to them was entirely inadequate to their wants, but if one-half was allowed, they would work as they had never worked before. Others wanted land on which to farm for themselves, paying the owner of the soil a fair proportion of the crop. After a free interchange of views among themselves and some very wholesome counsel from the military authorities, the dark billows of this human tide began to ebb, and by sundown the town was left to quiet and its rightful inhabitants. There was no disorder—no indications of turbulence.

With reference to their complaints: a planter informs me that he has contracted with twelve hands, and among these he will divide one-third of his crop ready for market. That this arrangement will give to each of them, at a low estimate, one bale of cotton (one hundred lbs. worth now two hundred dollars), from twenty-five to fifty bushels of corn, besides potatoes, peas, etc. He also says that other planters, proverbially more successful, will do more than this, and of course the more that is made, the richer the return to the laborer. Now with this statement, which is in every way reliable, it would appear that the conditions of the contract agreed upon generally in the middle country are equitable enough, unless an extraordinary bill of discount for expenses is brought against the laborer at the end of the year. In justice to the planters it should be added that some of them have cheerfully agreed to give one-half, and in some cases the freedmen have been established on lands where, without oversight, they are to farm for themselves, paying the rental with a part of the crop.

That this plan, which is so popular among the freedmen, has not been more generally adopted, is owing to the fact that it would involve the abandonment on the part of the planters themselves of their time-honored pursuits, leaving the entire area of arable lands in the hands of those whose undirected and uncontrolled energies might not be successfully applied to their culture. Enough, however, is certainly being done in this direction to fairly test the question whether or not the freedman, when thrown on his own resources, with land and everything furnished, is capable of such persistent industry as is necessary to insure success. And it might be considered as closely verging upon political folly to try the experiment upon any very extensive scale, at least for the present. Especially is this to be deprecated by those who like to hear favorable reports "from the land of cotton," and who know the importance to the South and the nation of a full crop the present year. In some things it is best to "hasten slowly," and this is doubtless one of them.

No class of people seems likely to be more benefited by the emancipation of the Negroes than the white mechanics. Some of them have said that they formerly desired (but in vain) legislative interference to save them from ruinous slave competition. But now they ask no favors, having full conviction that where all is free labor the white man's energy and superior skill must meet their merited patronage and appropriate reward. . . .

JUHL

SUMTER, S. C., January 5

. . . The first of May in New York might present some feeble picture of what is now transpiring among the freedmen of this country. A directory which might have correctly located them one month ago would scarcely enable you to find one of them now. Almost, if not quite, universally they have left their old plantations and secured new places, conceiving that their changed condition demanded a change in domicile and another field of labor. In all this they may be acting wisely, at least there are many planters who advocate and encourage the movement and believe it to be the best for both parties. These gentlemen exhibit a heroism which should at least command the respect and sympathy of the nation. As a class they were, of course, opposed to emancipation and never have believed that cotton could be raised profitably with free black labor. And yet they have submitted with a better grace to the loss of their slaves and the consequent revolution in labor, with all its present and prospective impoverishment, than did the English and New England handloom weavers to the introduction of steam and its laborsaving machinery. . . .

Many of our planters will probably run into the old error of planting too much cotton. Before the war they confessed their mistake in devoting all their best lands to its culture, to the fatal neglect of stock and the cereals. And yet they cling to the cotton as Burns did to his muse, though it makes them poor and keeps them so.

JUHL

Sumter, S. C., January 18

War depopulates, but the return of peace is attended with the usual arrangements for repairing the waste of the human material. Such is at least the case in this country judging from the number of matrimonial alliances recently consummated. Some of these have attracted unusual interest from the fact that they were celebrated in the churches—a circumstance which gives many an opportunity of attending who never could avail themselves of such a privilege if they waited for the formality of an invitation, and thereby insures a larger audience than could be possibly accommodated at a private house. In recent cases in this town, the parties have all been young, the brides beautiful and beautifully adorned, the grooms young men who fought gallantly in the late war and whose wounds attest their merit as soldiers in the southern armies, the "waiters," six bridesmaids, and an equal number of groomsmen appropriately costumed, these all arranged in front of the pulpit or altar, the minister performing the ceremony (perhaps joyous visions of the fee looming up before him), and the church well filled with sympathizing spectators (perhaps many of them wishing that his or her turn would come next); all these make a very interesting picture which reports say will probably be very often presented to the Sumter public during the present year. A pun may not be inadmissable—a pun may not be intended—but the remark may be ventured that the prevailing spirit at this time is in favor of *Union;* and, if that spirit is defeated by a congressional majority in the matter of states, it will not be in matters matrimonial—"the ladies go for Union to a man," and the soldier "hails with joy the cry, to arms! . . . "

A great change has come over the freedmen since the Christmas holidays. They very generously evince a willingness to work and are making arrangements to do so. Robberies in town and country are indeed rather frequent, but they may improve and do better. It is devoutly hoped that they may prove steady and faithful to their work, for, if the waste land of the world makes it picturesque, the waste labor makes it hideous.

The business of the town is in a thriving condition. Our stores are well supplied with all kinds of goods, and it is quite refreshing to examine their stock, provided one does not imbibe. If he does imbibe or is inclined thereto, it were better for him to keep in the suburbs. Certain it is that on Main Street you can buy anything from a candle to a coffin with cradles and whiskey, all along the route, and on Liberty (Cross Street) there are bakeries and barber shops and almost everything else from a wedding ring to a widow's cap.

Cotton is brisk and continues to be brought in. We can hardly imagine where it comes from, but the supply seems exhaustless. It is estimated that there are still two million bales in the South, and *De Bow's Review* is given as authority for the statement.

JUHL

SUMTER, S. C., January 22

"No! the Negro will not work. As a freedman he will inevitably indulge in idleness and sloth. He will steal, sir, and your barn and smokehouse and stock must suffer, for he must live, and if he doesn't work for bread he will steal it. Look, sir, at the West Indies and the various appanages of the British crown washed by the Caribbean Sea. See what ruin emancipation brought on that paradise of the tropics. And such will be our fate. The government has ruined us. It has turned loose upon the country millions of once useful laborers to starve themselves and to starve us. Sir, it is impossible with such a system to make cotton—we will hardly make bread."

"My dear sir, you are despondent. Believe me, the Negro will work, and cotton and bread both will be made. You should regard the South and the West Indies not in comparison, but in contrast. They are altogether different—soil, climate, productions, government, and people. The southern freedman is a different and superior man to his West Indian brother. He is more intelligent, more advanced in civilization, more energetic in every way. He has been accustomed to a more intimate association with the white race and has lost much of Africa in the engrafted principles of social and religious order which time and contact have effectually sealed. As a class they will disappoint you. Of course there will be many exceptions, and idle, vagrant Negroes will be seen. But the same may be said of our own race. Some of the laziest specimens of humanity I have ever seen were as white as either you or I."

But the shrill whistle of the engine reminded us that we were approaching our station, and, reluctantly leaving the two intelligent gentlemen to continue the discussion, a step from the platform placed us once more in the companionship of our own thoughts and the train rushed on.

It seems to be a conceded fact that in all countries where slavery has existed and been abolished the great difficulty in the way of improvement has been the very subject of labor. Those just ushered into the new estate can scarcely reconcile the idea of freedom with the idea of hard work. Some change from former life is so apt to be insisted on. And hence the freedmen "wish to work on their own land, if they work at all; and to be their own masters; to grow their own crops, be they ever so small; and to sit beneath their own vine, be the shade ever so limited." And unhappily for us, the most notable precedents which spring fresh to mind are precisely those less calculated to inspire hope—are precisely those in which "the struggle has produced idleness and sensuality, rather than prosperity and civilization."

In this district the freedmen will have a fair showing, as nearly all the planters have decided to depend on their labor, at least for the present. On some plantations, however, in the Mechanicsville neighborhood, and perhaps elsewhere, white labor is being introduced, and already a number of immigrants have arrived under contracts made with them in New York.

It is predicted that the Negroes will rapidly perish "by disease or the vices to which they are exposed." Heretofore they have been measurably free from eroding cares and anxious responsibilities. They could literally "take no thought for the morrow," as to what they should eat, or what they should drink, or wherewithal they should be clothed. But with freedom they became suddenly invested with those anxieties for which they are by temperament and education entirely unprepared. And as "care killed the cat," it may well have the same effect on them. Hon. John Bell of Tennessee in a recent letter says: "We may reasonably conjecture that within the next decade or ten years two and a half millions will have perished, and in the next succeeding decade, not more than half a million will survive." If this appalling prophecy should be realized, the South cannot too earnestly address itself to the encouragement of white immigration at once.

The country has long suffered from the unavoidable suspension of the courts. Crimes have been committed, but the offenders, although arrested and bound over to answer, have remained for years unwhipt of justice. Such will probably soon have an opportunity of passing through "the mill.". . . This will be gratifying intelligence, no doubt, to many who for years past have been losing cattle, hogs, and other property, and yet have thus far had no redress.

JUHL

SUMTER, S. C., January 26

. . . Major Lawrence of the United States Army, and now connected with the Freedmen's Bureau, writes from Fayetteville, North Carolina, December 14, 1865: "These people (the Negroes) must be allowed their civil rights: to sue and be sued and to testify in courts, but nineteen in twenty are no more fit for the political responsibilities and duties of a citizen than my horses." Perhaps when the Congressional Committee of Fifteen makes its contemplated visit of inspection South, it may reach the same conclusion.

The clamor for Negro suffrage at the South seems somewhat inconsistent, if not inexplicable, when it comes from a quarter where the privileges of the blacks are so essentially circumscribed. Here they are allowed a domicile, but in some of the northern states they are not; and, it is notorious that in schools, and carriages, and cars, and steamers, and hotels, all the distinction between the races is insisted on there which we have been accustomed to observe at the South. "Those whom God hath joined together let no man put asunder"; and those whom God hath separated by broad, distinct, and ineffaceable lines of distinction, let no man seek to amalgamate.

From all quarters encouraging reports are received as to readiness with which the freedmen have entered upon their work, mostly on the contract system. In this country extending from the Wateree River to the North Carolina line, it is believed that the planters have generally secured as many laborers as their lands require. And all the usual plantation work preparatory to planting is under full headway, the laborers cheerful and the planters hopeful. Step by step the system will be watched, and it will be subject of profound gratulation if encouraging reports can continuously be made.

General Richardson, commanding eastern South Carolina, has recently visited many prominent points in his district, and his report accords fully with the foregoing. One remark he makes cannot be too highly appreciated: "The quiet and orderly conduct of the people throughout the district, in the absence of the usual restraints of civil law, is truly astonishing. The roads are as safe for travelers by night or day, in any part of the district, as in any portion of the country, either North or South. . . . "

The 30th Massachusetts still has its headquarters at this place, although detachments from this command are on duty at Manning,

Cheraw, Camden, and perhaps other points. The men are comfortably camped in the suburbs and have no greater enemy with which to contend than ennui, the usual attendant of garrison life. Several members of the regiment have taken themselves wives in this town or vicinity and thereby may indicate a purpose to settle here permanently after their discharge from service. . . .

JUHL

SUMTER, S. C., January 29

. . . There is one great difficulty in the way of the country's hope and the freedmen's success: it is the idea which has been insidiously and sedulously instilled into the blacks that the government would give them lands and that each family should have its freehold possession—an idea which the military authorities have earnestly endeavored to remove, but which still pervades the mass and is cherished with a tenacity which nothing can overcome. To be an estated man is at present the height of the freedman's ambition—an ambition which Radical legislation seems disposed to gratify. If Congress persists in surrendering to them the Sea Islands and rice lands—the cream of the state—it will not only inflict irreparable injury upon individuals and the commonwealth to the full value of the estates involved, but it will by that one act give a galvanic shock to the entire labor system of the interior. It is yet an open question whether such a gift on the part of the government, whether for three years or in fee simple, would be a blessing to the recipients. Travelers—and only such travelers as are notoriously antislavery are referred to—tell us that the freeholding Negroes in Guiana and elsewhere "do not appear to answer." They quarrel about the division of the land, and, when this difficulty is settled by government interference, they utterly fail of success for the want of effort for the common good. . . .

As a faithful chronicler of the times, I am sorry to say that the close

73

of January finds the contract system sadly out of gear. As mentioned before, the planters found no difficulty in obtaining all the hands they required, and the written instrument of agreement was duly approved, signed, witnessed, and paid for. But already the freedmen have commenced deserting in squads of five or ten at a time, and some of the most humane and best-provided planters in Salem and Claremont are left with scarcely force enough to feed their stock and are now engaged hunting up another supply of laborers, who, when obtained, will probably play the same role. It may be well that this infraction of agreement has commenced so early in the season, as it will give the authorities time to adopt such measures as they may deem proper to arrest the evil—an evil which, if unchecked, will inevitably render hopeless any attempt to cultivate the lands with the present system of labor and lead to great want and suffering among the freedmen themselves.[1]

JUHL

SUMTER, S. C., February 1

. . . The return of peace has given a fresh impetus to the cause of education, and books have taken the place of bayonets, and satchels are carried instead of swords. In this town there are twelve schools— some of them of a high grade where young ladies are taught every accomplishment and young men are prepared for college. With this fact in view, may we not claim for Sumter the dignity of a university with its twelve professorships and schools under the same corporation of two miles square? The sentence with which this paragraph opens may be construed literally; for, among our teachers and their pupils

1. In the *Sumter Watchman* (January 31, 1866) Colonel Whittier warned against "enticing" freedmen from plantations where they have contracted to work, cautioning that such action was a "gross" offense and would be punished. In the next issue (February 7) General Richardson offered army provisions to planters who needed them for their freedmen—up to thirty days' food per man at cost.

alike may be found those who twelve months ago were in the trenches or on the weary march.

The *Watchman* makes its appearance this week considerably enlarged and improved in matter and appearance. . . . It is now published by Gilbert and [T. E.] Flowers, the former being its editor and the latter an excellent practical printer. It is in its sixteenth volume. Its publishers served in the artillery during the war, and its editor has since been rewarded by the people of the district with a seat in the legislature.

On the floor of Congress it continues to be asserted that the loyalty of the South is assumed and unreliable. That this is not true is somewhat remarkable, considering the persistent hostility and studied indignities shown towards us by the ruling majority. A course which would alienate and drive to madness and desperation almost any other people, it is hoped will have no other effect at the South than to fortify and confirm her people in that heroic endurance which calmly bides its time and at last takes hold on victory. Fiery impetuosity has long been our sectional characteristic—let nothing induce our people, at this juncture, to indulge in its exhibition.

JUHL

SUMTER, S. C., February 9

. . . Under the admirable administration of Col. F. H. Whittier, commanding this subdistrict, the labor of this country is being well regulated and judiciously controlled. Recent orders from his headquarters are calculated to enforce and secure fidelity to engagements voluntarily assumed, and the planters certainly feel more confidence and encouragement when such an authority stands ready to enforce obedience to contracts equitably made and properly approved.

The Right Way is the name of a paper published in Boston by G. L.

Stearns. Fifty-six thousand copies are sent weekly "free of all charge and postage paid" to persons all over the country whose address the generous publisher can obtain. Its motto is "Thou shalt love thy neighbor as thyself." Its object: to show "the utter unfitness of these (southern) states for admission to power in the Union they so lately sought to destroy and the extreme peril of this admission, at least without guarantees far beyond any which we have yet obtained." Its columns are filled with blasphemy and falsehood, and, although flying the golden rule at the masthead, the sheet, as a whole, is strongly redolent of sulphur and irresistibly suggestive of a place where temperature is unfavorable to congelation and water is not allowed.

Every wide-awake insurance company would consider any house in which its editor lives as "extrahazardous," and no man in his senses would venture to approach him with a lighted segar. It is annoying to have such a paper thrust upon the public. It is furnished gratuitously, it is true, but one does not like to have his house fumigated with brimstone or infested with polecats, even though it is done without charge.

JUHL

SUMTER, S. C., February 27

It is maintained in Washington that there is a reaction in public sentiment at the South, and in this the keen penetration of the government is not entirely at fault. The prompt and general acquiescence of the people in the result of the war and the earnest desire so sincerely evinced everywhere for the restoration of harmony and union has been followed by a course of Radical legislation calculated to wound and alienate almost any people. And yet our citizens are unquestionably loyal and true to the oath of allegiance to which they have subscribed, although they cannot easily discover wherein said oath has conferred any special benefits upon them. Taxation without representation, the suspension of the habeas corpus, and the prevalence of martial law in a time of peace were once thought repugnant to the Constitution and an unlawful invasion of popular rights, and no doubt the distinguished and patriotic statesman who presides over the Republic thinks so still, and perhaps the nation at large will ultimately agree with him and remove the burdens which now rest like an incubus upon the struggling energies of a suffering country. At least such is our hope.

But "where ignorance is bliss 'tis folly to be wise," and while the earnest student of our political situation is oftentimes most sadly depressed, it is comfortable to know that there are those among us who can afford to be jolly in spite of the times and whose spirits rise in proportion as social disorders multiply. Chief among this class may be mentioned old Shady, a notable freedman of this town, who in the dark days of bondage was attached to an estate beyond Turkey Creek, where he occasionally employed his time in making tar. Since emancipation he has become quite a character and holds a prominent place among the existing institutions of this honored corporation, cultivating music, in which he has become quite proficient, and giving examples of elocution and rhetoric which are certainly not to be found in books.

On the 22nd (a day which it has not been customary to celebrate outside of the large cities) our hero succeeded in running the flag to the head of the staff; and then, with book under his arm and bugle in hand, he honored the occasion by perambulating the streets and saluting with stage-horn music. We tried in vain to make out the tune; it may have been "Hail Columbia," "Yankee Doodle," or something of that loyal style, but if so it was so jumbled up with shakes and patriotic variations that it seemed very much like a mixture on the whole of the state of the Union. His venerable head was covered on the occasion with a veritable white beaver, which gave him a classic resemblance to Horace Greeley; and it was at once rumored on

Change Street that he had abandoned the Black Republican party and had become a head supporter of the white!

A heavy business is being done by our merchants. Stores are numerous and well stocked, and some of them have branch establishments in the country. Cotton and greenbacks are kept in motion, and a very handsome steam mill in the southeastern suburb converts corn into meal, grist, or horse feed with magical rapidity and will ere long have its powers applied to the no less important business of supplying the community with lumber. From all which you may infer that Sumter is on rising ground, although the sidewalks do not indicate it in wet weather. . . .

Mail contractors, mail agents, and qualified and paid postmasters continue among our forfeited blessings. Prominent places on the lines of railway or occupied by garrisons have the benefit of the military carriers, but a large part of the population remain without any mail facilities. This state of things must seriously affect the circulation of the district papers and injure them almost fatally as an advertising medium. Unlike the metropolitan journals, their circulation is strictly confined to the section where published and must be seriously circumscribed by the nonresumption of the country mails. And even the circulation of the *Courier*—large as it already is in this country—would be very much increased by the restoration of our former facilities, giving the planters regular mail communication.

Reports from the plantations are generally encouraging. Sometimes the indentured labor deserts his employer or throws other embarrassments in the way of the planter, but upon the whole the contract system may be considered successful thus far. Numbers of discharged colored soldiers have recently been added to our population; but, although many of them foolishly invested their funds in firearms and some of them have acted rudely, no case of serious disorder has yet been reported, and they will doubtless, from necessity, soon be peacefully and profitably employed. Many of their former owners are still their best friends; and, if extraneous influences are withdrawn, both classes will prosper.

Dr. Wiley McKain, a gentleman of large and influential family connections, died at his plantation near Mechanicsville on Wednesday last.

The early flowers, just blushing into existence, and the putting forth of the tender buds herald the coming spring. The fruit trees are not yet in bloom—a decidedly encouraging fact.

JUHL

SUMTER, S. C., March 8

Enough has already appeared in the massive columns of the *Courier*, vindicatory of the southern people, to correct many of the misrepresentations which have been assiduously circulated against us. And some slanders have been in this way so effectually nailed to the counter that one would suppose they never more could be circulated to our injury. And yet, in looking over a file of northern papers, it is impossible to resist the conclusion that in some places we are still regarded as semibarbarous, that ruffians abound in this country, and the lawless spirit of the people is only restrained by the presence of the military, and that the removal of the latter would be at once the signal for a reign of violence and outrage. Such reports not only do us a great wrong, but inflict upon us material injury. They discourage investments in a country which only requires capital and energy to develop its resources and enrich the world with its products, and they turn back the tide of immigration which the South so earnestly invites to furnish backbone and muscle to her struggling energies.

Now it is a notorious fact that since the cessation of hostilities the military forces of the United States have occupied this country, and it is an equally notorious fact that they have met with no resistance on the part of our citizens. While, from the circumstances of the case, an occasional collision would have seemed almost inevitable, quiet and order have prevailed, and the soldier and citizen can safely travel unarmed and unattended in any part of this country. An unarmed private, acting under authority, can make an arrest either of person or property with as little risk as an officer of rank supported by fifty muskets. Arms and ammunition are accessible to all and in the actual possession of many of the blacks as well as the white population, and yet the darker crimes are unknown among us, and on all our highways and byways the traveler meets with no let or hindrance, be the color of his face or of his clothing what it may. The commanding general of this part of the state has made a similar report after an extended tour of inspection—a report which does credit to its author and justice to our people. Ours is emphatically a law-abiding population—sustaining a position of humiliating embarrassment with a forbearance and respect for the laws which must eventually be recognized—and all the credit to which they are entitled should be cheerfully conceded as a matter of truth, right, and justice.

This much may be safely urged in vindication, especially of the white population of this country. And even the freedmen are orderly and well-behaved generally—although it must be admitted that larcenies are quite common, and burglaries are occasionally reported in which Negroes are the alleged offenders—but these offences are generally committed at night and are mostly confined to hen roosts and smokehouses.

The decline in cotton surprises no one, for there appears to be a great deal of it still in the country. A train of nine heavy wagons loaded with the staple rolling into town at one time would justify such a conclusion. The factories need certainly fear no stoppage for the want of the raw material. The prospect for a large crop the present year is encouraging. Plantation work progresses favorably, and from many neighborhoods highly flattering reports are received. A northern gentleman, who has taken a plantation on the Santee in the adjoining district of Clarendon, says the freedmen are working admirably in that section, and he entertains no fears of failure. He believes, however, that white labor would realize double the yield from the same area of land. It is very probable that European and northern farmers settling in this country would effect a very desirable revolution in its agricultural policy. They would plant cotton, it is true, inevitably and successfully plant cotton. But, they would first assign so much of land, manure, and labor to the culture of the cereals and would insure an abundance of provisions for all the occupants and dependents of the farm. Their cotton crop then would be clear gain— an annual net profit. This is the self-sustaining, home-enriching system by following which the farmer must be comfortable and independent. This is emphatically an agricultural country, and as such it appears almost a reproach to its planters that northern and eastern hay and western corn, at fabulous prices, are actually supporting the animals now ploughing the soil. Exhaustion caused by the late war may explain and excuse this the present year, but the same state of things existed before the war and may continue, although by common consent admitted to be a blunder.

The South invites immigration and offers its rich lands and admirable climate as inducements. And, if Congress will only endorse and carry out the president's views, the South will rejoice in a stable government affording every security to life, liberty, and property. In the meantime, many of our people are looking to Mexico and Brazil as their future homes—countries which doubtless possess many attractions, not the least among which may be considered the environment of unsolved political difficulties imperiling at every moment the stability of the empire and of estates acquired under it. But Americans are a migratory people, and constant motion prevents stagnation; and, while not unmindful of the question of profit, they sometimes dash into a venture for the venture's sake, even though it may fail to pay!

SUMTER, S. C., March 20

. . . Congress seems to have been impressed with the conviction that all its time and wisdom would be necessary to save the freedmen of the South from injustice and misrule, and such testimony as the Committee on Reconstruction has seen proper to publish would appear to justify this impression. Our own experience and observations are directly against any such conclusion, and our testimony, if credited, would relieve the national legislature of all further responsibility and concern in this direction. But in order to disarm those who would magnify our faults and rejoice in our continued humiliation, it is important that we as a people and a state should come up fairly and squarely to the requirements of the age. Place the black man in South Carolina on the same platform which he occupies in Pennsylvania, give him schools and churches of his own if he wants them, and encourage him in all his laudable undertakings and aspirations.

Let the same courts and the same laws take cognizance of crimes in both races alike, and justice be impartially meted out to all, and the voice of the frenzied fanatic and crazy Radical will have to find some other theme than the wrongs of the blacks. This will be giving substantial support to the president. This will create confusion in the ranks of his opponents, and will work no serious detriment to the commonwealth. South Carolina is the only state which has pursued a distinct legislation for the Negroes. No other state has followed her example. And it is very probable that the freedmen's code and district courts which thus far are entirely inoperative will be abolished when the next legislature meets. Otherwise, we shall be kept in the rear of our sister states, and our state laws and courts of sessions have no jurisdiction in cases where freedmen are parties litigant. Our ablest southern statesmen entertain and have made public the very views herein expressed. The prejudices of the past must be abandoned—they are the fungi of slavery; and, as the tempest has swept away the stem, the excrescence which grew from it must likewise disappear.

The discontinuance of martial law and the military courts would, on the supposition of equal rights, be also of decided benefit to the freedmen. For while at present in some cases, as in an action for debt against an employer, an idle, trifling freedman may recover from the provost more than he deserves and throw heavy costs upon the defendant, already victimized by the negligence and desertion of the plaintiff; yet, in other cases, the Negro does not recover in this court such damages as a southern jury would inevitably award. . . .

The present state of things is decidedly anomalous and hurtful; wheels within wheels, Blackstone hemmed with bayonets, and clients and counsel sadly bewildered. And while the country is quiet and the people are regarding themselves as models of patience and good citizenship, the mails bring us intelligence of the statements which continue to be officially made at Washington that we are disloyal and bitter in our hatred to the government. Can it be that the design of such misrepresentations is to make us what really at present we are not? The private madhouses of England contained many who were entirely sane when they entered those prisons, but when day after day they listened to the insulting assurances of their keepers in the face of the poor victim's solemn protest, and when day after day they were compelled to undergo the discipline of the madhouse, reason finally gave way and became a wreck, and they were mad indeed.

How many of the young and the gifted and the beautiful have thus been sacrificed by those anxious to control and enjoy their estates! Alas! Shall this be our history and our fate, to have the cry of "disloyal" repeated in defiance of all our protests until madness shall seize upon the brain, and every emotion of the heart and every purpose of the life develop an undissembled hatred as implacable and fearless as the present friendly and loyal avowals of the South are sincere?

Receipts of cotton light. Trade of the town continues well sustained. A gentleman who has recently visited Florence, Darlington, Cheraw, Chesterfield, and Bennettsville says Sumter has more trade than all those places combined. Our merchants are receiving large stocks from your city. After telegraphing to friends in Baltimore and New York and comparing figures, their decision is they can do better in Charleston this season than by going North. Merchants in the South generally may find it to their interest to make a note of this.

Juhl

Sumter, S. C., March 22

... Under the direction of the Freedmen's Bureau, schools and churches are being established at various points in this department for the blacks. The various denominations at the South cannot be charged with remissness or want of attention to the religious instruction of the Negroes, for, in addition to all the privileges which the white members enjoyed, there was one service on every Sabbath specially devoted to the colored people. But under the new regime the freedmen of the Methodist persuasion particularly exhibit an ambition to establish churches for their own race exclusively and have already taken the initiatory steps at this and some other points. Schools will also be connected with these establishments, and the *programme* includes a corps of northern teachers and preachers for their benefit.

Bishop [Osmond C.] Baker of the Northern Methodists will probably soon land in your city, whence he will make a tour through this part of the moral vineyard. The design seems to be to make these

African churches and schools missionary stations of the northern church—and, while recognizing the importance of educating the blacks with reference both to their own interests and the future welfare of this country, the expediency of the contemplated arrangement may well be doubted. The M. E. Church North cherishes no very fraternal feelings towards the Southern Methodists—and such sentiments are generally reciprocated; and, therefore that church seems less adapted than any other to this work. Its teachers and preachers will not, therefore, find a protracted residence in this country pleasant or agreeable, and any ostracism to which they might be socially subjected could easily be construed and reported as proofs of our hostility to the government and to the blacks. In this way, it would damage us politically, disturb the harmony and peace we now enjoy, and tend to perpetuate a sectional bitterness which the good men of every state would gladly see eradicated forever.

It is a fact, not likely soon to be forgotten, that in all the voluminous testimony before the Reconstruction Committee the most offensive and (as we think) untruthful allegations against the South were made by men rejoicing in the clerical prefix to their names. So much so, indeed, that the moment a witness is introduced as Reverend we prepare at once for a chapter of horrors. . . .

Private intelligence from Anderson C.H. states that at the recent session of the common pleas a man was convicted for horse-stealing (a capital felony by late statute) but strongly recommended to mercy. From the same reliable source we learn that the gangs of "Slicks" and "Regulators" disturbing that and the adjoining districts are mostly composed of men from other states, who have selected our upper districts as the theatre for their lawless performances.

JUHL

SUMTER, S. C., April 7

. . . Harmony Presbytery held its late session at Reedy Creek Church in Marion District. . . . This presbytery will have ten mission stations within its bounds supplied by an educated ministry for the special benefit of the colored people. With such an application of money and ministerial effort on the part of a single denomination within the contracted territorial limits of one presbytery, it is difficult to perceive upon what grounds any northern church or society can persist in regarding this as a missionary field demanding their ghostly intervention in behalf of the blacks. This is no Boo-rah-borrah-gah; and if it was, there are some persons who believe that it has within itself such means for its own enlightenment as the emancipated blacks of Jamaica have never received and the freedmen of the South do not require from their so-called friends abroad. . . . The late session possessed no unusual interest. Reedy Creek settlement is within a few miles of the North Carolina line—freedmen doing well in the field—a few cases of smallpox here and there through the country—and some difficulties between the Negroes and the late garrison of Marion village.

The Order of the Sons of Temperance is being revived here and elsewhere—a gratifying fact to every lover of peace and good order. A barkeeper not long since, having indulged rather freely in what he had so often furnished in customers, delivered an eloquent address on Main Street in which he declared "the grog-shop to be the antechamber of hell." From his long practice at the bar he claimed to be competent to decide the point and warned his hearers to "flee from the wrath to come." In vino veritas.

As the warm weather is now upon us, the people of this department would like to exercise the usual privilege of the season and dispense with fires. But even in this it seems they are not to be gratified. Fires in Marion—incendiary. Fires in Darlington, sweeping away much of that beautiful village—accidental in one instance, doubtful in another. Fire in Lynchburg, destroying a valuable store and its contents—clearly incendiary. Fires in Sumter, Spann's Mills seven miles from town; and last night, at eleven o'clock, an outbuilding on the premises of Mrs. Harvin in the western suburbs—clearly incendiary. The sufferers in some of these cases have little doubt as to the parties to whom they are indebted for these unwelcome attentions, but thus far there is no proof to convict. Such frequent fires in city and country would almost indicate a degree of concert amounting to conspiracy. Vigilance and the summary execution of the first offender whose guilt shall be clearly established may arrest the evil. . . .

JUHL

SUMTER, S. C., April 14

In reporting some observations on the course of the Radicals, a gentleman of great weight recently remarked, "After sitting for four years on a barrel of powder, I am not now to be scared by a squib; after having so many waves break over me, I am not now to be frightened by a ripple." A sentiment which may indicate a degree of sang froid and a philosophy very desirable at this time, and almost equaling in its nonchalance the reply of a skeletal antediluvian to Noah's refusal to take him on board, when standing up to his neck in water he shouted, "You may go to———(sea?) with your old hulk; it's only a shower!"

There may be something more than a squib or a ripple in that deluge of wrath which a Congress seems inclined to rain down upon this country. Ten righteous men would have saved the cities of the plains, but inversion of the rule is insisted on with regard to the South. During the war the press and politicians of the North persistently maintained that the Union element in all the seceding states was large and respectable and in many even had a large and respectable majority, that the people had no desire to abandon the old government, but

87

had been engineered into rebellion by the craftiness and ambition of their leaders. Now it is insisted that the masses are disloyal, bitter in their hostility, and anxious for another opportunity to plunge the whole country into revolution. Such consistency would be remarkable were it not that of late years that virtue has become so common among parties and politics that its exhibition even by Radicals and fanatics occasions no surprise.

Waving all claims to generosity or magnanimity on the part of the ruling power, the South would be amply satisfied with a dispensation of exact justice. And it cannot be regarded as just and right to construe the ill-temper, hasty language, or impudent conduct of a few individuals as the correct exposition of the sentiment of large communities or states. There are men in this country who always were Union men—who never wandered from their political faith, but tenaciously held fast to their confidence during the long and troublesome years of the war and openly avowed their preference for the old government and its Constitution. There are others who are still bitter in their feelings and although rendering political allegiance have no love for the Union nor wish for its continuance.

Both of these classes are small in numbers, however respectable by position. But the masses—the people at large—are such as went with the states into secession and war, but have acquiesced in the result with no lingering thought or desire to renew the experiment; and they are as good citizens today and as much entitled to the sheltering wings and friendly nod of the American eagle as any others, north, east, or west. Yet all these are included in the same category, visited with the same proscription, and wronged by the same hostile enactments; and to all of them alike, however variant in sentiment or feeling, is ruthlessly applied the radical apparatus of torture and death.

The [Civil Rights] Bill has passed. In vain the president's veto. In vain the voice of reason and the protest of patriotism. It has become a law—a law specially obnoxious and known to be so to the very states excluded from representation and allowed no voice in its passage. A measure pronounced by prominent statesmen to be most fatal to liberty and certainly most damaging to our great unrepresented southern domain. Its leading provisions regarded by learned jurists as directly at war with the first principles of this government, and likely so to be declared by the Supreme Court, the only remaining barrier to the progressive waves of fanaticism. But the Radical purpose has been consummated and becomes the law of the land.

This will necessitate additional state legislation. Our own legislature must undo much of its last winter's work. The freedmen's code and its adjunct machinery, considered by some at the time an abortion, must be decently buried. Under the high pressure now brought to bear, we have no option. No state law must be left on the statute which does not accord with the express will and decree of Congress. There must be no more class legislation, no discrimination in codes or courts on account of color, but equality before the law must be everywhere recognized. Georgia anticipated—looked ahead—and by wise legislation has met the difficulty; the provost courts are there discontinued and the jurisdiction of the state courts fully recognized over all classes and colors alike. The Civil Rights Bill finds but little to do in that state. Alex. Stephens pointed out the course, and the legislature followed his counsels and now realize their wisdom; and it devolves upon us to fall in promptly at the word of congressional command and occupy a similar platform. An extra session may be called for this purpose; but the governor may defer convening the legislature until he ascertains that the Rump Congress has reached its *ne plus ultra*, at least for the present year. . . .

JUHL

SUMTER, S. C., April 21

Rev. George Brown is dead. A long and mournful funeral cortege slowly advancing up Main Street a few days since was to many the first announcement of the fact. He has obeyed that fiat to which even "the tall, the wise, the reverend head" must bow. His educational advantages in early life were necessarily limited, and he made no pretensions to superior classical or theological attainments. But he generally followed the thread of his discourses and clothed his subjects in the most fitting attire. He was calm, grave, dignified, and practical, but sedulously avoided that exciting department of clerical practice. "Cut your coat according to your cloth" was a maxim which he not only professionally pressed upon others, but followed himself. For many years he sat upon the Board, of which he was a conspicuous member, his window looking down that great thoroughfare known as Liberty Street. A careful genealogical investigation establishes the gratifying fact that he bore no relationship, lineal or collateral, to John Brown of Harper's Ferry notoriety. His career was uneventful; he did nothing to make himself famous or infamous, and partly on this account and partly perhaps from the spread of the Radical contagion, the people here have a higher respect for black George than for white John. The latter may be celebrated in song, but was hung for his crimes. The former lived and died in peace and was followed to the grave by a very large procession of his clerical and lay brethren of the colored persuasion. *Obit*, April 18, A.D. 1866, and A.L., 1.[2]

The interests of this state are very materially affected by its legislation. It has often been considered a matter of small amount who were sent to Columbia, and personal consideration very generally decided the question. The vote has been given as a matter of compliment and with little or no regard to the qualifications necessary to meet such responsibilities. The result is seen in the past history and present

2. "A.L." probably can be interpreted as "After Lincoln."

condition of the state. All is confusion—a tangled mass of complications which it will require skillful manipulations to unravel. We are not abreast of the times; we are drifting leeward, while our associates in the sufferings of the past are working up to windward gaining an offing and have before them an opening sea. The Savannah River divides two states, and how do they compare? In Georgia the civil courts have undisturbed jurisdiction over all classes alike, and the usual remedies which the law provides are accessible to all, and the provost courts are discontinued. In this state there is no operative law for the freedmen, except that of the bureau, and a citizen may be arrested on information or complaint made and taken a hundred miles if there is no post nearer to answer before the provost. It is needless to enlarge upon the embarrassments which must be occasioned and already have been experienced by citizens upon accusations which could not be sustained, but which required their absence from home and neglect of business at a time when such absence was (especially in the case of planters) fatal to their interests. The two contiguous commonwealths are separated by something more than the Savannah River. The people begin to feel this. Where is the palmetto drifting? The question is pertinent. . . .

The 30th Massachusetts Regiment, which has held military occupation of this section for eight months past, is under marching orders.[3] Considering the very delicate duty assigned to these troops and the peculiar circumstances under which they came and have remained among us, they have done remarkably well. Some of the decisions of the provost courts have not met with outside approval, and military rule is not desirable in time of peace; but nowhere has better order been maintained, and the regiment is entitled to this endorsement. Col. F. H. Whittier, the commanding officer, has mani-

---

3. The *Sumter Watchman* (May 2, 1866) reported that "on Wednesday last" the regiment departed for Unionville.

fested a prudence, firmness and impartiality which insure him a successful administration. The regiment will occupy Union, Chester, and Spartanburg—the colonel's headquarters will be at the former place. What troops, if any, are to come here has not transpired.

Would it not be wisdom in the government to release Mr. Davis and allow him to join his family in Canada? Will not his continued imprisonment increase and strengthen a sympathy which attaches to misfortune, while his liberation would tend greatly to withdraw him from the public attention?

The railroad schedules are now admirably arranged to avoid connections. Going or coming, the traveler is allowed an abundance of time to become thoroughly acquainted with Florence and Kingville. Thirty hours is the mail time from your city to Sumter.

JUHL

SUMTER, S. C., April 30

Estimating the maximum cotton crop of the South, under the most favorable circumstances, at from 3 to 4 millions of bales and making a discount on those figures of from 50 to 65 percent and you have the probable yield for 1866. But why the discount?

The lands are not in the condition in which they were five years ago. They are more exhausted. During the war they were devoted to provisions and deprived of those foreign fertilizers with which they had formerly been supplied. . . .

The seed is generally defective and unreliable. This is no unimportant consideration. The anxiety evinced and the high prices paid by planters in former years for choice seed attest their conviction of its influence on the crop. They have not now even good seed of ordinary cotton, but are obliged to use such as has been greatly injured by age. By actual experiment a large percentage of it has lost the germ. And from this may result a bad stand, sickly plants, and multiplied chances for such diseases or other fatal visitants as . . . baffle the best skill of the planter and render fruitless all his toil.

The area in cotton is certainly less than formerly. For very many reasons there are thousands of acres which will not be planted this year, and but few plantations will be worked up to their highest capacity. And in some cases even the land which was devoted to cotton will now be applied to grain—especially where the cotton seed has proved defective and a stand has not been obtained.

The required labor is neither abundant nor as reliable as formerly. While some planters have obtained a full force, others have not been so fortunate, and cases have been reported (though rarely) of land owners who have utterly failed to secure a single laborer. Cases abound, however, of planters who, from choice, have declined employing more than from one-third to one-half as many hands as they formerly worked, and this will, of course, proportionately reduce their crops. And the labor now employed under the contract system is somewhat uncertain. Kind and experienced planters declare that while the freedmen generally behave well, they do not exhibit the energy or industry which would entitle them to rate as full hands; and, as the temperature rises with the advancing season, it is apprehended that in many places the crops will suffer from their indifference and neglect. However partially this may be realized, its effect will be to reduce the crops.

Congressional action, past and prospective, is also having a damaging influence on this great agricultural and commercial interest. A tax of two cents on the pound is a check on its production. An increase of this tax to five cents, as recommended and perhaps determined, will be still more fatal. . . .

The foregoing remarks apply to the entire cotton-growing region and are deduced from statements deemed accurate and trustworthy, as well as from personal observation. There are, doubtless, particular neighborhoods which may furnish exceptions to some one or all of them. But, in general, the facts assumed are believed to be correct, and if so the inference is plain.

In this section the present season has been very unfavorable for cotton. Heavy and continuous rains have interfered seriously with plantation work, and high winds have whipt the young and tender plants into a sickly condition which must injure and retard their growth. The last week in April was far more blustering than March.

Since the departure for the upper districts of the troops so long in garrison here, the usual good order has prevailed in our community. Our position is somewhat anomalous, but the good sense which seems to prevail among all classes will probably insure us a continuance of quiet. Occasionally an incident like the following occurs, suggesting the importance of the early reestablishment of civil law. An Irishman, living one mile from town and depending on a small farm and blacksmith shop for his support, while absent from home one day last week was robbed by a Negro man and woman in his employ, who, taking advantage of his absence, loaded a cart with sundry chattels to the said employer belonging, and with the only horse on the place incontinently decamped. We have heard of no efforts to arrest the fugitives and to recover the stolen property, other than a posted notice in rather rude chirography offering a reward of twenty dollars for the same.

The rapid decline in cotton has unpleasantly affected the planters who still have it on hand, having declined selling when the market was buoyant. The article will not now command more than one-half the prices ruling a few months ago. Eighteen to twenty-two note present extremes.

As an indication of how much our people suffer from the inattention of the government to the reopening of the post routes, the citizens of Camden pay one hundred dollars a month, in addition to regular postage, to get their mails from this point. Twelve hundred dollars a year by private subscription is a heavy tax on a small community for the performance of a service which properly appertains to the post office department. And this in our present impoverished condition. The same is true of other places. When will fall the last feather which is to break the camel's back? Or, when will dawn the bright and glorious day when heated passions of men shall subside to rest, and all the states be enfolded in one bond of Union knowing no North, South, East, or West in unfriendly political array, but the flag which protects and floats over our commerce will truly symbolize the government which first unfurled it to the breeze with its *e pluribus unum*, "distinct as the billows, yet one as the sea"?

JUHL

SUMTER, S. C., May 4

Sumter, with its floral wreaths and gush of merriment, is by no means an unpleasant place on the first of May. The air is laden with the delicious breath of a thousand flowers, and the dark shadows of anxious thought which wear so heavily on heart and brain are, for the time, dispelled by the contemplation of youthful loveliness in the rapture of careless happiness. Many parties may have honored the occasion and if all were as pleasant as the one given by Miss [C.] Morgan's school, they have no cause to regret the trouble incurred. In the immediate suburbs a grove of stately oaks sheltered the large assemblage of young ladies and children and teachers with their invited guests who witnessed the crowning of the beauteous May queen and all the ceremonies usual to such coronation. Not the least interesting part of the entertainment was the presentation of the rainbow photographed in lines of living beauty on the stage by a well-informed arch of little fairies who gracefully celebrated in mellifluous verse its varied hues and sacred mission. The long tables were bountifully supplied with such things as only a good caterer knows how to select and serve up, not excepting ice cream and other luxuries, and the company passed a most agreeable day without an accident to mar its enjoyment. . . .

The weather continues to be cool for the season, and reports just received from a number of plantations are very unfavorable. The cotton in many fields is a total failure and is being ploughed up and planted in grain. Much of the seed used has proved entirely worthless. In one field of forty acres there were not plants enough to make a good stand on an area of twenty feet square. And the effect of the unfriendly attitude which Congress assumes towards the South and its great agricultural interests is seen in the calmness and indifference with which the planter contemplates what, under a more equitable rule, they would regard as a calamity.

The recent arrival of an officer and ten men of the 15th Maine, who have established their quarters in this place, has thus far had no other results than the increase of our population to that extent. It is impossible to resist the conclusion that the government is needlessly expending a great deal of money in continuing military establishments where the civil law, if allowed, would be amply sufficient. And, of course, our people are not blind to the fact that such expenditures must be ultimately met out of the already depleted and well-nigh exhausted resources of the South.

JUHL

SUMTER, S. C., June 27

On Sunday, the 17th inst., the Reverend Mr. [H. H.] Corbett, a local Methodist preacher, officiated at the Spring Hill Church in the upper part of the district. The neighborhood has a large white population made up, for the most part, of poor but industrious, hard-working people. Very few of them have ever owned a slave. Topographically, the country in the vicinity is rolling and hilly—in all essential respects a continuation of the high hills of Santee. Agriculturally, the lands are poor and the crops generally light.

The house of worship occupied by the Spring Hill Methodists has no galleries, but the entire congregation occupy the same floor; the whites in front and to the right of the pulpit and the blacks to the left. On the day of the occurrence, while the minister was proceeding with the service, three Negro women left their own proper seats and, crossing the church, deliberately crowded into seats among the ladies.

A gentleman at once went to them, and after some time spent in remonstrances, succeeded in inducing them to return to their own side of the house. A Negro man in the congregation, seeing all this, left his seat and passing out at the side door came around to the front and, entering in a very bold and defiant manner, took a seat among the white men. It seemed evident to everyone that there was a design, a settled premeditated purpose to create a difficulty by asserting the right to violate all decorum and trample upon the order which has been observed in this church since its first establishment. But still the white congregation remained calm, no attempt was made to eject the offending Negroes by force, and from the most reliable sources it is clearly ascertained that no other language was employed than that of kind expostulation and remonstrance. This at length succeeded in inducing the freedman to leave his seat among the white men; but instead of quietly returning to his seat among those of his own color, he walked out and standing at the door indulged and vented his wrath in the most horrible blasphemies and abuse, maintaining his right to sit where he pleased and cursing the whole concern in terms and tones which effectually defeated all attempts at worship.

This in itself was a most grave offence against the law for the protection of churches and congregations engaged in worship, an offence for which a white man would be indicted and upon conviction be severely punished. But, with a forbearance which is almost inexplicable, no attempt was made to arrest, detain or punish the offender; but two men, Mr. Charles Britton and Mr. Corbett, leaving the house, addressed themselves in words of kind remonstrance to the belligerent freedman and after some time succeeded in restoring quiet. Scarcely, however, had this been done when another freedman, who was sitting at the root of a tree, a spectator and witness of what had passed, rising from his seat, advanced in a most menacing style towards young Britton, and with uplifted club in his right hand and his left hand concealed in his right breast, and saying, with an oath, "I am ready to meet you with any weapon," aimed a severe blow at Britton's head, which he received in full force on his left arm ... paralyzing that member. Whereupon ... Britton drew his pistol and fired. The Negro ran a few hundred yards to the office of Dr. Daniel Reynolds in front of which he fell and very soon expired.

Of course, this tragedy, however unavoidable it may be regarded, abruptly closed the services of the day, scattered the congregation like leaves before the tempest, and produced a feeling of uneasiness and regret which has not yet worn away. Britton at once rode to this place and stating the facts surrendered himself to Captain [M.] Boyce, then in command of this post. But, as the latter was about leaving to be mustered out, he conceived that he had no jurisdiction in the premises and turned him over to the civil authorities. If this arrangement had been undisturbed, he would have been tried at the fall term of the sessions with scarcely the shadow of a doubt as to what would be the jury's verdict, even though the victim of the homicide had been a white man. But a late military order from Columbia resumes martial control of the case, and the man-slayer must go to those headquarters where, no doubt, the evidence will fully substantiate the foregoing statement. And, as there will now be no jury in the case to be affected by it, there can be no impropriety in giving the facts as your correspondent has carefully collated them from sources worthy of absolute confidence.

It seems to be the unanimous opinion of the people that in all which preceded the dread catastrophe of the day the Negroes (first the women and then the men) were clearly and designedly the aggressors; a most unhappy fact, for however tolerant and even kindly disposed the white population may be, there is a point beyond which forbearance ceases to be a virtue and when that is reached outrage on one side must be attended with retribution on the other. Especially is this to be anticipated so long as the civil law is silent, and we remain, through all this rich and populous country of which this town is the grand business centre, without a garrison or even a provost court. When it is remembered that there is now no redress short of Columbia, and when the expense, fatigue, and inconvenience attending a journey there are considered, the temptation to settle disputes or to resent indignity and outrage on the spot is very strong and by some persons cannot be resisted.

Accordingly a detachment of regular U.S. Cavalry from Columbia has, this week, swooped down upon our district and been actively engaged arresting alleged offenders, white and black, and marching them off to Columbia. And such armed courtesies, rendered necessary by our present anomalous and wretched political condition, will be repeated time and again so long as any are found to violate the law and no local tribunal exists to adjust the damages.

It is worthy to remark that a night or two after the Springfield tragedy Corbett's kitchen, with hog pen attached, was set on fire and burnt to the ground; and the fire was raging with such fury when discovered that it was found impossible to save the hogs, and he lost them all. Being a poor man, he feels the loss severely.

Notwithstanding all these unfavorable reflective facts, as an indication of a forgiving charity ennobling its possessor, it is understood that Colonel Reynolds, a planter in the Spring Hill neighborhood, has, since the homicide of the freedman, given the Negroes land on which to build a church for themselves. An arrangement which will render it less likely that disturbances and collisions will occur in future, and one which, perhaps, will have to be adopted everywhere under the sudden bursting of freedom upon those who seem blinded by its blaze and whose untaught and unbalanced brains will lead them, if unrestrained, to intolerable excesses and ultimately to every species of degradation and disaster which can curse mankind. Hope looks for better things; may hope be realized.

JUHL

SUMTER, S. C., June 30

From the tower of Nickerson's Hotel, Columbia, a view is presented of our desolated capital which cannot be had at any other point. Looking to the north, east, and south, there is a sea of foliage beneath you interspersed with elegant private residences and massive public buildings; and this part of the city seems reposing in undisturbed beauty, retaining all its former attractiveness and looking as if war with its withering breath had never ploughed its way through these peaceful shades. Turning away, however, to the west balustrade and looking in the direction of the river, and the eye is pained and the heart grows sick. There may have been beauty there once, but it is gone; there were shade trees and shrubbery and the choicest exotics and all the sweet fragrance of flowers, but they are gone; the torch has done its work, and a vast area once beautified by all that wealth and taste could create is seen covered with crumbling walls and piles of rubbish and a forest of burnt chimneys and withered and decaying trees.

The opportunity of enjoying this view of Columbia and taking in at a glance all its beauty and its desolation is enough in itself to make Nickerson's Hotel a place of attraction to his guests. The tower is reached by an ascent so gradual and well arranged that even an invalid can visit it with little fatigue and no risk. A well-served table, attentive waiters, pleasant rooms, and a kind and accomplished host render this hotel the next thing to home. . . .

Main Street—the once great thoroughfare and business mart—is deserted. Its sidewalks are obstructed by huge mounds of bricks and mortar, and we watched with sympathizing interest some of the lovely houris of the place on their evening promenade as they pursued their serpentine course, alternating from the sidewalk to the middle of the street. The navigation is difficult and not without danger after dark. The stores and businesses, of course, are confined principally to the streets leading from Main to the river and a street running parallel with the west of Main Street. The people seem hopeful. They are displaying considerable energy in their efforts to recuperate and build up their broken fortunes, but long years will elapse before they recover from Sherman's desolating march and Columbia regains all its former loveliness and unaffected grandeur.

Such are some of the notes of your correspondent's sojourn in May last during the appeal court session in the wrecked and shattered city by the ever murmuring, rolling, rushing, ever beauteous Congaree.[4]

JUHL

SUMTER, S. C., July 4

A number of outrages have recently been committed in this district which are well calculated to take from us the good reputation we have heretofore enjoyed for obedience to the laws. And, in vindication of the white population, it should not be forgotten that when the military forces were withdrawn from this section we were left without the authority or power to interfere in the enforcement of law or in the punishment of offences in any case in which freedmen were involved; and where a people are thus rendered powerless, their own courts and laws denied jurisdiction and wrapped in a silence as profound as the grave, they cannot fairly be chargeable, as a people or as a community, with outrages committed by a few individuals, resulting almost inevitably from the wretched condition to which we have been re-

4. Court records reveal Julius was in Columbia to qualify as an attorney. He registered with the South Carolina Supreme Court on May 9, 1866.

duced—outrages which neither the people nor the civil courts of the country are allowed to investigate or punish.

Again, it is not to be denied that the Negroes who, while the garrison was here, behaved generally well and by their good conduct were rapidly gaining the approbation of the country, have since behaved badly in many instances in the rural districts and provoked results which otherwise would have been avoided. . . .

But, on the other hand, it is not pretended that equal provocation has been given in all cases in which offenders have been roughly handled. There is no doubt that in some cases deadly weapons have been used in punishing insolence or in attempts to enforce plantation or domestic discipline, in violation of the well-known sentiment as well as of the law of the land. And it is also probable that one or two persons in secluded neighborhoods may have resorted to punishments no longer allowed by the government. All this would be corrected by our own courts, if they were not denied the right to interfere. But, as it is, our people can only look on and regret what they cannot remedy.

In our goodly town, where the freedmen have been treated well and where they have generally behaved well, we have recently been brought to the verge of serious disturbances. On Saturday night last an intoxicated freedman and his friends had some difficulty with the police in which shots were exchanged, but no damage done. And, on Sunday night the freedmen's religious meeting near the depot had armed pickets, and at the close of the services some fifty or sixty Negroes with their guns and pistols marched up Main Street. No one interfered with or opposed them, and the night passed off quietly. But the act was justly considered as an unprovoked violation of the decorum and good order which have always prevailed in this community and as an open challenge and act of defiance to the authorities of the town. Nothing but the moderation and good sense of the citizens prevented a serious collision. The meetings which on every Sunday and repeatedly at night bring together large masses of these people have never in any way been disturbed. Their schools are largely attended, and there has been no impediment thrown in their way. And today they had a great celebration here in which a long procession of the scholars and teachers participated, marching the streets in perfect peace with no molestation whatever. With such a record in our favor it may well be claimed that our community has not deserved such a gratuitous insult as the marching of armed bands of belligerent Negroes through the heart of the town in the closing hours of a peaceful Sabbath day.

It is understood that tomorrow will bring a force of regulars here from Columbia who will no doubt terminate the reign of anarchy upon which we seemed to be rapidly entering and restore peace and quiet to our beautiful town. And here it is devoutly hoped they will be permitted to remain until the state is permitted to resume the control of its entire population. The short interregnum under which we have lived without the presence of the military on the one hand or civil law for the freedmen on the other has doubtless satisfied all parties that while our political *status* remains as it is, a garrison must be here.

A recent military order published in the *Courier* requiring contract laborers to remain on their plantations, establishing an island prison, and ordering the arrest of all vagrants was most imperatively demanded.[5] It would have been still better had it come sooner. Unless

5. This order, general order #9 from Lt. Col. H. W. Smith of the U.S. Army Headquarters, Charleston, can be found in the *Sumter News* (July 5, 1866). It makes these points: vagrancy and idleness among freedmen will not be tolerated. Freedmen deserting legal employment will be arrested and put to work on the roads, and plantation owners are urged to report freedmen not working according to their contracts. Children of such freedmen will be bound "to such persons as will take care of them and learn them the habits of industry." An island prison will be established for vagrants where they will work from "sunrise to sunset." Anyone selling liquor illegally to Negroes will be fined from twenty-five dollars to one hundred dollars. These regulations were to be read in all Negro churches in the coastal region.

such an order is enforced, starvation and ruin must ensue. The planters uniformly report that the freedmen are not doing more than half work and that in a very careless and unsatisfactory manner. The consequence is the crops are injured materially for the want of work. Reports from the largest plantations in the different parts of the district concur in limiting the cotton and provisions to half crop; and, if the present drought continues, it will be necessarily still less. In some neighborhoods the Negroes are committing sad depredations, killing the stock, even including milch cattle, breaking into barns and smoke houses, and carrying off everything eatable.

JUHL

SUMTER, S. C., July 17

. . . A circuit provost court has been in session here for a week or two past. It is composed of two citizens, one of Columbia, the other of this place, without the usual (and heretofore believed to be necessary) presence and presidency of an army officer.[6] The complaints brought in from the country have been numerous, and such as have received any attention have developed a state of things which must be corrected if this country would enjoy prosperity and peace. To say that dissatisfaction exists among the freedmen is to use a very mild term to express existing facts of the case. We have unquestionably reached a point in our history when neither wisdom nor good sense are evidenced by ignoring their [the Negroes'] importance as the laboring population of the country. And, whatever social distinctions exist between the two races, which may and doubtless will be perpetuated, emancipation has certainly changed their political condition, and Congress claims for them equality before the law. And this must not

6. A local provost court which met late in May was composed of Fleming and R. M. Thompson, Sumter magistrates, and Capt. M. Boyce, U.S. Army (*Sumter News,* June 7, 1866).

only be conceded and recognized in theory, but must be illustrated in the record and findings of the courts. Recent occurrences in some sections have inflicted a fatal blow upon the contract system. The freedmen regard it as a vehicle of injustice, and some other plan will have to be adopted to secure their labor for another year. And this conclusion may be noted as the result of innumerable unpleasant details whose introduction here neither time nor space will allow.

Aside from the alleged inefficiency of the labor, this year has been a most unfavorable one for the planter. The spring was unusually cold and wet, and the summer has brought us intensely hot weather with a drought which has well nigh destroyed the crops. There is much suffering among the inhabitants of the land, and there are hundreds of poor white persons in this district who have not tasted meat for months and who are dragging through the season on half rations of bread alone. Something will have to be done to relieve the distress of the country, and the state should interpose at once to save the destitute and starving poor. Occasional appeals are made from the pulpit and the press, and meetings are suggested and perhaps held to consider the subject, but it all amounts to nothing—the suffering still exists. A stronger and more general remedy is demanded, and this the state alone can supply by pledging the public credit as Georgia has done and importing large supplies of provisions for distribution among the needy.

There are thousands of acres in this country which will not produce the present season three bushels of corn to the acre, and much of that will be stolen from the fields before the time for harvesting arrives. To crown our happiness, the taxes—town, state, and federal—are heaped upon us. . . . Instead of foolishly persisting in keeping us *out of the Union* Congress had much better go to work to devise some plan to keep us *out of the grave*.

JUHL

Sumter, S. C., July 21

The extra court for Clarendon was held at Manning on Wednesday and Thursday of this week, Judge Aldrich presiding. The juries were discharged the first day, and the principal business consisted in the renewal of lost records. Manning is usually a very quiet village presenting little or no attraction to a stranger, but on this occasion was crowded with people from the surrounding country. With but few exceptions the planters gave very discouraging reports of the crops; and the drive of twenty miles from this place to the Clarendon court furnishes abundant ocular demonstration of the truth of their statements. . . . It is said and believed that if the fields had been properly worked, the hot weather would have been much less injurious. But all agree that the freedmen have been careless—doing less work and that less thoroughly than in former days—and that such labor cannot be relied upon for agricultural purposes on anything like a large scale. . . .

Our courthouse square is now occupied by the horses of the cavalry. The grand jury rooms are used as barracks for the men, and the shrill notes of the bugle remind us from time to time of the condition to which we are reduced—a condition which renders the presence of a garrison necessary to the peace and security of the country. And all this in the very land in which Sumter and Marion lived—where they performed their heroic achievements and where they made the name of Carolinian a synonym for valor, patriotism, and noble endurance. They were rebels, but they were successful, and even the starry flag twines round their memories and calls them its patriot heroes. They belonged to a rebellion into which our ancestors plunged—a rebellion which gave to the world a Washington—which gave to the family of nations this great republic—which gave to history some of its proudest names and most glowing pages. But that rebellion was successful.

Ours was a failure, and hence a thundering crime—to be forgiven? nevermore?

1866

July 23

JUHL

SUMTER, S. C., July 23

According to a previous announcement, a public meeting was held today at the courthouse to appoint delegates to the convention which is shortly to meet in Columbia to select a representation for the state in the approaching National Union Convention. Rev. H. D. Green was chairman and A. A. Gilbert, J. S. Richardson, Jr., and J. J. Fleming, secretaries. The following gentlemen were appointed delegates: J. N. Frierson, A. A. Gilbert, J. T. Green, J. S. Richardson, Jr., R. B. Cain, G. W. Cooper, T. M. Muldrow, Dr. J. M. Sanders, Dr. W. S. Burgess, Wm. Burrows, F. J. Moses, Jr., and J. W. Rembert.

The absence of all enthusiasm and the apathetic indifference manifested by our people in all matters relating to our national politics need occasion no surprise, for so many efforts have already been made to comply with the demands of Congress in order to conciliate the dominant party and so little success has attended these efforts that the people of this country are losing all faith in their power to effect in any way the ponderous machinery of a government which allows them no votes in its councils—and, yet the convention may do some good.

Refreshing rains have visited some parts of the districts, but they have been partial. The provost court has now an officer presiding, and the complaints of and against the freedmen are by no means diminishing. In this particular the market may be reported brisk, buoyant, lively, advancing.

JUHL

SUMTER, S. C., August 7

A barren, desolated, impoverished, uncultivated South! A fruitful, renovated, peaceful, prosperous, prolific South! How to escape the former condition and secure the latter is with us the great, vital, all-absorbing problem of the age. . . . Labor is unquestionably the keystone to the imposing arch of our agricultural and commercial strength and importance. Labor is the backbone of our country. Break this and our energies and strength are gone, and life itself must waste away. All pursuits, all interests are dependent upon it. . . .

Slavery is gone. It came under the condemnation of the civilized world, and the late war opened the prison doors and gave the captives liberty. As a system of labor it was tractable, easily managed, and profitable. Besides sugar, rice, tobacco, and provisions, it raised at the South from 2 to 4 million bales of cotton annually, according to the seasons. Can such crops be raised again?

Evidently white labor cannot accomplish this. It cannot cultivate the tide-swamp rice lands or the sugar plantations of the Southwest; and years must intervene before such an immigration can be secured as will supersede the necessity of Negro labor in the most healthy sections of the cotton region. The richest lands in this state will not suit the Celt or Saxon laborer, and the most we can reasonably anticipate from white immigration will be but a partial relief.

To the Negro, then, we must look for the cultivation of the soil. He is no longer a slave; Congress has made him a citizen, but he is no less destined to be a laborer. In the professions, in the counting house, in the workshops of the artisan, in the factory, and on the wave, the white man is his superior; but, in the field as a cultivator of the great southern staples, he is unequalled for skill and endurance. He is the laborer for the South, and it is useless at present to look for a substitute. As such, his importance to the state cannot be safely overlooked. His money value as a human chattel is indeed destroyed, but he represents the wealth of muscle and skill which made him, when a slave, invaluable to the planter and which—if properly directed and encouraged—will still make him an important contributor to the general prosperity.

Can this be done? It must be done. Admitting the experiment this year to be a partial failure and to have resulted in confirming the doubts of many as to the success of free labor—the freedmen are still among us; they constitute a large part of the population; no provision has been made for reducing their numbers by colonization or emigration on a large scale; they must live and to live they must labor—and how can they labor in this country as a race otherwise than as tillers of the soil for which they have been trained and for which business alone they are at present qualified?

This year can scarcely be considered a fair test. The country has not had the time to shake off the angry feelings inspired by war. The Negroes in the infancy of their freedom entered upon their work under contracts which they could not read and which they imperfectly understood; contracts, too, which betray more than the usual imperfection incident to all innovations upon long-established usage. The planters, irritated by defeat and heavy losses, were called on for the first time to recognize and manage as freedmen those whom they had always been accustomed to command as slaves. The seasons were remarkably unpropitious, and hence the pro rata of the crop allowed for the labor must create dissatisfaction from its very inadequacy— while the planter's share in many cases will not cover the outlay extended. And to this must be added the presence and sometimes injudicious interference of the [Freedmen's] Bureau or the military, with inflammatory visits from strolling preachers—all which conspired to make up a chapter of trials and embarrassments which neither race will desire to travel over again.

The contracts of 1866 will scarcely be renewed. The freedmen have serious objections to the terms and conditions which give rise to acts of injustice against which in many cases there is really no redress. And the difficulties and disabilities under which they labor in their attempts to obtain legal indemnity against a wrong does constitute another and very reasonable ground for complaint. All which will be more fully considered when the subject is resumed.

We feel safe in saying that the freedmen form no contemptible part of the state; that their emancipation has been too sudden for their own good and for ours; that their labor is vitally necessary to our prosperity and cannot be superseded or dispensed with; that the highest interest of the country demands that they should be treated with humanity, forbearance, and equal justice; that we, as a people, should lose sight of the fact that they once were slaves and encourage them in every good word and work; and that thus we should impress upon them, not in word, but in deed that their best friends are to be found, not among those who hail from a colder clime, but among those who were born on the same old plantations, long, long ago.

A public meeting yesterday at this courthouse adopted the usual resolutions in favor of legislative interference in behalf of debtors. This sentence expresses the whole affair.

JUHL

SUMTER, S. C., August 11

Contracts for labor in this section allowing to the freedmen a proportion of the crop for services rendered generally include a proviso that if the laborer leaves before the end of the year he is only to be paid four dollars a month, and from this is to be deducted whatever has been furnished him by the employer. This proviso may have been designed as a check to vacillation and as an inducement to fidelity and perseverance. But how does it operate? A Negro makes this agreement on the first of January. From his absolute want of means he is compelled to draw on his employer for all he needs for himself and family. Lost time and other contingencies are carefully noted against him. After the crop has been laid by and before it is harvested, an interruption occurs which ends in a separation. A settlement takes place, and when the planter's advancements even for corn and bacon at market prices are brought against the four dollars a month—which is all the contract allows in such a case—the balance is found in favor of the employer, and the employee finds that he has actually worked himself into debt.

In addition to this, the Negro may have cultivated on his own account and in his own time a few acres of corn, rice, and potatoes, which he is likewise required to abandon; for until ready for the harvest, the crop is part of the soil and adheres to the land and the landowner. The breach of contract and the dismissal of the laborer is generally attended with such circumstances of irritation as involve and include an order from the planter excluding the obnoxious freedman from the premises. . . . Such an interruption may occur at any time during the year. It may be occasioned by the misconduct of the laborer, and in such an event he has no right to complain. But it may arise from the action of the planter and is then a great wrong—a wrong which inflames the sufferer. And yet might be considered a small matter when viewed in its immediate results; but, unhappily, like the pebble falling upon the placid waters, its influence widens and spreads and creates a general feeling of distrust and discouragement exceedingly damaging in the end. It is even possible that some men may create difficulties in order to discharge the hands under circumstances and at a time most favorable to the employer.

And this is no reflection upon the planters as a class, for, conceding to them all they can possibly claim, they are certainly no better than other men. And, if they could rival the apostles in purity of character, they might still find some in their company (as the apostles did) who would do naughty deeds for money's sake. It is undeniable that many such labor engagements have been abruptly terminated this year by acts of violence or of injustice on the part of the employers—and certainly, in every such instance, provision should be made not only for the punishment of the wrongdoer, but for the remuneration of the laborer's toil. . . .

When these people were slaves it very rarely happened that deadly weapons were used against them, either in punishing insolence or enforcing domestic discipline. On the contrary, even when they became amenable to the law by the perpetration of the most atrocious crimes the interest of the master opposed the execution of justice, and the ablest counsel were employed for the defence. In this way it is notorious that felons were fastened upon communities where they continued to live unfettered and unpunished, although clearly guilty of crimes which would have brought a white man's neck to the rope. And as a last resort, when the most ingenious legal finesse could accomplish nothing more, the criminal was sold and sent off into some other state and foisted upon some unsuspecting community. Then he was property, the representative of a specific sum in hard cash, and the public sentiment and safety of communities—as well as the requirements of the law—were unblushingly trampled upon and disregarded in order to save his guilty life. Now that he is free he seems with many to have lost his value. The advocate who pleads his cause when he seeks redress for wrongs done him often feels that he is on the unpopular side. He is without a master. He is really without a home. As one of them on a western steamer said to an English traveler (Mr. [Laurence] Oliphant, M.P.): "If, when I was a slave I had tumbled overboard, the boat would have been stopped, and I should have been picked up and put by the fire to dry, because I was property; now, if I fall overboard, the cry would be, O! it's only a nigger, go ahead!"

Is there not a grave political blunder visible in all this? Is not the black man still a valuable component of the state? Is not his brawny arm necessary to develop our resources? And would not the sudden withdrawal of the entire Negro population be an actual calamity? Would it not be equally calamitous to have their confidence in us destroyed by any apparent sanction on our part of acts of injustice and oppression against them?

The extent to which our every interest depends upon the popular replies to these questions can scarcely be exaggerated. And hence the subject is earnestly pressed upon the attention of the state as one intimately and indissolubly associated with the prosperity of the people. If the contracts of 1866 will not do, then let labor be untrammelled as in other lands and let every man make his own bargain. Where specific wages are agreed upon by the week or month, there is little room for dispute, and the result is far more satisfactory—the planter owns the entire crop and the laborer receives his fixed reward.

The most effectual way to disarm the Radicals of their power to harm us and to divert the bureau of every plea for its interference or continuance is for southerners themselves, in their legislatures and courts as well as in domestic and plantation service, to adopt these unhappy people as their wards, apprentices and servants, and inflexibly to insist upon their full employment of every right—including proper remuneration for their labor and ample legal protection against injustice, violence, and wrong. With this flag at the masthead, we can confidently rely on a successful future—but on any other platform we are doomed to continued disappointment, humiliation, and defeat. These are the convictions of a native Carolinian and a former slaveholder and are the result of careful thought based upon a long practical experience in the field involved.[7] That they are just and applicable to present surroundings and future hopes time will doubtless fully demonstrate. May our people realize their importance and be wise in time. . . .

---

7. Since Fleming himself was a native South Carolinian and owned two household servants prior to the war, he may be expressing here a personal opinion.

A very handsome picture of the freedmen in their improved condition may be seen daily on our Main Street, a chain gang of culprits under sentence of the provost carrying bricks on hand-barrows and so hampered in their movements by fetters around their ankles that the camp meeting chorus of "Move along" would be madness to their ears.

JUHL

SUMTER, S. C., August 16

... The crops are light. The provision crop of this district, it is estimated, will barely sustain the population until March next. The corn seems to have had no ambition to rise in the world, nubbins prevail, and full ears are few and far between. Many fields are valueless except for the fodder, and this may occasion some serious disputes. It seems to have been omitted in most of the contracts in the list of field products to be divided with the laborers, and these latter now claim their share or a recognition of their right to it. . . . When the harvest is over the division of the crop will almost invariably result in much disappointment, angry disputes, and vexatious litigation and will thus add another argument in favor of specific wages. The cotton fields are very much improved in appearance and, if we do not have an early frost, will yield much more heavily than was anticipated six weeks ago.

We are without a jail, but not without jailbirds. Small covies of these latter are often seen here and appear to be perfectly tame, showing no signs of alarm even when approached very near. Certain precautions adopted as impediments to their flight and which are quite visible without a glass may account for their apparent passivity. But, we need a jail, and we are to have one—a veritable *log* jail in place of the costly and capacious prison which was swept away by the war. A *log* jail for this stately town and proud district! Where will the builder find a model or plan short of the outposts of Kansas! Pioneer life and pioneer creations in this country had become obsolete; but a *log* jail—shall we, with all our retrograding, have to go back so far?

From statements in a number of papers it is evident that government officials have sometimes interfered injudiciously with the popular demonstrations of affection for the southern dead. . . . Secession may be denounced, slavery abandoned, and everything else given up, but the images and memories of the dear ones swept away by the hot breath of battle must cling to their kindred and country still. And the government should honor and respect this sentiment; for the tears of the mourner and the meanings of the bereft have no treason in them—but if they were wanting it would be treason to the dead.

JUHL

1866
August 27

SUMTER, S. C., August 27

One of the surest indications of the prosperity of this town is in its retaining a full population, notwithstanding all the changes through which it has passed. It is a rare thing at any time to find vacant stores or dwellings to rent. During the war, when it became a place of refuge, many old residents sold out at high figures for Confederate paper and gave way to newcomers from Charleston and elsewhere. It was then said that whenever our refugee population left us on the return of peace, the town would be deserted. But our low country friends are gone and their late residences here are occupied by others, and the population seems rather to increase than diminish. In defiance of corporation taxes, high enough to swamp almost any inland community, Sumter seems to hold its own amidst the ebb and flow of the changing tide.

It would be gratifying if the same report could be made of the surrounding country. But such cannot be truthfully done. Planters of thirty years' experience pronounce this the worst crop season within

115

their knowledge. As to the labor, it seems to be generally ridiculed. Employers and laborers are alike disgusted with the present contracts and declare their purpose to avoid all such engagements in the future. Some planters despair of making a crop with free Negro labor under any circumstances or on any terms. How we are to weather the point and pass safely through the harvest and its division and launch away successfully on the work of another year is more than the wisest among us can at present discover.

That there is much irritation in the country is understandable. The planter who stands in the midst of his parched fields and looks upon the failure of his hopes is not in a condition meekly to submit to the chance insolence of those to whose neglect he in part ascribes his misfortune. And the freedman is disappointed with the prospect ahead and ready to give or take offence at the slightest provocation. Dismissals from the plantation, attended with forfeiture of interest in the crop, turn out upon the country at large many who believe that they have been tortuously discharged from their places and wrongfully deprived of the fruits of their toil. These form a growing class of vagrants soured in temper and ready to make reprisals out of anything which may come to hand. And if one vagrant is a nuisance, a number of vagrants is a curse.

It is said that there is no law to prevent a planter from dismissing obnoxious employees, that he is the owner of the soil and has the right to discharge at any time those in his employ. But this measure, however necessary and unavoidable in some cases it may be, is injurious in its influence upon the public. And if carried to any very great extent, it must inevitably result in the most serious social disorders. Many cases of insolence or laziness might be corrected by lighter penalties; and at best, there certainly is nothing gained by converting even an inefficient laborer into an idle and reckless vagabond.

The stillborn enactments of last winter known as the Negro Code will no doubt be repealed at the approaching extra session. And it is the earnest wish and hope of many that the legislature will confine itself to such action and leave the entire population of the state under the same laws and courts, at least for the present. While the bureau exists, it is needless for the state to undertake any special legislation for the freedmen, other than such measures as the Civil Rights Bill requires. Any new measures at this time would be against the temper and judgment of the people and subject to another counterblast from Congress.

During the past week the mission superintendent of the African Methodists has been preaching nightly to large congregations near the depot. He is a black man (the Reverend Mr. [Richard] Cain) from your city, educated, it is said, in Massachusetts. He made a favorable impression here and on Sunday afternoon preached to a large congregation in the Reverend Mr. [D. J.] Simmon's (Meth.) Church on the "Spread and Conquests of Messiah's Kingdom," drawing freely from sacred and profane history in illustrating his subject. Among his hearers were a number of ladies, lawyers, preachers, editors, etc., the body of the church, however, being closely packed with an audience of a darker hue. The Northern M. E. Church has for some time had a mission station and school at this place, but the African Methodists seem likely to take the wind out of its sails. The colored wigwam, as seen from any standpoint which may be selected, certainly presents just now a scene of confusion which no human voice could suddenly bring to order. . . .

JUHL

Sumter, S. C., September 2

In former years the helpless and decrepit Negro was supported by his owner, and the white pauper found an asylum in the district poorhouse. Now, when the state is like a dismantled ship—deprived of all control in many important particulars, its treasury exhausted and its people impoverished, its lands imperfectly tilled and its crops greatly reduced—it is not in a condition to provide for its poor. And the destitute and suffering form a much larger class than ever before.

A notice from the officer commanding this post that rations would be distributed on Friday brought together quite a number of the lame, blind, and aged destitute whites and blacks, and our courtroom presented a novel and stirring scene while the numerous applications were considered and decided, and the rations of meal, meat, molasses, and salt were distributed to such as passed muster and obtained tickets. Some of these people had come fifteen or twenty miles on foot, a wearisome pilgrimage to the infirm and half-starved, in order to obtain this temporary relief. And, when they succeeded in crawling out of the courthouse with their bundles, it appeared very doubtful in some cases whether they would be able to reach home again with the load of provisions they had so earnestly craved. They belong, of course, to the poorest class of our population and really need all the aid which can be given. . . .

Our town is being greatly improved by private enterprise. Paint and whitewash are liberally used, and the trowel and hammer, saw and plane are actively and noisily employed. Gangs of athletic freedmen, under sentence for various offences, are usefully engaged in improving Main Street. Occasionally there is an escape of a few prisoners under cover of night, but the provost court very soon supplies their places with new recruits.

The homespun and sombre shades of Confederate times are rapidly disappearing, and the ladies appear in all the tints of the rainbow.

And their bonnets—what is the style? No two alike in shape, material, size, trimming—who can decide what is the fashion? Fashion is a divinity at whose shrine so many bow that it may be hazardous even to whisper a criticism.

But take a rear view of the bonnets in any large assembly, and it will remind you of a tableaux of roosters preparing to crow, with here and there a few cooters in tremulous repose, and any quantity of dishcovers ready to be removed. A rear view exhibits a ludicrous variety, almost a burlesque on fashion. Take a front view and the effect is somewhat different, for no man of sense will think of the bonnet when the eyes of the wearer look back into his own. From recent observations it is concluded that no particular shape or style is required, but that to be in the fashion demands that you get something different from what you had before, something which may look and feel horrible and frightful at first, but to which you may in time become accustomed—something which came from Paris or London, Boston, or New York.

JUHL

SUMTER, S. C., September 18

The position assumed is that popular education lessens crime and pauperism; and, wherever statistics on the subject have been collected, the fact is established by figures, and figures generally prevail where other argument is controverted. That this is a subject of great practical, social, political, financial, and moral importance to us is evident from the large proportion of our population recently delivered from bondage, untaught in letters, uneducated in the great principles of self-government, and ushered suddenly into a new position where they are to constitute an intelligent, useful, and happy peasantry or a vast hive of ignorance, vice, and vagrancy from which the jails and poorhouses of the future are to be filled. . . .

The Negroes are ignorant. It was against the policy of the country in former years that they should be otherwise. This policy was only justified by the necessity which inspired it and which has now passed away. The public safety may have required that the Negro, as a slave, should be ignorant; the public safety requires that the Negro, as a freeman, should be enlightened. The spelling book and the testament can do him no harm. Notwithstanding all that may be done in the way of education, moral and religious influences, and magnifying the terrors of the law, his race will inevitably tax heavily the country by its pauperism and crimes. And a wise statesmanship will gladly adopt any suggestion or system which affords substantial promise of relief by reducing the criminal calendar and the roll call of the poorhouse and penitentiary. . . .

An ignorant voter exerts with us a dangerous power. Hence, some of the wisest statesmen object to an extension of this franchise. Hence, the undissembled horror with which Negro suffrage is regarded at the South. An untaught and unprincipled multitude would be a hard master, worse than a drunken pilot or crazy engineer. "The greatest despotism on earth," says De Tocqueville, "is an excited, untaught public sentiment; and we should hate not only despots, but despotism. When I feel the hand of power lie heavy on my brow, I care not to know who oppresses me; the yoke is not the easier because it is held out to me by a million of men." In the absence of general education this tremendous power of suffrage is something frightful to contemplate. And yet, the tendency of the age is to force it on this country. The result of recent elections and the disgraceful demonstrations attending the president's tour sufficiently indicate the strength of the Radical purpose. The millions of the North show no signs of receding. Their programme in all its fullness may not be achieved this year or the next, but if in ten or twenty years it may possibly be realized, it will be wise to prepare.

Those rights of citizenship which have already been conferred on the freedmen would be more cheerfully conceded if they had some knowledge of letters. A witness is scarcely to be feared if he has an intelligent appreciation of the sanctity of an oath and a proper horror of the guilt of perjury. And, if a new and enlarged position is assigned to these people, irrevocably and beyond recall, then the highest political wisdom will demand that they be qualified safely to occupy it and that the state therein shall suffer no detriment.

Freedmen's schools are springing up all around us. There are several here and in Camden, Darlington, Florence, Lynchburg, and various other points. They may be in part self-sustaining. They may be in part supported by northern societies. Some of them have native colored teachers. Others are taught by regular "Down Easters." But, *n'importe*, so long as the young are instructed even in the simplest rudiments of an education, it is a service rendered to the state. An occasional newspaper fling at the "Boston schoolmarms" is not in the best taste, for they certainly do no harm to us in teaching the Negro to read. These volunteer efforts to establish schools among the blacks should be encouraged, as they have been and are by some of the most distinguished southern gentlemen. And, looking to the future, it cannot be doubted that this question will assume an increasing importance; and that the state itself, when it rises once more from its ashes, will find it wisdom to assume the direction and aid in carrying on the work.

JUHL

SUMTER, S. C., September 19

I know not that the *Courier* can do a better or more timely service to the state than by ventilating in its columns the following objections to the suspension of the courts by the legislature:

1. It is clearly unconstitutional, as much so as the Stay Law itself.
2. As a measure of relief it is partial and confines its benefits to such

debtors only as are embraced in the jurisdiction of the common pleas, leaving the magistrates (and district courts if established) with full powers to enforce payment of all smaller debts, thus shielding the rich and leaving the poor at the mercy of their creditors.

3. It discriminates with suicidal folly against the home creditor, as the foreign creditor will have—and doubtless exercise—the rights to sue in the United States courts and thus will gain priority of judgment and preference of lien.

4. Its tendency will be to postpone the reestablishment of civil law and perhaps furnish a plea for the continuance of military courts with an enlargement of their jurisdiction. For what right, it may be asked, has any state to claim jurisdiction for its own courts over its own citizens when it voluntarily stops the wheels of justice and leaves its people substantially without law and without the remedies for wrongs which the Constitution guarantees?

Any legislation so palpably against the Constitution—protecting the rich and deserting the poor—favoring the foreign and crushing the home creditor—and militating against the earnestly desired restoration of civil rule—must be mischievous. Will the governor interpose his veto?

JUHL

SUMTER, S. C., September 21

It may be said that the laboring class requires very little general intelligence to fit them for their work. But some years ago many curious and instructive facts were collected in the factories of New England. As a general thing it was found that those operatives who could sign their names were able to do one-third more work and to do it better than those who made their mark. The industry even of a common laborer is rendered more effective and valuable by education, and an intelligent mechanic is said to be worth twice as much as one ignorant and stupid. . . .

The education of the masses exerts a most potent and salutary influence on the common industries of life in all the departments upon which the wealth of a state depends. Even agriculture, the basis of all the other arts and the leading source of southern prosperity, is greatly promoted by it. Chemical knowledge is doing for the production powers of the soil what the application of steam has done for the increase of mechanical power. The farmer who wishes to double his crops finds the means of doing so, not in multiplying his acres, but in applying a knowledge of the laws of chemistry to the cultivation of the soil already possessed.

Universities and colleges are not alone sufficient to meet the wants of the country. They are only accessible to the wealthy and serve their purpose in qualifying for the professions and the higher walks of literature and scholarship. They leave the great arch of heaven dark and gloomy with here and there a hand-breadth of clear sky through which a few brilliant stars are visible. But common schools instruct the masses and roll away the clouds of ignorance and leave an entire and glorious azure, lit up with myriads of stars of every grade.

As an indication of the progressive march of a healthy sentiment on this subject, it may be stated that wealthy native planters of the highest character, formerly large slaveholders and some of them distinguished during the war as officers of high rank in the southern armies, are at this time aiding and encouraging freedmen's schools in their respective neighborhoods, and applications have been forwarded from such sources for New England teachers. As a free state (if Congress will concede us the privilege) it is folly to suppose that we can suffer any detriment from the universal diffusion of knowledge among all classes of the people.

We are having abundant rains. Cotton picking progresses. The common law prevails—common to all races and classes alike. The magistrate and sheriff are kept much more actively than profitably employed. The freedmen express a decided preference for the civil rule. In this they are sensible. There is no doubt that they fare much better under a judicious and impartial civil administration than under military rule. There are some cases which of course find no timely remedy at hand—but all this will be doubtless provided for in the future. Prejudices of the past must give way, and impartial justice be administered. The great wave which had volume enough to sweep away slavery with all the treasure and capital included in it has not lost its momentum and will inevitably sweep away also the prejudices which were fostered by that institution.

A barn was burned last night near Manchester by incendiary freedmen. A Negro man recently lost a leg by being accidentally run over on the Wilmington and Manchester Railroad. A slim mulatto stole over a hundred dollars from the cash box of a store in Kingville, came on to Sumter where he indulged his fancy in a number of purchases, bored into a store here on Saturday night and replenished his funds, was arrested on Tuesday and the stolen property mostly recovered, and made his escape the night after, and will no doubt be soon practicing his craft in other quarters.

JUHL

SUMTER, S. C., October 7

The sun shines as gloriously as ever upon the land of Sumter and reveals the same beauty in the varying foliage of swamp and forest, but all else is sadly changed. A ride of ten miles in any direction and in almost any section of our country will present a picture whose every shade is sombre and depressing. Immense clearings covered with grass through which stunted corn and sickly cotton here and there appear, and out-buildings and fences in a dilapidated condition exert no very inspiring influence upon the mind. The planter is ready to demonstrate the absolute worthlessness of the present system of labor and to enlarge upon the laziness, impudence, and dishonesty of the Negroes.

The freedmen are equally well prepared to prove the unfairness of the present contracts and the grievances and wrongs to which they are sometimes subjected. Occasionally an instance occurs, like an oasis in the desert, in which an old planter is found gathering around him again his former slaves, who, after having been wafted by the first breath of freedom to a new field of labor where they have worked through the crop, have voluntarily gone back and successfully sought restoration to their old homes. The ineradicable sentiment of the human heart, so touchingly presented in the wanderer's cry, "O carry me back to old Virginny," may ultimately result in returning very many families to their old familiar places of labor and abode.

While the dreary and wretched appearance of the plantation must be measurably ascribed to the want of proper culture, it is not to be denied that with the season of 1866 no kind of labor could have achieved a much more satisfactory result. Such a season does not probably occur more than thrice a century, and it seems peculiarly unfortunate that so great a disaster should have befallen us upon our first entrance on the experiment of free labor. It will certainly be pleaded by the friends of the system as a bar to any unfavorable verdict which this year's trial would otherwise give. The cotton crop of the district will probably reach—in proportion to the land planted—at least half an average, but the provision crop is certainly a failure, already producing distress and threatening still more serious suffering.

If there are any persons at the North who still entertain vindictive sentiments towards us, it must be because they are desperately ignorant of the sad condition to which we have been reduced. If they regard the South as a criminal convicted of treason, by what code can they demand the infliction of heavier penalties than the inhabitants of this land have already suffered? Punishment should never be inordinate and excessive. A serious breach of the law is often considered atoned for by the imposition of a heavy fine; but, what shall be said of the tribunal which, after exhausting in this way the offender and his family, continues to pursue its victims in their wretchedness with insatiable hate? But the rebellion must be punished and treason made odious! This is still the cry. Do they forget the millions of money swept away by the Act of Emancipation, the hecatombs of noble dead, the thousands of bereaved families, the widespread desolation which has visited states and cities, the staggering blows given to the agricultural interests of the country, and the general impoverishment of a whole people, groaning under an accumulation of debts and taxes and deprived in some places of even the means of present sustenance? Does all this amount to no punishment, and can a civilized people whose past national history has identified them with the enemies of oppression consent to play the part of the oppressor and treat a subdued and suffering section with an implacable ferocity which can find no excuse and no justification? This might be expected of eastern despotisms, but is a blot upon the proud record of free and enlightened America.

In a like manner the continued imprisonment of Jefferson Davis and the many evasions by which his trial is deferred and his liberation on bail refused will be marked in the pages of future history as a disgrace to our national character. St. Helena seems to be repeated in Fortress Monroe, but in the one case the repose of a continent seemed to demand and justify captivity and death in exile, while in the other no such exterminating plea can possibly be urged. If "the blood of the martyrs is the seed of the church," no possible gain to the Union sentiment can be anticipated by persecuting a man whose offence consists in having occupied a position in which one-third of the states placed him when they engaged in a struggle for a separate and independent nationality—a struggle of which he was by no means the initial and upon which he only entered when his state recalled him from his place in Washington. The struggle is over, its decision accepted, and he and the country over which he presided for four years have suffered enough to entitle them now at least to some degree of moderation and forbearance from the rulers of the land.

A revival meeting is in progress in the Baptist Church of this town. From a meeting of days it is likely to be marked by weeks in its duration. This morning the pastor, Reverend Dr. R[ichard] Furman, after an earnest and able discourse to a very large congregation, baptized eight converts. Among the number were two ex-Confederate soldiers, one of whom served for a long time as major of artillery in Charleston harbor and was afterwards severely wounded in North Carolina. Leading him into the water, Dr. Furman said: "I hold by the hand a brave soldier of our fallen Confederacy. He now joins a service which shall know no defeat." Five of the converts were in the lovely bloom of early womanhood. The ordinance was administered in a most impressive manner, and tears attested the sacred interest with which it was witnessed. Revivals are reported among the different denominations in various parts of the state, and it may be that the trials through which we are passing as a people will be thus blest of God to our spiritual and eternal good.

Several plantations have recently changed hands at very fair prices, and a town lot on Main Street (thirty-three feet front by sixty-three feet deep) with a three-story wooden building in a tumbling uninhabitable condition brought last week at public sale five thousand dollars! This certainly indicates no disposition to "despair of the Republic."

JUHL

SUMTER, S. C., October 11

When Congress meets again it should not overlook the fact that the population of the South has undergone a great change since the war. Very many of those who were most influential in the prosecution of the struggle have sold their estates and migrated. Some are in Europe and others have removed to Mexico, Brazil, or Canada. A great many have gone North. The population of New York City alone has received (so the papers affirm) an accession of twenty thousand from this source. Washington and northern papers frequently allude to the numerous arrivals of Southerners with their effects, seeking homes among *the free*. On the other hand, large numbers of northern men have settled at the South, planting cotton, making turpentine, running mills and factories, and merchandizing.

In this way, the two sections have so far exchanged population that the Radicals may well pause before proceeding against the South, lest peradventure they damage their own friends. Very many of those who first drew their fire have judiciously flanked their batteries and are actually in their rear or otherwise out of range. Hence, if Mr. [Thaddeus] Stevens or Mr. [Charles] Sumner have more shells to throw in this direction they should be reminded of the fact that they are more likely to blow up some of their late constituents than any of the principal "rebs." What a subject for a comic painter! Scene: Washington City; a long line of Radical batteries with guns all pointing South and manned by honorable members; in the rear, as lookers-on, crowds of former Southerners, once known as prominent "rebs," smoking and gaily commenting on the performance; in the distance the shells are seen bursting among New Englanders, freedmen, and a few poor natives "away down South in Dixie." How long before reason, policy, humanity, and the general good shall successfully command these madmen to "cease firing"?

Political liberty may be a great blessing, and slavery may be an unmitigated evil, but it is maintained that the sudden emancipation of the millions of southern Negroes was a mistake and must work injuriously to both races. It has certainly impoverished the former masters and demoralized the entire labor of the cotton states, and it has withdrawn from the former slaves the care and protection they once enjoyed and thrown around them responsibilities for which they were not mentally prepared. And it is maintained, with equal confidence, that any further unfriendly legislation by Congress, impairing confidence in southern securities and discouraging enterprise and investments at the South, will deprive the Negro of his last hope of profiting by his newly acquired freedom. Give prosperity to this country once more, and the freedmen may find remunerative labor, homes, and sustenance; but, otherwise, their fate is and must be deplorable. To use the figure, the southern ship carries a great variety of passengers, and an enemy whose only aim is to destroy the occupants of the cabin must remember that when the vessel sinks, the steerage goes down with it. And, even if we are kept at sea with scanty supplies, it is not difficult to decide which class will be the principal sufferers.

Again, cotton may not be king in an absolute sense, but that it exerts a vast and potential influence upon the commerce, manufactures, and traffic of the world is undeniable. The North itself gives proof of this in the nervous anxiety with which it watches the slightest fluctuation in the market. A sudden rise or decline at Liverpool makes or breaks fortunes thousands of miles away. And the South is emphatically the land of cotton. Encourage its production and wealth flows through all the channels of northern trade. And Congress can do this by allowing reason and humanity to control its legislation. It need not sacrifice any important principle, nor make any unreasonable concession to southern politics or prejudices. It need only be just in giving to the South what it requires the South to give to its own population—equal laws.

But neither cotton culture nor any other pursuit can thrive in the face of persistent and relentless war waged by the government against those engaged in it. Hence Congress really and alone must decide whether much or little cotton shall hereafter be raised in this country. Rebuke fanaticism, restore reason to her throne in the national councils, and give just and beneficial laws to this land, and the whole country—North and South—will feel the benefit in revived prosperity and renewed energy and hope. For such a result ought not an American Congress to waive its past antipathies and astonish the world by the unexpected display of good sense and a sound political philosophy?

Sumter has become a very important cotton market, and the new crop is coming in rapidly. Trains of wagons roll into town laden with cotton and leave well freighted with family supplies. Our stores are numerous and still increasing, and the immense stock of goods collected here and constantly replenished by fresh arrivals attracts the trade of a very large scope of the surrounding country. Peace and good order seem to prevail throughout the country, interrupted occasionally by an assault and battery or other light cases for the courts.

A planter who employs forty hands reports forty bales of cotton. Another reports one bale to every five acres planted. Another, with seventeen hands, makes three bales and a failure of provisions. Some few have done even worse than this, but many others will, doubtless, be able to make a better report than any of the foregoing. The average freedmen's share in this district, after deducting advances, will hardly furnish these people with their winter blankets and shoes.

The court of appeals deserves the thanks of the state, and especially of the poor, for postponing the district courts to another year—thus giving even to the humbler debtor a chance for one more Christmas before the screw pressure can be applied.

JUHL

SUMTER, S. C., November 7

Among the many enterprises arrested by the war the South Carolina Railroad was not among the least important. No railway project probably occasioned greater enthusiasm among the people occupying the line of its proposed route or promised greater results in proportion to the outlay required. Deflecting from Gourdin's Station on the

Northeastern Railroad, it was to traverse Clarendon, Sumter, Kershaw, and Lancaster Districts via Manning, Sumter, Mechanicsville, Bishopville, and Lancaster Courthouse and find its upper terminus at Charlotte.

By an arrangement with the Northeastern Road, trains leaving Charlotte were to run through to Charleston without changing cars. The route was surveyed and approved, a route involving less grading, bridging, and trestlework than any other of the same length and affording an abundance of timber for all the purposes acquired in its construction. A charter may have been obtained, but whether or not, the enterprise was brought suddenly to a deadlock by the breaking out of the war. Shall it so remain, or shall it spring up again with renewed vitality and eventuate in a glorious success?

It will appear, at a glance, that it would be a most important feeder to the Northeastern Road—a fact fully recognized by the directory of that corporation. Its influence upon the city of Charleston would be vast and permanent, as it would effectually tap a large extent of country, the business of which is now vigorously diverted from you by other lines and by the want of a direct and continuous railway from this section to your wharves. And the entire route is through a great agricultural region whose productive energies have, indeed, of late been partially checked, but only to be profitably resumed, it is hoped. Passengers and freight would make it a paying concern—a good investment to the stockholders and no mean tributary to the commercial prosperity of Charleston. In our present circumstances we may not be able to undertake, without foreign assistance, this great work, but the attention of capitalists might be invited to the subject with the best results.

The revolution in the labor of the country will necessitate a great change in the planting interest. The old plantation system which with slave labor enabled a single proprietor to cultivate profitably an immense area of land will, under the new order of things, have to be abandoned in a great measure; for the best managers despair of employing free labor successfully beyond a certain limit. But, if our former mammoth estates disappear, it will only be by their subdivision into smaller farms, whose aggregate of production under improved culture may actually exceed the former yield of the same land.

The land in the immediate suburbs of this town is naturally as barren as almost any in this section, and yet seven acres of it with a bad stand and such a season as the present made four bales of cotton (more than some planters in the country made with seventeen hands), and one mere acre produced 21 bushels of rice, and this result would have been at least doubled by a more favorable season. One acre of similar land in this district has produced in a favorable year, by accurate measurement, 100½ bushels corn, the fodder of which fully paid for all the manure applied to the acre. Emigrants, therefore, securing small farms anywhere on the proposed route, would find abundant remuneration for their labors. And the country is perfectly healthy at all seasons and in every respect adapted to white labor. Thus it would probably result that the employees engaged in the construction of the road would meet with sufficient inducements to become permanent settlers and in a few years, by their field products, add largely to the business of the line.

It is no time for us to despair. We may be shattered in fortune, but we are yet not destroyed. Great as have been our reverses, they may yet find ultimate reparation in hope, energy, and enterprise. The leader of the Radicals in the United States Senate has recently advised the South to let politics alone for the present and to go manfully to work in rebuilding her waste places. And this counsel, although unsolicited, and coming from a source scarcely entitled to our confidence, it may be to our interest to follow. In politics we are (*nolens, volens*) voiceless and powerless, but no law or imperial edict as yet forbids our earnest efforts to clothe this land again in beauty and open up fresh avenues to trade, commerce, and wealth.

In order to succeed, however, we must exhibit somewhat more of energy and promptness than have been displayed by the commissioners of public buildings for this district. We still have no jail, very much to the comfort of a very considerable number of rogues and to the great annoyance and damage of the honest and suffering public. Proposals for a *log* jail were sometime ago invited, but the idea of such a backwoods contrivance was properly repudiated as unworthy the dignity of this gay and growing town. Some months of exhausting meditation resulted in the conversion of the grand jury rooms (basement of the courthouse) into a temporary lock-up, and the entrance and rear were made to look quite formidable with heavy iron gratings.

By a happy oversight no attempt was made to secure the fireplaces with which both rooms are furnished, and hence the first prisoners lodged there remained but one night, finding no difficulty in removing the hearth and making their escape. Both were for capital felonies, incorrigible in crime, and will soon make the public the sufferers for their enlargement. A magistrate soon after having to commit another culprit to the safe keeping of the sheriff, somewhat facetiously advised the prisoner to remain where the sheriff placed him, lest his escape should furnish a presumption of guilt. We are not ashamed of our sheriff, but our sheriff is of his jail.

JUHL

SUMTER, S. C., November 16

... Mr. Richardson has returned from his visit to Washington, having failed to obtain the land scrip appropriated by an act of Congress for agricultural colleges in the several states. Before the said land grant can be made available, it will be necessary for the state to give security that the proceeds shall be applied to the purpose named in the act; and, as our legislature seems to have been ignorant of this important prerequisite and therefore made no arrangements for complying with such condition precedent, the mission of the state agent was not entirely successful. Other states will do well to note the fact and profit by our experience.

As the year draws towards its close, the usual stir begins to manifest itself among the freedmen, some of whom still entertain visions of land and homesteads and high wages and halcyon days, indiscriminately to be bestowed on all without consideration and without labor. Mass meetings are being held by them in this district with a view to regulate wages for another year and to arrange for the emigration of such of their numbers as may be anxious to try their fortunes in Liberia or the West.

The vast majority, however, of our colored population have too much good sense to seek any such change, and with good conduct and proper industry they will certainly do as well here as anywhere else. It is neither our wish nor our interest to encourage their removal. As a race, they behaved well during the war, and under a sudden emancipation they have preserved an equilibrium worthy of praise, and we see no reason why, with proper encouragement and counsel, they should not become an industrious, useful, and well-behaved part of the population. . . .

JUHL

SUMTER, S. C., November 17

A very large assemblage of the colored people met here today at the Freedmen's Tabernacle located in the southern suburbs. The exercises were opened with singing and prayer, after which a number of addresses were delivered setting forth the absolute inadequacy of one-third of the crop as a just remuneration for the labor of the year. The speakers dwelt upon the present condition of the freedmen without land, without homes, and without resources, and in many cases, unsupplied with shoes and clothing with the winter close at hand.

They expressed the conviction that the only safe conditions on which they could make engagements for the future would be for the land and labor to divide the field products share and share alike. The speakers were intelligent freedmen, and all belonged to this state and district, and the immense audience not only behaved with utmost decorum, but appeared unanimous and deeply in earnest.

A local magistrate [probably Fleming himself], who was present by special invitation, being called on for his counsel embraced the opportunity of impressing upon their minds the real causes of their present destitution. The contracts of the present year were an experiment—adopted and approved by the military and the bureau—and were unequal in their operation and productive, in some cases, of great injustice, hardships, and dissatisfaction. The seasons, too, had been so remarkably unpropitious that planters and employers were alike involved in a common disappointment and common suffering. The system of a pro rata of the crop was liable to very grave objections, while stated wages would ensure to every man, in proportion to his skill, character, and capacity, a certain compensation easily defined and ascertained. On this plan, whenever an employer and employee concluded to part company during the year, it would be easy for the former to ascertain his dues to the latter and to pay the same either in money or by note maturing at the end of the year. The entire crop would then belong to the planter, and all disputes about its division be entirely avoided.

The freedmen were earnestly advised to act calmly, prudently, and in obedience to law; and it is due to them to say that thus far they have shown no disposition to act otherwise. And although this meeting assumed, in some of its features, the character of a strike for higher wages, there really seems no ground for apprehension that the movement will eventuate in any serious interruption of the planting interest, especially if their claims are met with that kind indulgence which their present helpless condition should inspire.

The meeting also resolved to appeal to the general government for aid in behalf of the destitute. It was stated that this appeal would have been made to the state, but it was well known to them that South Carolina was at present too poor to meet so great an emergency. And, truly, the government should send material aid to these people at once. Will not some of the rich men of the North enter this wide field for the exercise of a substantial benevolence and a real philanthropy? While spending millions in advocating the political regeneration of these people, a few thousands invested in brogans, blankets, and bread for the blacks would be much more sensibly and profitably applied.

It is worthy of note that during the four hours of this gathering of freedmen not a word was said about political rights, Negro suffrage, or Negro equality. The first and last note of the occasion was on the same chord, a fair and remunerative return for the services of the laborer and the ways and means of saving the destitute multitude from starvation and death.

The Southerner is impoverished. He may give these people his sympathies, but he has nothing else to give. The government has deprived them of a master's care. Should not the government interpose to save them from the inevitable disasters of this year's failure in the crop and at least enable them to live until they can gather another harvest? Will private northern munificence attest an undissembled interest in the black man's welfare by contributing promptly and liberally to his relief?

This meeting is but one of many which have been held in various parts of the country for a like purpose. There is no doubt that the movement is a general one, and when the character, numbers, and position of the freedmen are considered, the matter assumes an importance which may claim the attention of the state.

Your correspondent has carefully watched the animus of this movement and has been unable to detect in it anything like defiance or disrespect towards the superior race. The labor question in its new phase is attended with difficulties which no popular combinations or even astute legislation can immediately remove. But it must be palpable to all that humanity and the public good demand that every reasonable effort shall be made to reconcile these people to the necessities of their condition by furnishing such inducements to renewed industry as will make them cheerful, useful, and contented cultivators of the soil. This may be impossible with some of them, but with many others it will be no very difficult task.

JUHL

1867

UNSETTLED CONDITIONS continued in South Carolina throughout much of 1867. The year opened with hundreds of Negroes leaving for other sections, especially Florida. The Radicals were busy stirring up trouble for the South; and, surprisingly enough, Juhl concluded that Thad Stevens with his plan for territorial governments, may have the right idea after all. If Congress was intent on a vindictive policy and would not permit the southern states the freedom to conduct their own affairs as states, then maybe the former Confederacy should be carved up into territories. If Congress was determined to run roughshod over everything south of the Potomac, let it have whatever responsibility and glory that went with such a program. The year closed in a welter of incendiary fires, robberies, and shooting affrays. What was needed, commented Juhl, was "a little more peace and little less politics."

However, all was not chaos and confusion. Although the legislature failed to reappoint Fleming as a magistrate (absence of wartime military service undoubtedly accounts for this turn of events), Juhl pointed with pride and satisfaction to his columns reproduced in other newspapers, a growing legal practice, and correspondence with national figures such as Horace Greeley. In the late spring he took a trip to New York City and southern New England, returning to Sumter with numerous notions about scientific farming, the development of small industries, and the need for a land grant college in South Carolina.

In keeping with his benevolent, humane attitude toward the black man, Juhl presided at a Fourth of July celebration attended by a mixed audience of several thousand. It is apparent that despite frequent disturbances—prior to the upheaval of the Ku Klux Klan and the turmoil of the presidential campaign of 1868—relations between the races were relatively cordial. Residents of Sumter were not yet blaming the freedmen as a class for these outrages. Instead, they vented their anger upon certain ignorant, truculent blacks, Yankee

1867 bureau agents, and a frail, ineffective system of courts and police officers.

... There is at this time an extensive exodus of the colored population of this district. Large numbers of them are encamped near Mayesville, this place, and perhaps other points along the line of railroad. They are bound for the land of flowers [Florida], and it is understood are moving under government supervision and with government assistance, having the promise of transportation and six months' rations. The trains are to move them off on Thursday, and it is very probable that the night following Captain [L. M.] Coxetter will have as many of them on board the *Dictator* as his noble ship can accommodate.

We cannot look with indifference upon this wholesale emigration. In a politico-economical sense we cannot but believe that it will sensibly and injuriously affect the material interests of the district. Certain it is that in the past the lands in this section have furnished employment and support to all of these laborers. The lands still remain, but it is evident that with so great a subtraction of labor the area cultivated must be, and will be, very much reduced.

The freedmen are leaving reluctantly. They cannot forget that they are turning away, probably forever, from the homes of their childhood and the graves of their fathers. But last year's experience, which after all their toil brought them to its close without money, without provisions, without blankets, shoes, and clothing, they are not willing to repeat. They desired more favorable terms for the present year. In some cases they have obtained them and remain—but where they have failed to do so, they emigrate. A proper effort would doubtless have secured and retained them all.

The Christmas festivities passed off with unusual hilarity—fantastics, fireworks, balloon ascensions, and a tripping it on the light fantastic toe. But, as another year opens upon us, with our still unsettled conditions, a heavy fog resting upon our political horizons, and some of the best labor of the country on the wing, graver thoughts obtrude themselves, and the eyes which look into the future are marked with anxiety and deep concern.

JUHL

SUMTER, S. C., January 18

The colored population continues to occupy a large share of the public attention; for even such persons as care nothing about their political status and aspirations and their mental and moral improvement cannot be unmindful of the fact that they constitute the operative force in what has always been and must continue to be a strictly agricultural country. The failure in many instances to make satisfactory arrangements here for the current year, coupled with the most seductive inducements presented by planters from Florida and the West, has been and still is reducing our Negro population to such an extent that there must be a very serious scarcity of labor in this section in the future.

On many plantations in this district the Negro houses are empty, and there seems no reasonable prospect of finding tenants to occupy them again; and on some places, it is said, not enough have remained to perform the duties required of house servants for the planter's family. Other planters have obtained all the hands they required— the Negroes doubtless having been largely influenced by the reports of those who worked on the different plantations last year, as to the manner in which they were treated and the remuneration they received. Large numbers of freedmen, who as yet have made no arrangements to emigrate, are still disengaged and ready to accept a suitable offer; but in the meantime the winter is gliding away, and the important plantation work which should be attended to at this season remaining neglected.

There are still numbers of emigrants here "waiting for the wagon that they may all take a ride," but the government has not come up to time, and their hopes of a speedy migration are growing "small by degrees and beautifully less." To a calm and impartial looker-on, it would seem a matter of first moment that this labor should be retained in this country and that every reasonable encouragement necessary to secure it should be given. A strike among factory operatives may stop the engines and looms for a few days or weeks, but the work can then be resumed without serious damage to anyone. But the suspension of labor in an agricultural region for a month or two is quite a different affair, and plantations left without laborers for such a period must suffer. . . .

To those who are disposed to be despondent in view of the present state of the country, there is some little solace found in the fact that the legislature has adjourned to meet no more until the people shall have an opportunity of making some changes in its membership. In all the history of the state there never has been a greater amount of useless, expensive, and unwise legislation than the past two years have witnessed in this state.[1] The time and money consumed in framing, discussing, passing, and exploding the Negro Code may be taken as a specimen. The tax bill for 1867 may be considered a model (?) of its kind, especially in view of the flourishing condition of the state. And as to courts, we have enough of them for six states as large as South Carolina—a circumstance which does not even please the lawyers, for these gentlemen are sharp enough to deprecate too large an increase of business where their clients are already reduced so low that it would be folly to expect them to pay much of a fee. . . .

The popular sentiment here and through the state is, of course, adverse to the increased degradation implied in Mr. Stevens's bill for the establishment of territorial governments in this and the other southern states. And yet there are gentlemen of unquestioned re-

---

1. Fleming was personally unhappy because the legislators failed to reappoint him as magistrate and coroner for the Sumter region.

spectability to whom the apparently fixed purpose of Congress in this particular occasions no alarm and but little if any regret. As they say, we now have the name and expenses of a state government without the position and powers and privileges of a state, and a military force and a national legislature supervising and overriding the whole of it, from the governor down. Either let them give us all that a state has a right to claim, or let them have the undivided glory of running the machine themselves. They will find it rather rusty and with many a screw loose, but perhaps Yankee enterprise and ingenuity would be able once more to place it in good running order, and the *new territories* be found keeping pace with the progressive spirit of the age, if no obstructions are thrown upon the track. . . .

JUHL

SUMTER, S. C., February 5

The January term of the district court for Sumter has been held. The business of the session was confined to state cases and excited little interest. This court is a novelty and seems to have but few friends. It has but one jury, and when that body retires to make up a verdict, the court must take a recess or resolve itself into a Quaker's meeting until they return. Working through a heavy docket with so many stoppages of the machinery would be somewhat tedious, especially when the jury consumed much time in coming to an agreement.

The panel consists of eight men. By the new constitution, the convention gave the legislature the power to reduce the number of jurors in the inferior courts, and the legislature has done so. This might be a matter of no importance, if such courts were confined to the trial of causes "small and mean." But the district courts have jurisdiction in cases in which character itself is swept away by the verdict. As far back as feudal times in France, Germany, and Italy, the jury consisted of twelve men. And in the English and American courts it has always been the rule that the panel should consist of the same number, and their unanimous concurrence has been necessary to divest a citizen of life, reputation, or estate. It is but natural that any innovation on this time-honored and priceless privilege should be regarded with distrust; for, if a reduction to a panel of eight is sanctioned, why may not the jury (?) in time be restricted to three or even two?

Another innovation is the trial of a citizen upon an indictment which had not been committed to a grand jury and upon which no "true bill" had been found and without any presentment by such jury. The constitution of this state does not authorize the legislature to dispense with a grand jury in the inferior and district court. On this ground, appeals have been taken in cases tried here last week, and motions will be made before the appeal court in May in arrest of judgment or for new trials. A people jealous of their liberties cannot see, without concern, those great safeguards swept away which have heretofore been thrown around their rights. It is one thing for franchises and privileges to be abolished by a conqueror; it is quite another thing for the safeguards of a people to be broken down and destroyed by their own legislature.

The winter has been unusually severe with more snow than is generally seen in this latitude, and by common consent it seems decided that we are to have favorable seasons and a heavy crop. The freedmen who have not migrated to other sections (*States*, we would say, but don't like to use a word so nearly obsolete) have made engagements and gone to work. And it is not amiss to express the hope that there will be such an improvement in their treatment and compensation this year that no further and future emigration will take place, and that this important part of our population will be retained in numbers sufficient successfully to cultivate the soil.

JUHL

SUMTER, S. C., February 15

... Rumors are rife that the legislature is to be convened again in extra session. From different sources we have a very emphatic "God forbid." Its past sessions have brought no relief, affected no improvement in our condition, but cost an impoverished constituency immense sums, which would have been much better applied in bread for the poor. And, now with Elliott's [Thomas D. Eliot] bill and other measures indicating the settled purpose of Congress to establish military and provisional governments at the South, it would appear little less than insane folly to attempt any further legislation. But, if such should be resolved on, it is hoped that in mercy to the state, the members will defray their own expenses.

Captain [Samuel] Place of the United States Army is now at this station distributing rations to the suffering and helpless poor.[2] There is considerable destitution in some parts of the district, and the relief thus afforded by the government cannot fully meet the demand for aid. There are some farms which will have to be abandoned unless the laborers can obtain an advance of provisions. Are there none of your factors able to advance supplies on lien of crops and thus insure larger shipments of cotton to Charleston next fall . . . ?

JUHL

SUMTER, S. C., March 23

There are those who think that the more rapidly the reconstruction plan is carried into execution, the better for the state. The restoration now offered may be attended with unpopular or unpleasant conditions; but, evidently, until such restoration is effected, we are actually under military rule with a quasi-civil government resting under its

2. During the week of February 11–17, Place distributed 1,515 pounds of pork, 1,200 pounds of corn meal, and 20 bushels of corn to 301 persons—155 of them Negroes (*Sumter Watchman*, February 20, 1867).

shadow. Delay certainly holds out no promise of better terms, but may aggravate our distress and humiliation.

The present transitory state of the country and the uncertainty in which everything seems involved affects injuriously all the various branches of industry and raises a formidable barrier to enterprise and trade. Hence, planters with large unencumbered estates find it exceedingly difficult to secure advances necessary to success in making another crop from the want of confidence in southern securities. Mortgages, liens, assignments, all the usually accepted guarantees of payment are rejected and dishonored, and capital looks upon our entire section with a nervousness which is fatal to its investment.

Passing recently over miles of trestle crossing some of the largest swamps in the state, our attention was given to the variety of remarks which the occasion excited among the passengers. To some it was an agreeable change from the pine land to swamp scenery; to others it brought expressions of uneasiness and a desire to be safely over; but to certain travelers from the North, it unfolded a world of wealth in its vast supplies of the choicest material for manufactures in which they were interested. An interchange of views with these latter brought from them the assurance that there was not only capital ready, but actually companies formed for the establishment of various kinds of manufactories at the South. They were only waiting for the country to settle down on a fixed and secure platform.

The wealth of our country is by no means confined to its cotton and rice lands. Many of these are well-nigh exhausted by a long continued system of improvident culture and require the yearly application of expensive fertilizers, and are chiefly adapted to Negro labor. But the mineral resources of the state invite development, and the woods and swamps abound in timber, whose value can scarcely be estimated in figures. The immense factories at the North, where furniture of every style and quality is made, consume annually millions of feet of lumber, which costs—when delivered—about one-half of what is realized for it after it is made up for use. This is owing to the distance and expense of transportation, which would render similar factories near the source of supply more successful competitors—a consideration urged by our northern travelers, at considerable length and with much earnestness, as an evidence that extensive establishments for a variety of manufactures would spring up in our midst as soon as capital could feel secure in such undertakings. Nothing less, however, than the full and successful inauguration of the new regime will satisfy these parties; and, until such consummation, it seems as if a kind of deadlock must attach to every such enterprise in which northern craft and capital are required.

There is no doubt of the fact that many planters will have to discharge at least a part of their hands for want of provisions. And the friends (?) of the freedmen may note the fact that there are farms in the district entirely under colored control and management, which will almost certainly have to be soon abandoned for want of corn. One hundred bushels advanced on lien of the crop would be amply sufficient in each case to carry them through; and, yet all their efforts through the bureau and otherwise to obtain such assistance have thus far resulted in failure. It is very much to be regretted that such well-directed and commendable efforts on the part of these people should be doomed to disappointment.

The new tide of politics upon which Congress has launched the state is one which may lead us on to peace and prosperity, but it certainly will require cautious navigation. Passivity itself would be far better for us than opposition. The latter will do no good. An exciting campaign of opposing parties would intensify an antagonism which now only partially exists. And, after all, there is only one platform presented as essential to restoration—there is really no choice and therefore should be no contest. With all our privations and disappointments, let us at least have peace. If we have but a handful left, let it be "a handful with quietness."

JUHL

. . . The season thus far has been very favorable to the planting season. We have had a plenty of rain, and yet not too much, and the temperature and the weather have been all that could be desired. In some parts of the district the people have lost their slips, the seed banks when opened disclosing the rottenness of the contents. Hence sweet potatoes may be expected to rule high in the fall, if to be had at all. But much of the fruit seems to have escaped, and of berries we have every promise of an abundant yield.

The largest congregation at this place is that which is connected with the M.E. Church and must number its membership and adherents by the thousand. It has native colored pastors and owns a very large house of worship in the suburbs. . . . Connected with the church there is a very flourishing school under the tuition of two Massachusetts ladies and attended by crowds of colored children. It is sustained by northern societies; and it is unquestionably true that, as the North has given freedom to these people and made them full citizens, it should complete the work of educating them for a proper appreciation and enjoyment of their new estate. We certainly have not at present the means to do so.

The African Methodists also have a church here, and the Baptists have a small society with colored preachers. There are some private schools for colored children, and such ample opportunities thus furnished to this class of the population that any of them may acquire the rudiments of an education. The religious divisions indicated in the foregoing enumeration of sects are very apt to be followed and perpetuated in every future political canvass upon which this country may enter. Bread and hard work now absorb the attention, and we hear little of politics; but, we cannot expect the same indifference to continue when election agitations commence.

A new paper has just been issued in Manning. It is called the

Clarendon Press, is published by [M. B.] Lucas, [E. Manly] David and [E. P.] Lucas, three energetic and deserving young printers from this place, and is edited by J. W. Ervin, Esq., an earnest and gifted writer, who has had good experience as an editor, and in the line of the *nouvellette* has acquired some fame. No enterprise of the kind has probably commenced its career under more favorable auspices or with better promise of success—a result which all concerned with it richly deserve.

JUHL

SUMTER, S. C., April 22

... In the present starving condition of the country it is vitally important that our provision crop this year should be a good one. To insure this, even with good seasons and proper culture, it is necessary that reliable seed shall be used. And there is reason to fear that—on account of the difficulty of obtaining Carolina corn—many have planted the northern or western. It may not be known to them that such seed is utterly unreliable, at least in our soil and climate; that persons who tried it last year say that, with all the stimulant which the best fertilizers could give, it produced a diminutive stock and worthless nubbins. ...

While a small farmer living about a mile from this place was engaged a few days since at work in the field, with the small force in his employ, a freedman was discovered in the rear of the barn attempting to force an entrance. The alarm unfortunately was prematurely given, and the Negro escaped. On repairing to the spot, it was discovered that the daring rogue had succeeded in removing three pieces of the weather-boarding and but for the timely discovery would have soon obtained the coveted supply of grain. This occurred near midday, and the audacity of the attempt shows the necessity for strong measures for the suppression of disorder and crime if we would escape a general system of plunder between now and harvest.

The inflammatory addresses reported to have been made at meetings of the freedmen recently held in various places have occasioned unfeigned regret among some of the best friends of the colored race. And it is still more to be regretted that such addresses were received with favor. There is no necessity for this. There is no fitness, propriety, nor sound policy in such a course. In the exercise of their newly acquired rights, they have been undisturbed. They are organizing everywhere as a Union Republican party, and we hear of no opposition or counterdemonstration. Their platform, however intensely radical, and proceedings however open to criticism are published in the leading southern journals, generally without censure or comment. Under these circumstances, there is no excuse for bitterness. They have the right to organize and to vote for such men and such measures as they approve; but the more peaceably and amicably they proceed, the better for them and for the nation at large.

It is worthy of remark that even Governor Perry in his recent letter neither suggests nor recommends any opposing party organization, his nearest approach to it being in the advice to the white population to register as voters and simply to express on their tickets their nonconcurrence in the reconstruction of the state on the congressional basis. Many may differ with Governor Perry, and good and true men may believe it best to restore the state as soon as practicable to its civil functions, but certainly he has furnished in his late letter another evidence of fearless independence of character, and the words which come from his mountain home will derive additional force from his well-known antecedent history. There is scarcely a doubt, however, that the congressional plan *will* be carried out in this state, and opposition to that which is inevitable would not only be fruitless, but harmful in every way. "It takes two to make a quarrel."

The North desired and accomplished emancipation, but it is not to be supposed that its intelligent population will sustain either race at the South in any course which reason and justice do not approve. Even the Hon. Horace Greeley, the well-known advocate of freedom, in a private letter to your correspondent relating to the efforts now being made in New York for the relief of the South, says: "I beg you to believe that no one here asks whether the needy be white or black." And they are now generously engaged in supplying with food the very people over whom they so recently prevailed in arms.

JUHL

SUMTER, S. C., April 29

General [R. K.] Scott and the Reverend Mr. French [officials of the Freedmen's Bureau] have been on a visit to this place. On Saturday they had several conferences with white and colored citizens. On Sunday (yesterday) they visited the Sunday School of the Emanuel M.E. Church (colored) and expressed, in appropriate addresses, their gratification at the neat and tidy appearance of the scholars and the proficiency they exhibited in their various recitations. These consisted of catechism, Bible questions, and hymns recited. The whole school united in the song "America, My Country 'Tis of Thee," which was executed with spirit and harmony. Handsomely printed certificates and copies of a Sunday School paper were distributed, and the school then retired in platoons with the utmost order. Miss E. C. Breck and Miss Jane B. Smith, the ladies in charge, are from Massachusetts and seem devoted to the really missionary and noble work in which they are engaged. Before the war many of the first families in the state introduced into their domestic circles northern governesses to whom the education of their children was confided, and we cannot see why the same class of teachers should lose caste and be socially ostracized when they come among us as teachers of colored schools.

At 11 A.M. an immense congregation had assembled, and, as they could not be accommodated indoors, the seats were removed outside to a platform hastily erected in the open air. A number of white persons were present, but the vast majority of the audience were of the other race. The hymn "Try us, O God, and Search the Ground" was read by Chaplain French and sung by the choir and congregation. Prayer was offered by Rev. B. Lawson (colored) and addresses were made in the order named by General Scott, Mr. French, the Reverend Mr. Whittemore . . . J. J. Fleming, Esq. (in response to repeated calls from the meeting), and Rev. Scipio Horry (colored). The topics principally urged in these speeches were temperance, economy, industry, conjugal fidelity, harmony, and peace.

It was stated by authority from General Sickles that the registration of voters would not commence in the Second Military District before the last of June, in order to avoid any interruption of plantation work at this busy season. It was also said, on the same authority, that when competent colored men could be found to act as registrars, or in other capacity, the commanding general would not hesitate to include them in such appointments. The last named speaker is familiarly known among the freedmen as "the Bishop," and his address was in behalf of his numerous adherents, avowing their absolute want of confidence in the administration of bureau affairs in this district and urging on General Scott the necessity of a change. . . .

JUHL

Sumter, S. C., May 7

On Friday evening last a freedman was shot at Lynchburg in this district and severely if not mortally wounded by a white man named Morris or Morrissey. The freedman was a local preacher of the Methodist Episcopal Church and had participated as one of the speakers at several recent meetings of the colored people at that place, and it is said that the shooting was occasioned by remarks made on those occasions. We have heard of no other cause being assigned for the act. The affair has produced much excitement and will no doubt receive the attention it demands on the part of the authorities. Such outrages are inexcusable, and for the good of both races it is all-important that prompt and wholesome measures should be adopted to restrain the lawless. A thorough investigation may give a somewhat different complexion to this unfortunate occurrence—but the foregoing is a correct version as now generally reported, and we have heard no other or contrary statement.

JUHL

SUMTER, S. C., May 28

The steam ship *Saragossa* left Charleston on Saturday last, about midday, and landed her passengers in New York soon after breakfast on Tuesday morning. The run from your bar to Hatteras was magnificent. The barometer was sinking steadily, the sea and wind rising, and the weather threatening, and as the ship went rushing through the huge rollers, the scene presented was grand indeed. No vessel could have behaved better, none could have been managed more beautifully. Capt. M. B. Crowell, who commands this ship, is one of the most careful, watchful, and skillful commanders—an old navigator and a most uniformly fortunate one. . . .

The transition from South Carolina to this region is a great one—from poverty to wealth, from disorganized society to an established order of things in which the civil administration of the country is undisturbed. The city of New York is a great Babel of business, noise, and confusion. Its wealth is vast—its shipping almost innumerable—its businessmen untiring and energetic—it has much of which it may justly be proud. And yet, it has much of which it should be ashamed. Its charities to the South have not exceeded three hundred thousand dollars, and yet two-thirds of that sum has been sent to Carolina. Vice, dissipation, and the most degrading immoralities abound. "The Black Crook," as a dramatic performance, is contemptible; the recitation absolutely on the schoolboy order, and nothing redeems it but the music, the scenery, and the dancing. That such an exhibition should have such a protracted run among a people boasting of their intelligence is strange indeed. Last night, as usual, Niblo's was crowded.[3] Today I looked in at Trinity Church when it lacked but ten minutes of the time for service, and there were *three* persons in the pews. Such is New York. If half its secret history could be disclosed, a picture would be presented on which no man who loves his race would like to look.

JUHL

SUMTER, S. C., June 26

The rain falls piteously day after day, and the husbandman looks on with an anxiety which cannot be concealed on his inundated fields so lately full of glorious promise. Cotton looks sickly under such persistent and extravagant hydropathic treatment, and the corn in its soft and watery bed is prostrated and uprooted by the driving wind. At any time this would be cause enough for apprehensions; but now it is peculiarly so, when an impoverished and starving population recognize in an abundant harvest their only hope of escape from absolute ruin. But the summer is not yet ended, nor is the harvest past, and *ergo* even we may yet be saved. Strange to say, despite the recent rains, from some neighborhoods most favorable reports of the crops continue to be received, and if we escape a drought after so much wet weather, an abundant harvest may yet crown the labors of the year. At all events, there is no use in crossing a river until we reach it, and the evil of today is sufficient without plunging by anticipation into the possible evil of the morrow.

There is nothing more fatal to local prejudice than travel. "Can any

3. Niblo's was a famous amusement spot which included a theatre, gardens, and a refreshment pavilion.

good come out of Nazareth? Come and see." Personal observation often reverses our former opinions, especially where the mind is ready to welcome and approve and imitate that which is excellent, wherever and in whomsoever it may be found. If we have nothing to learn, we have reached a perfection of which no other people can boast. If we have yet much to learn, we should not object to profitable instruction, even though the tutor may not have been born in our own parish. In a country naturally rocky and barren in many places, it is certain the Yankee has managed to create around him an amount of wealth and comfort, of refinement and elegance, for which nothing but indomitable energy and perseverance can account. Intelligent labor, mechanical skill, a genius for invention, and a uniform and universal habit of industry can accomplish almost anything. Labor is honorable and honored in all its departments, and idleness is almost regarded as the synonym for crime. In such a society few "gentlemen of elegant leisure" can be found and a still smaller number of loafers about the corners and store steps.

Where land is unsuitable for any other purpose, it is "seeded down," and the result is a profitable crop of clover and hay and a pasturage which insures a rich and exhaustless dairy. If the land is covered with stumps, Yankee genius furnishes the machine by which they are quickly uprooted and ranged in barricade, fencing the field. If rocks abound, the same genius comes to the rescue, and by a cheap and simple contrivance removes them from their bed with much the same facility a dentist performs his delightful task. A tract of land is so poor that its inhabitants seriously regard a general exodus as inevitable, but one of them "guesses" that a little run of water as wide as a lady's fan, though at some distance off, might do something for them; the idea is communicated, and the rivulet is conducted to a basin, where it soon forms a clear and beautiful lake, supplying an unfailing water power, and a village springs up with its schoolhouses and church spires, and its factories are now worth several millions.

Connecticut has two capitals—Hartford and New Haven—between which the legislature alternates in its annual sessions. This year the lawmakers were at work in the former city, which is beautifully situated on the Connecticut River at the head of navigation. The senate chamber is suitable in size and appointments for the body which occupies it. The walls are adorned with portraits of past governors, including Jonathan Trumbull, from whom the great American family derives the name of Brother Jonathan. The presiding officer occupies a chair of charter oak and over him is a full-length portrait of Washington by Trumbull, originally intended for South Carolina, but relinquished by this state for the purpose of securing another in military costume—the one at Hartford being in civilian dress.

The representatives occupy a room having all the appearances of an ordinary lecture room, the speaker's chair not being elevated, and the members having no desks or tables. The hall is absolutely destitute of ornament and will not accommodate more than 150 persons, including the members. The same building contains a valuable library, the law department including the most complete collection of law reports extant. The librarian is something of an antiquarian and, among many other rare old writings, exhibited specimens of South Carolina colonial issues with autographs of the illustrious men of the olden time.

Juhl

Sumter, S. C., June 29

The accident on the Wilmington road has cut us off from the rest of mankind for nearly a week, during which time there have been no trains and no mails. This is refreshing—especially to one who has just returned from a section where lightning trains leave every hour, and where damages to the track are repaired in a very short time. But our railroads, as well as our people, feel the embarrassments of the times and are doubtless doing the best they can.

The effects of the late rains on the crops can scarcely yet be fully estimated. Some experienced planters place the damage to the cotton at 10 percent. This, however, may be no ultimate injury as the previous estimate would have given an unusually heavy crop, which being somewhat reduced may enhance the value proportionally. The provision crop, except in the bottom lands, may yet do well.

But to resume our notes of travel. . . . The [Connecticut] Democrats endorse Governor Perry's "no convention" policy. They say the South seceded without cause, but now has abundant cause for revolution, and ought not, by any acquiescence, to virtually endorse the Radical measures. They bitterly denounce the military governments now ruling with despotic sway over once proud and sovereign states and are especially severe upon that hyperexcessive negrophilism which gives everything to gentlemen of color and practically maintains that "*white* is no color at all—at all."

To all this we had but one reply: Gentlemen, it may do very well for you to talk of revolution, but *we* have had enough of it. We have not the power, if we had the desire, to repeat any such experiment. Our policy and our desire is peace, and the arts of peace we would cultivate. If there is to be any more revolution, you must kick it up among yourselves. The man who has his hand in the lion's mouth, if a sensible man, will do nothing to irritate the animal. If military governments are obnoxious, we can be relieved of their presence only by the restoration of civil rule; this can only be effected by our return to the Union, and for this there is but one road open—"all others lead astray."

It is a pleasure to record the fact that a Southerner with proper letters of introduction is well received at the North, and particularly so in New England, and hears nothing to grate harshly on his feelings or to remind him that he belongs to a conquered section. . . .

Taking one of the many steamers which ply daily between Hartford and New York, we enjoyed a delightful trip down the Connecticut for thirty miles: fare fifty cents. The scenery is beautiful, the river alive with small craft, the shad fisheries in active operation, the rock quarries with hundreds of workmen making music with their chisels, and [there are] the various towns at which the boat touches. Wethersfield, with its grim looking penitentiary and its suggestions of garden-sass, onion patches, and Sam Slick [Thomas C. Haliburton] humor; Middletown, in whose classic halls the gifted [Stephen] Olin has left the impress of a noble piety and a pure and consecrated learning; and Middlehaddam, where lies the old blockade-runner, *Ceres*, an iron steamer captured and sold by the government and afterwards accidentally burnt, all except the iron hull, which still looks defiant, although divested of motive power and dismantled.

Here we land and, leaving the river, with fast horses and light wheels pass over three and a half miles of magnificent hills and ever-varying landscapes to the beautiful village of East Hampton. The dwellings combine the useful and ornamental; the spires of two handsome churches rise high above the surrounding habitations; various schoolhouses, inseparable from every New England village, appear at convenient distances, and the factories of Bevin Brothers, Nichols & Watson, and others give employment to a large community in the manufacture of gongs and bells for sleighs, cars, hotels, steamboats, and factories, house bells, and in fact any and every kind of bell under two hundred pounds weight.[4]

The bells made here are preferred to all others for tone and power. A short but very agreeable sojourn at this place, embracing a visit to Pocotopaug (Clear Water) Lake, and the traveler leaves with an increasing suspicion that there is something else in Connecticut be-

4. "The Sisters of Mercy take this public method of returning their thanks to Julius J. Fleming, Esq., for his welcome donation of two handsome 'gong bells' and one beautiful 'call bell' for use in their new building" [*Sumter News*, July 6, 1867].

sides wooden nutmegs and peddlers of unreliable clocks. Yale College at New Haven (the alma mater of many a Southron in former days), the asylums for the insane and the deaf and dumb at Hartford, and the liberal provisions made by the state for the poor and for the education of the masses are monuments of a noble civilization to which this commonwealth can point with pride.

JUHL

SUMTER, S. C., July 5

Yesterday was duly celebrated here by a procession, addresses, and a public dinner. The procession was composed entirely of colored men and was an immense affair for this country, the numbers in ranks being estimated as high as five thousand, and there must have been at least half as many more (men, women, and children) present on the occasion who did not join in the march. The column was preceded by drum, fife, and bugle; in the centre was carried the United States flag, under the direction of numerous colored marshals, appropriately designated; and starting from Emanuel Church in the southern suburbs [the column] passed up Main Street and returned by Washington and Liberty and Main Streets to the grove near the depot, where a carpeted stand was erected for the speakers and a long line of tables for the dinner.

According to previous arrangements of the central committee having charge of the matter, Julius J. Fleming of Sumter presided, and the immense assembly was addressed in the order named by Messrs. Fleming, John T. Green, Rev. W. E. Johnson, John S. Richardson, Jr., Rev. Burrell James, T. J. McCants, and Rev. John B. Burroughs— those with the clerical prefix being colored. Rev. Scipio Horry (the Bishop) and Rev. Ben Lawson were also on the platform and took part in the exercises. Quite a number of white citizens of town and country were included in the audience, and the best of order prevailed throughout all the exercises of the day. Not a drunken man was visible, not a breach of the peace occurred. The dinner was a liberal one, provided by general contribution and amply sufficient for a very large crowd. But such a multitude defeated all previous calculations, and some, no doubt, went hungry away. By sundown our streets presented their usual quiet appearance—the multitude had departed, every man to his tent.

The freedmen certainly deserve great credit for their uniform good deportment. They have been visited and addressed by all classes of speakers and been subjected to various and conflicting influences, but they seem determined to pursue the even tenor of their way and, for so doing, deserve well of the country.

The weather is now intensely hot and too dry for crops.

J<small>UHL</small>

SUMTER, S. C., July 8

... The present stagnation in business, so generally deprecated, may be productive of good in the end by driving many from the ways of traffic to those of production. Numbers of persons, discouraged or disgusted last year with the change of labor, gave up planting and resorted to merchandizing. Hence, we have stores at almost every crossroad, and at the railway stations and villages they have multiplied beyond precedent. There has been no corresponding increase of population or of production to justify this, and it requires no very high development of prophetic vision to predict the inevitable result. Neither the country nor the men concerned are benefited when good farmers become small shopkeepers and give up the plough for the yard-stock and scales. ...

J<small>UHL</small>

Sumter, S. C., July 24

The new mail arrangement from Charleston to Sumter indicates progress, but does it in a way not very acceptable to the public or favorable to the press. The Charleston papers now reach us about 1 o'clock, P.M., on the day after publication, and Baltimore papers are received here two hours in advance of your city papers of the same date. Think of it; the running time per mail schedule between Sumter and Baltimore actually two hours less than between Sumter and Charleston!

It is a fact worthy of note that Georgia, long considered the Empire State of the South, exhibits more decided and influential opposition to the congressional reconstruction measures than can be found in probably any other. Among the leading minds of South Carolina, Mr. Perry seems to have stood almost alone in his "no convention" policy. And yet he is not without admirers, and it is not at all improbable that the intelligent white population of the upper districts will endorse his views at the ballot box. These views will also derive additional strength and popularity from the recent acts of Congress. . . .

The political apathy evinced by many is increased by the growing conviction that Congress has not yet reached a finality, and that all the coming programme of registration and elections will really in the end amount to nothing; that Congress will retain its present control and empire, and these states remain military districts for at least a year or two to come.

Sumter has another garrison. Company G, 29th Infantry, is encamped in the Academy Grove. Major [Lyman] Bissell of the regular army has taken command of this post, and a provost court is organized and established by an order from the commanding general. . . . The district court, now in session here, may consider its days numbered, and it has so few friends that its demise will not cause a very general lamentation. Under existing circumstances it is very hard on an impoverished people to have to support the expensive machinery of a state government, which is but a shadow and a name at best.

The arrival of a garrison is timely. The lovers of good order will not object to the presence of a force which will be respected even when bad whiskey and bad men come in contact and threaten the peace.

The weather is sultry and the crops suffering.

Another change in the mail schedule today, the mail coming from your city by the Northeastern Railroad . . . lands here side by side with the Baltimore mail of the same date.

JUHL

SUMTER, S. C., July 29

Prospecting may pay better than retrospecting, but when the surroundings are gloomy and the future dark, a swoop into the past or a flight into the far away may furnish such mental diversion from graver thoughts as the "political summer heat" demands. . . . We are a great people as well as a great country and can furnish the greatest political problem of the age—the problem of reconstruction. Congress has taken a grand hunt and captured the elephant, and the animal wearied with his past struggles stands quiet enough, subdued in spirit and awaiting the action of his keepers. But the keepers seem to require much time for deliberation, and the poor brute awaits in anxious suspense their decision. How shall the elephant be disposed of? That's the problem which, if solved speedily and well, will throw in the shade all past achievements of political necromancy.

In the book line, the wonder of the age is the new revised and enlarged edition of Webster's dictionary. . . . In its etymologies, synonyms, illustrations, and definitions it is the best manual extant to the student who wishes to acquire the multifarious wealth of the composite English tongue. There is more real education in it than in any other single work. The sum total of great libraries may be found in the three books: the Bible, Shakespeare, and Webster's royal quarto.

In our recent rambles in and around Springfield, Massachusetts, many places, persons, and things of interest were found which deserved attention. There was the armory with its spacious buildings and beautiful grounds, its lofty cupola commanding an extensive and charming view of city and country, its three hundred thousand splendid muskets ranged in racks with mathematical precision, and its curiosity room in which numberless specimens of broken, bent, and busted guns were exposed to view, and guns dented or perforated with shot, and guns with various devices and inscriptions carved into the stocks by southern and Union soldiers whose names they bore, all these having been gathered on the battlefields of the late war.

And there was the cemetery rivalling Mt. Auburn and Greenwood in its monuments, its fountains, its drives, and its shrubbery and trees—on a small scale, it is true, but none the less beautiful for that. And there was the immense establishment of the Union Paper Company with its genial and generous proprietors, Dickenson & Taylor, filling large southern orders for printing and writing paper of every description with as much satisfaction to their customers as if they were present to select for themselves; and the Columbia Paper Company and the Paper Collar Factories with their wonderful array of machinery and operatives, and Morgan's Manufactory of Envelopes putting up a superb article in a style which cannot be surpassed and stamping your initials on paper and envelopes if you desire it. But all these would leave a visit to Springfield incomplete, if there was not included an hour spent with the Merriams, the publishers of Webster. . . .

On Saturday last, two of the town police of Sumter were arrested by the post commander under an order from General [Daniel E.] Sickles for alleged unnecessary severity towards some disorderly freedmen in this town. The occurrence which occasions this military process is not a very recent one, and the parties concerned were certainly surprised and startled by being so suddenly withdrawn from their guardianship of this august corporation and consigned to jail. An ineffectual effort was made by the intendant to obtain their release on the usual recognizance, but the accused will probably be arraigned today before the provost court and shortly disposed of. This hath a moral, which your readers can supply.

JUHL

SUMTER, S. C., August 26

... We are passing through the initial steps in the reconstruction programme; the work of registration proceeds quietly and appears to occasion no excitement. Very many of the white population are excluded from the privilege, which will necessarily make the colored majority larger than it really is in proportion to the population. Among the disfranchised there are, doubtless, some who are still hostile to the government, but there are many others who would cheerfully cooperate in restoring the state to civil rule and her rightful position in the Union, if they were allowed to do so, whose participation in the work would make it more satisfactory, durable, and complete.

But Congress has decided the question and there is no appeal. Even wise men may err, and measures which in their general features seem unassailable may in some of the details involve a political mistake, a blunder, a crime—a crime against the genius of a free government, a crime against the country's good. If this be so, time will demonstrate the fact, and even the national legislature may see cause to remove all such civil disabilities and restore our disfranchised fellow-citizens to at least equal rights with all other colors and classes whatsoever. Unless these states are well governed, we certainly cannot expect the intelligent and enterprising white men of the North to trust either themselves or their capital at the South. And yet there are many such now waiting and ready to come, but they wish first to see what kind of government we are to have before they make the venture.

The provost court continues its sessions from day to day. It is expeditious, but costly. It dispenses with the jury and, therefore, is no tax on the time of the people, except the parties and witnesses in each particular case. Its decisions may be considered final—substantially without appeal, in view of the costs attending such process under the general orders establishing the court. The decision of the Supreme Court *in re* Milligan might be considered adverse to the legality or constitutionality of such courts in time of peace, but in this latitude it would be a waste of time to urge any such plea to the jurisdiction. Perhaps if we had no such court we might have something worse. Certainly, the only civil tribunal (the district courts) which the late legislature gave us, having concurrent jurisdiction with the provost court, is liable to grave objections and is by no means popular. It remains to be seen how the present military arrangement will work.

Two freedmen, recently sentenced respectively to twelve and six months' imprisonment, "at such place as the commanding general may direct," made their escape a few nights afterwards, doubtless preferring to select for themselves their place of residence for the allotted period. At first view, such conduct might seem disloyal; but, on the other hand, it indicated great reliance on their own judgment.

JUHL

SUMTER, S. C., September 2

. . . Careless, ignorant, and unscientific farming is so often seen throughout the South that its rough and wasteful and offensive features need not be described. A picture of the opposite kind is presented in the view from Mount Holyoke in western Massachusetts. A very good road with an easy ascent leads up the mountain to within six hundred feet of the summit, and this latter distance is traversed in a small car up a covered railway at an inclination of about forty-five degrees. This lands the tourist in a very good hotel, which furnishes, *inter alia*, the requisite glasses for the eye to "view the landscape o'er." The landscape includes the beautiful villages of Amherst, Northampton, Hadley, etc., a long stretch of the richest meadows through which the Connecticut pursues its serpentine course, and innumerable factories, villas, and glistening spires interspersed. Seen on a bright day in June, nothing in the way of landscape can be more charming—a natural paradise with all the exquisite embellishments of art. Jenny Lind, who spent her summers in Northampton, declared there was nothing in Europe to equal it; neither Italy nor the Rhine could surpass it in loveliness. The meadows are in the grasses and sometimes the small cereals, and at that season present a rich carpeting of green, whose continuity is unbroken by fencing of any kind, for cattle are not allowed to run at large.

The farms are small, but are admirably cultivated, and every acre is made to respond most liberally in tons of hay or other products by the most approved system of dressing and tillage. And all the appendants of the farm indicate this. The horses are large, substantial animals, with glossy skins, well-fed and well-groomed, and uniformly in admirable condition. The same is true of cattle and other stock. The farm implements are also of the most improved patents. The buildings are neat and often elegant, and the agricultural works on the library shelves give evidence that they have often been handled during the long winters. The refinement and comfort and plenty everywhere are the fruits and rewards of intelligent, educated labor. It has made an Eden of a land naturally poor, and where winters are long and rigorously severe. What would the application of the same principles, energy, intelligence, and systematic and scientific efforts make of South Carolina, with such a soil as we have and such a climate all the year? Governor [Henry A.] Wise tells the Virginians:

We must change our whole system of labor. The agricultural interest especially must renounce its old routine of planting the large staple crops, and culture must be more varied, on a smaller scale, and on a more improved system, or a system more improving. Arboriculture, horticulture, gardening, and trucking, and grasses, and stock raising must be substituted for the one idea of wheat and tobacco, and the mechanic arts must be substituted for the "soft places" of clerking and drumming, and bookkeeping, and town employments of irregular loungers about a trade and commerce which have not pabulum enough to support them. We must teach our children to labor and love and honor labor by going to work ourselves, earnestly, honestly, hopefully.

Such words are like "apples of gold in pitchers of silver," and the reader will find in them wholesome food for thought until the subject herein being considered shall be resumed.

Juhl

Sumter, S. C., September 4

. . . When Congress made a grant of lands to the states for agricultural schools, three hundred and sixty thousand acres were assigned to Massachusetts and were subject to entry at $1.25 per acre. The scrip was sold at $.80 per acre, and the money applied at an agricultural college which has been located near Amherst. Connecticut assigned the scrip to Yale College, which will receive the benefit of the prospective rise in the land; and this, it is said, will eventually be worth $5.00 an acre. In New York, Ezra Cornell offered $500,000 for the scrip, if they would take the agricultural college of that place which had been a failure and locate it at Ithaca. He has located the scrip and is selling it at $5.00 an acre.

South Carolina would have received one hundred and eighty thousand acres of the public lands for the same purpose; but, under an act of Congress the secretary of the interior was instructed not to deliver any of the scrip to unrepresented states until further orders. The further orders will no doubt be given as soon as approved state governments are established, and it will become then the duty of "the powers that be" to secure and apply this fund, either in attaching an agricultural department to the university or—what may be better—in establishing a separate school in which a thorough course of instruction shall be given in scientific and practical agriculture, in physical geography, agricultural chemistry, zoology, botany, structural anatomy, reproduction, and rural architecture. The model farm connected with such a school may not only present the leading southern staples in the highest state of development and cultivation, but materially contribute to the annual revenues of the institution.

It is worthy of remark that even in New England this subject has assumed an importance second only to its great and leading manufacturing interests and has already made its bleak and naturally barren hills yield the most astonishing returns to the husbandman. How much more pressing are its claims upon us, who are preëminently an agricultural people, and who have no pursuits whatever to which can subordinate the cultivation of the soil? Germany has thirty-two universities, and yet all Germany and indeed all Europe has but one Liebig. America has a multitude of colleges and but one Agassiz, and he is not of native growth! But the world moves on, and the brotherhood of scholars—the highest freemasonry on earth—is at work. And the time may soon come when South Carolina will be connected by the wires of thought with the best chemists and savants and scientific men of New and old England and France and Germany—wires which will be worth more to us than any cable the *Great Eastern* laid, and which can never suffer break or interruption, except from prejudice, and the day has come when prejudice should be buried as deep as the cable beneath the sea.

JUHL

Sumter, S. C., September 6

What's in a name? A rose would smell as sweet by any other; and, when a rose is despoiled of all its other charms, the stealing of its name should pass without indictment. The South has lost much; shall it also lose its favorite sobriquet of Dixie? A writer in the *New Orleans Delta* says:

I do not wish to spoil a pretty illusion, but the real truth is that "Dixie" is an indigenous northern Negro refrain, as common to the writer as the lampposts in New York City, seventy or seventy-five years ago. It was one of the everyday allusions of boys at that time in all their outdoor sports. And no one ever heard of Dixie's land being other than Manhattan Island, until recently, when it has been erroneously supposed to refer to the South from its connection with pathetic Negro allegory. When slavery existed in New York, one "Dixy" owned a large tract of land on Manhattan Island and a large number of slaves. The increase of the slaves and the increase of the abolition sentiment caused an emigration of the slaves to more thorough and more secure slave sections, and the Negroes who were thus sent off naturally looked back to their old homes where they had lived in clover, with feelings of regret, as they could not imagine any place like Dixy's.

Hence it becomes synonymous with an ideal locality, combining ease, comfort, and material happiness of every description. In those days Negro singing and minstrelsy were in their infancy, and any subject that could be wrought into a ballad was eagerly picked up. This was the case with "Dixie." It originated in New York and assumed the proportions of a song there. In its travels it has been enlarged and has gathered moss. It has picked up a note here and a note there. A chorus has been added to it, and from an indistinct chant of two or three notes it has become an elaborate melody. But the fact that it is not a Southern song cannot be rubbed out. The fallacy is so popular to the contrary, that I have thus been at pains to state the real origin of it.

The South has suffered so much in the way of real disaster and spoliation that this additional bereavement will scarcely deepen the shadows of her children's grief. Besides, there is some satisfaction in knowing that if Boston is the "hub," New York is "Dixie." And again, if this is no "Southern song," there is nothing disloyal in it. Webster defines Dixie: "An imaginary place somewhere in the southern states of America, celebrated in a popular Negro melody as a perfect paradise of luxurious ease and enjoyment." Perhaps New York may have been such a place to the Negro in the olden time; perhaps it is no longer such, especially in midwinter! Seven cities may have quarreled over Homer; we have no disposition to quarrel over anything. "The empire is peace." If any man "take away thy coat, let him have thy cloak also." Is not this the logic and the philosophy of the hour? . . .

The spirit of unrest still exists among our population. The emigration fever has not yet subsided. Mexico and Brazil have been tried with no encouraging results. Now Honduras looms up as the land of promise, and parties in this and Darlington District are preparing to move. In a population of twenty-five thousand it has only about two thousand whites; the rest are Mexicans, Negroes, Spaniards, and Indians. The British flag may float there, but does the red cross of St. George promise any more to us than the stars and stripes? Besides, what's the use of moving at so much expense, danger, and trouble when the Second Adventists have announced that positively next year will be the last in the calendar, and immense multitudes are encamped in various places at the North waiting the grand event? [William] Miller, it is true, tried this twenty-five years ago and, although greatly encouraged and assisted by an immense comet, failed—but now? Well, now, even now there are skeptics. . . .

JUHL

SUMTER, S. C., September 13

Among other items showing the importance of the early reestablishment of civil rule is the war of opinion at present existing with reference to the courts. The district or county courts created by the late legislature by no means meet the demands of the country and cannot give satisfaction. The U.S. Provost Court, established at this post by General Sickles, is declared in the local press to be unpopular with all classes. What the country seems to demand is a uniform system for the administration of justice for all classes alike. With the turbulent elements at work and with irresponsible and ignorant and often unprincipled men assuming the direction of political affairs, who among us can venture to say what will be the issue, and when, if ever, we will emerge from shadow into sunshine again? "When the pot boils, the scum floats"—thus hath it ever been, thus shall it ever be.

The provost court, which in the short space of six weeks has managed to wake up the districts of Sumter and Clarendon and create an excitement far more extensive than agreeable, has taken a short vacation in order to accommodate with the courtroom the equity court now in session here.[5] Chancellor [W. D.] Johnson, calm, patient, attentive, presides and looks down benignantly and encouragingly upon the bar. And the bar indicates business—the decks are cleared for action—the tables are covered with papers and long rows of equity reports, and the chairs are occupied by the learned solicitors, whose delight it is to unravel the mysteries of the chancery practice. . . .

JUHL

5. During these weeks F. J. Moses, Jr., one of three men on the provost court, severed his editorial connections with the *Sumter News* and began a career which would make him governor of South Carolina, 1872–1874. However, in the *News* (September 21, 1867) Moses vowed he was still not a Radical in the usual sense of the word.

On Sunday afternoon, September 22, a very interesting meeting was held at the Emmanuel (colored) Church in this place. After appropriate introductory services by colored preachers, three large volumes containing the Psalms and New Testament scriptures in raised letters for the blind were presented to the pastor, the Rev. Scipio Horry, a blind freedman, who uniformly sustained a good character while a slave, and who, since emancipation, has exerted a very great influence over his own race.

The presentation was made by Mr. J. J. Fleming in the name and behalf of the American Bible Society, and responses were made by Rev. Scipio Horry, J. B. Burroughs, and Burrell James. A rising vote of thanks was given by the entire congregation to the American Bible Society, to Mr. Fleming, on whose recommendation and application the gift was secured, to Messrs. John and Lewis Tappan of New York for their kind offices in the same direction, and to Miss Jane B. Smith, the teacher who instructed the preacher in the alphabet and rudiments and thus furnished him the key with which to unlock this rich treasure house of knowledge, to Messrs. Ravenel & Co., of Charleston, for obtaining free transportation by steamship and express from New York to Sumter of the package containing these large and handsome volumes.

Mr. T. J. Coughlan, United States marshal and provost judge, also addressed the meeting at some length in general advice as to conduct and expressed his great gratification at what he had witnessed on that occasion. The music was furnished by the choir with melodeon accompaniment, and the entire services were invested with unusual interest, and all classes of the population were represented and appeared to take pleasure in the same.

JUHL

SUMTER, S. C., November 22

The English Parliament, in emancipating the slaves in the Windward Isles, voted and paid a handsome sum in compensation to the owners. It neither disfranchised the white inhabitants nor raised the blacks to political supremacy. It did not require the untutored Negro to suddenly assume the intelligence of the politician and the wisdom of the lawmaker. But Congress recognizes the necessity of outstripping its British rival and, in its determination to revive the age of miracles, "laughs at impossibilities, and cries, it must be done." Humanity may say the Negro is a man; philanthropy may recognize in him a brother; but how can the statesman discern in him already every qualification of citizenship and every capacity for the government of states?

And yet what are we required to witness? All the formalities of an election for a convention in which the people of South Carolina are to be considered represented in solemn assembly and from which the white population—the taxpayers and property holders, the real supporters of the government—have been ingeniously, involuntarily, and maliciously excluded![6] It matters not how various their views, whether they are with or against the national legislature, whether always Union men or the most determined "rebels," whether allowed to register or not, they are equally voiceless, unless they can adopt the extreme Union League platform, consent to Negro supremacy, and impose upon their own race the most degrading disabilities.

Men in this section have been bitterly denounced by the party leaders because they maintained that it was neither wise nor proper to go beyond Congress in reconstructing the state. What Congress required might be considered unavoidable, but to transcend even its radicalism was considered more than any party had a right to ask of

6. According to the *Sumter News* (September 28, 1867), there were 3,288 qualified Negro voters in Sumter District and 1,191 qualified white voters. In the town of Sumter registration totals showed 1,029 Negroes and 317 whites.

the honest white men of the state. And yet the party which has managed and controlled the only vote polled in the present election did ask and insist on more than Congress required, and the consequence is that the entire mass of intelligent citizens of native or northern or even foreign birth have had to stand aloof. The Negroes have been duped by designing leaders, and it is no slander to say that these latter—as far as known to the country—are entitled to neither confidence nor respect. Certainly they have done no service or kindness to the freedmen in arraying them in disastrous hostility to the other race.

And what shall be said of a party which in its very triumph involves everything in desolation? And who will say that the colored race can find in any political franchise or fraudulent victory an offset and compensation for the general impoverishment which, as a consequence, everywhere threatens? When was this country poorer than it is today? All its industrial energies brought to a deadlock, its labor fatally demoralized, its business reduced to stagnation, and its people plunged in despondency and gloom! Can anyone doubt that this is the result of Radical rule and the continued agitation of the country by political demagogues? Who can look ahead and arrange for the future?

And where must the agricultural interest, upon which all other interests in this country depend, look for encouragement and protection when the laborer is filled with the wildest notions and alienated not only from his employer, but from his accustomed pursuits? Crazy legislation when thus carried out to its legitimate results brings ruin and death in its train. The tables have turned, but they have turned too far—and the party *regnant* in its attempts to hoist the Negro into the saddle has performed the part of the clown who, in assisting an awkward rider to mount his horse, had pushed him too far to the other side and brought him to the ground again. The clown was greeted with laughter and shouts; the party is repudiated by the white population and will in time receive the anathemas of the black man himself.

A company of white emigrants left this place on Monday last for Honduras; men, women, and children, eleven in number. Others had previously left for North Carolina. *Sic transit.*

Robberies are frequent, some of them very daring and some even sacrilegious. On last Sunday, during the Sabbath School services in the Episcopal Church, the surplices and other regalia of the priesthood were stolen from the vestry room, and the minister had to officiate in the usual citizen's dress. Cotton, in bales, is stolen from the depot, although under the care of paid watchmen, and the stock of the country is rapidly disappearing to meet the cormorant demands of irrepressible marauders. . . .

JUHL

SUMTER, S. C., December 8

In France stagnation of trade, depression of the leading industrial interests, disordered finances, and a scarcity of breadstuffs are considered evidence of bad government and, when not promptly remedied, lead to a popular revolution. These proofs of political misrule all exist in this country to an extent which in England would force a change of ministry and render in France a revolution inevitable. And such must be the result in the United States, for it cannot be doubted that when the great intelligent masses of the North are forced to realize the extent of the ruin which is now being brought upon this country, they will hurl from power the reckless men who have wrought the mischief.

The present condition of the southern trade is not without voice and meaning to the capitalists of the North. It has been confidently anticipated by its great and varied manufacturing interests that if the South could survive the famine and other discouragements of the present year, the new crop would usher in a revival of trade and the southern people become buyers on a large scale of northern and eastern wares as in olden times. But these anticipations have not been realized. There is scarcely an article manufactured in the mills and factories of New York and New England but what is wanted at the South, but our people are too poor to buy. Another year of free Negro labor, under all the demoralization which persistent party training could accomplish, has left the planters without money and without hope. Their uniform testimony is against a renewal of the experiment. It will not pay. There is no money in it, but any amount of vexation, annoyance, and harassing care.

The South under the existing regime is utterly unable to contribute to the national wealth—whatever may be extorted from it in the way of revenue—but is, and must continue to be, a tax and a burden upon the national energies; and, as to its trade, every year must witness its continued decline under the mad legislation which keeps the country in commotion and unrest. So far from encouraging southern agriculture, checked as it was known to be by a most damaging change in its system of labor, Congress has this year extorted 20 millions of dollars in one item from the impoverished, unrepresented, and persecuted cotton producers of the South. In this one sentence, announcing as it does a stern and living fact, there is a volume of rebuke. The entire cotton region, but recently overrun by hostile armies and wasted under the desolating fires of war, scourged by famine during the year, and thousands suffering and some actually dying from starvation, baffled in its best efforts by unreliable labor which eats up the planter's substance, preys upon his property, and defies his authority, reaches the close of another troublous year still unrepresented and voiceless in its woe, and from its leading staple alone is required to pay 20 millions to the revenue. Vive la Republique!

The necessary result of such legislation will soon be painfully visible. The continued political disturbance of the country, keeping up a state of feverish excitement among the blacks by all the ingenious campaign appliances which party chicanery can contrive and party funds support, has brought them, as laborers, into such low repute that there will be an exceedingly limited demand for them in the future. White men in cities and elsewhere who frequent barrooms and run wild over elections, losing time from their work, are soon turned adrift; prudent businessmen are afraid of them. And this is a principle which will apply generally. The northern farmer would insist on it, and the southern farmer must do the same. Hence, very many in this section, from the want of means as well as the want of confidence, will plant less and depend on their own labor and such exceptional cases of steady old hands as they may be able to obtain and to trust. The Negroes, as usual, exhibit a sublime indifference to the future. Of course, the bureau and the party will supply their wants.

Those who early in emancipation looked on the freedmen with kindness and sympathy and Christian hope have been greatly disappointed. And this, not so much in the freedmen themselves, as in the concurrence of so many poisonous influences to ruin them and the country. Who can say that the experiment of free labor has had a fair trial? Who can doubt that everything would have worked well if these people had been undisturbed by party emissaries, religious fanatics, Union Leagues, and political harangues? If friendship, peace, and habits of industry had been inculcated with half the zeal with which the very opposites are daily taught by those who came among them with hatred in their hearts to the white race of the South, how different would have been the condition of this country today and how much happier the future!

Even a few months ago our most gifted citizens did not hesitate to attend and address the meetings of the freedmen, thus recognizing their new position and cheerfully conceding to them every accruing right. But others, of a different stamp, have since poisoned the minds of these people against those who were too honorable to resort to the same measure of low craft and duplicity to retain their influence, and a marked line of separation now appears. Is the freedmen or the country benefited by the change? And will not the colored race, if ever properly enlightened, abhor and condemn these agents of evil, whether native or imported?

No remedy for existing evils will be afforded by the simple removal of the cotton tax. If Congress has determined on its programme and will give us at once such constitutions as it demands, dispensing with all farther farcical pretences of popular elections and popular ratifications and thus saving the laboring population from any more political fomentation, the country may resume its former quiet and go to work again. A little more peace and a little less politics, or our ruin is complete.

Private advices from Florida represent that territory as eaten out and ruined by the depredations of the freedmen; one lady is said to have lost during the year, in this way, her entire stock of sheep, amounting to fifteen hundred. This section is also suffering greatly and the plunderers hold high carnival. Occasionally, a detachment of hog-stealers leave for the penitentiary, but the evil is in no wise abated, as there always seem to be "a few more of the same sort" left.

JUHL

1868

Juhl's correspondence for 1868 opened on a happy note. Christmas of 1867 had been a joyous occasion with a parade, a mock pageant, hand-organ and monkey, and lots of firecrackers. Hundreds of citizens thronged the street of Sumter to join in the fun, "without reference to race, color or previous condition." Then a few weeks later Fleming was off to Florida for an extensive tour of Fernandina, Jacksonville, and St. Augustine. His eleven comprehensive letters not only tell about these cities, but also describe a stopover in Savannah and give on-the-spot accounts of Reconstruction in two more southern states.

Perhaps the two most important developments in the life of Sumter during these months were both of a disturbing nature: the presidential canvass and the beginning of Ku Klux Klan activity. Throughout September and October Negro voters were kept at almost a fever pitch by a variety of rabble-rousers. The Klan, which first appeared in April of 1868, was never very potent in Sumter, but presented a constant threat to order. The reasons why this organization had few recruits are all too obvious. The white segment of the population was in a distinct minority, and the Freedmen's Bureau and its agents were unusually prominent in this region.

In November Juhl visited briefly at Walhalla in the northwestern corner of the state and sent the *Courier* a trio of intriguing letters about that thriving community composed mostly of German immigrants. Also during the last months of 1868 and the opening weeks of 1869 he contributed several articles to the *New York World*. This brief connection was undoubtedly prompted by the Grant-Seymour election battle. The *World*, a Democratic organ, wanted as dismal a picture as possible of life in South Carolina, and Juhl did his best. In a letter written on December 4 and signed merely "F," he told readers of the *World*,

> The lower half of this state is completely Africanized and under the absolute control of the carpetbaggers. Idle and ragged Negroes abound, and no kind of movable property is safe. Cotton, provisions, cattle, hogs, poultry are often swept away at night. Into the up-country the more notorious adventurers are afraid to go; the Negro leagues have been broken up, and a better state of things exists; and there the Negro is better clothed and better off, and seems happier, and is certainly well treated wherever I have traveled and observed his condition. If he has less politics, he has better clothes, better food, and a more fixed and comfortable home than his low-country brother.

This letter and others which Fleming contributed to the *World* told of corrupt government at every level, predicted that the Citadel would shortly become a Negro school (Jefferson College), and emphasized the moral and economic decline of his native state.

It is interesting to note that his columns appearing in the *Courier* during those same weeks painted a somewhat more hopeful picture. The weather had been propitious, crops good, and money circulated freely in Sumter. Apparently Juhl was neither the first nor the last correspondent to write what he believed an editor wanted his readers to see. And in his last column of the year Juhl again hammered away at the absolute necessity for a balanced economy in the South:

> To say that the South ought to be and can be self-sustaining is to reiterate a declaration which was by no means new fifty years ago. It has the power to manufacture and raise a multitude of articles which it now imports from other sections, and by so doing could retain much

of the money now sent away, and greatly improve, embellish, and beautify its homes with such surplus capital. But argument is wasted on this subject; the principle is admitted, the fault confessed, but the practice remains unchanged from generation to generation, and the country grows older day by day without its landscape evincing any of the ripening influences of taste, culture, and wealth, which mark and attend maturity in other lands.

SUMTER, S. C., January 2

The twenty-fifth was balmy and bright as a spring day. Our streets were thronged with people, and all seemed determined, without reference to "race, color or previous condition," to enjoy the Christmas fun. The "Fantastics," grotesque in dress and character, paraded at noon and with bugle, hand-organ and monkey, followed by a long cavalcade of funny fellows, and caused shouts of merriment wherever they appeared. The ladies crowded the courthouse steps and balcony, forming an arch of beauty, before which the mock pageant halted more than once in rapt admiration. Firecrackers, Christmas trees, balloons, and the ladies' supper for the benefit of the Presbyterian Church all received due attention, and no accident or disturbance marred the pleasures of the day.

The holidays have not been without accident. The town tanner has had another visit from the robbers, who, this time, completed the job and carried off the balance of his stock. The small room used as a jail is crowded with inmates, with a loyal indifference to color; and, as these were debarred the usual pyrotechnic privileges of the season, they broke the lamps furnished by the sheriff, scattered the kerosene over the floor, set it on fire, gave the alarm, and expected of course to scatter themselves as soon as the door was opened. In this, however, they were disappointed, the fire was soon extinguished, and quiet restored with the prisoners all safe. One of them, at another time, while bringing water attempted an escape, was pursued by the guard who indulged in some very bad pistol practice on the occasion, and after a long chase the prisoner was recaptured, handcuffed and locked up, but during the night one of his comrades broke off the handcuffs and threw them in the stove where they were soon rendered worthless. All this is very pleasant to the sheriff whose term expires in March and who will most gladly hand over the office to one of the several candidates now urging their claims with the commanding general.

The provost court owes its existence to the reported unfairness of the civil courts in cases where freedmen are concerned. That it works charmingly in behalf of these people or in behalf of somebody is evidenced from the fact that a Negro committed on any charge, however trivial, and whose friends desire his release or bail, has to pay five dollars for his bail bond (exclusive of any other costs) whereas under civil or state process the magistrate was not allowed to charge a tenth of that sum, and even this charge had to be made against the state and not against the prisoner. How far such a statement may invalidate the only plea or pretext for the continuance of such courts, it is for others to judge.

It is too early yet to report how much of the laboring population will obtain engagements, or how much land compared with last year will be planted. In general it may be safely assumed that there will be a great falling off in the area planted and in the number of hands employed.

JUHL

FLORIDA IN FEBRUARY   1[1]

The great body of travelers making their way to Florida—whether for business, pleasure, or health—will naturally seek Charleston as a convenient and desirable point of departure. There are numerous steamers leaving that port for all points on the southern Atlantic coast almost daily, and among these there is none which offers more in the way of comfort, speed, and safety than the *City Point* and the *Dictator*. The former is in size and in all her appointments unquestionably the finest and fastest vessel of the kind in our southern waters. The *City Point* is commanded by Capt. Sim Adkins, of whom it may be enough to say that he smokes the biggest pipe, wears the jolliest face, and drinks less and sleeps less than almost any other man in his profession.

1. These Florida letters, bearing no dateline, appeared in various issues of the *Courier*, February 25–March 25, 1868.

But more may be added, for the observant passenger will soon discover that this rotund and wide-awake captain is thoroughly "reconstructed," albeit he has no special fondness for carpetbag politicians, bureau agents, and Negro conventions, and that he will hardly yield the palm to G. F. Train[2] himself in vivacity of conception and the rapidity and eloquence with which he unfolds some of the magnificent enterprises which occupy his thoughts. Not the least among these may be named a city at Picolata, a line of steamships from Europe to Port Royal, building up a second New York there, and filling the country with emigrants in a few voyages, and by consequence making the desolated land of the palmetto once more blossom as the rose. But the discussion of these magnificent schemes is not the object and design of these papers, and therefore any who may feel a special interest in them are advised to take a trip on the *City Point* and have it all served up by a master hand, with the turtle soup and venison steaks, and other delicacies which grace that steamer's mahogany.

Leaving Charleston at nine o'clock Friday night, the water distance of 112 miles to Savannah is accomplished in eight hours. Although this is called the outside passage, it really presents little, if any, more of the perils and discomforts of a sea voyage than a trip on one of the New York and Albany night boats on the Hudson or a night in good weather on one of the Sound boats between New York and Boston. It embraces a night view of Charleston harbor, with its numerous lights from city and shore and fortress and beacon, a few hours of "a life on the ocean wave," and then Savannah River from Tybee to the city.

Arriving at Savannah soon after daybreak, the steamer remains at

2. George Francis Train (1829–1904), an exotic, superactive New Englander whose career spanned several continents and numerous causes, was much in the news for his espousal of the Fenians and his unorthodox political views.

the wharf there until 3 P.M. This gives ample time for a tramp over the city and a view of the surroundings. The city itself presents much the same appearance it did before the war, but the surroundings mark the sad results of the late terrible struggle. Standing on the high bluff which overlooks the river, the immense area of rice lands on the South Carolina side are in full view. These were formerly immensely valuable and were under the most admirable culture, but they appear now like a vast waste of prairie, and the stately mansions with their surroundings of neat cottages, barns, and rice mills are no longer visible. Their cultivation involved a system of embankments, dykes, and drainage which doubtless contributed to the health of Savannah, and their present abandoned or partially neglected condition will probably create a miasma which will largely increase the bills of mortality in the future. At the Screven ferry slips there was a closely packed collection of small boats, canoes, yawls, batteaux, etc., of the roughest description, owned and occupied by Negroes, and laden with oysters and an occasional bundle of rice straw, wood, etc. Inquiry settled the point that numbers of these people who had been raised to the hoe had abandoned their old habits and taken to the water, where they eke out a precarious existence.

Inquiry established the additional fact that the most of the oysters were taken in fresh or brackish water, and that many who had used their bivalves had already died from cholera, and the disease was quite prevalent in the surrounding population. The rice fields required continuous labor, and this the freedman has now the right to shun. The river and the roughest old boat sends freedom on a cruise, and a boatload of oysters landed at the wharf gives the boatman rest and a frolic while the money lasts. There is a philosophy in this which, however obnoxious to the commerce and wealth of the country, finds a ready disciple and convert in the emancipated Negro, and no bureau nor formidable order from headquarters can change his opinion. General [John] Pope had the right to have his "headquarters in the saddle," and Cuffy has the right to have his headquarters on the oyster banks. There may be some difference between canoe loads of oysters and casks of rice inviting the commerce of the world, but political economy is a dry subject, and well-nigh obsolete, and if its teachings are still followed elsewhere, it certainly is not in this latitude.

Large plantations must give way to a system of small farms. Such seems the sentiment and decree of the age. It has been by no means difficult to give a fatal blow to the plantation system of the South; it may not be quite so easy to expand into full bloom the small farms, which are to be established in lieu thereof. The bureau alone was sufficient to give a quietus to the former, but neither bureau nor its masters can vitalize the latter. Cotton, sugar cane, and tobacco may be cultivated in patches, but how about rice in the richest tide-swamp lands in our country? The small farm system here must be a failure, and these lands with all their exhaustless fertility must be thrown away and reduced to waste marshlands again, cursing the country with their malaria instead of blessing the country with their rich products, unless they at least can be restored to their plantation power and culture. Every rice planter on the Savannah River and everyone accustomed to the tide culture anywhere will attest the truth of these remarks.

JUHL

FLORIDA IN FEBRUARY 2

Leaving Savannah at three o'clock in the afternoon, the *City Point* pursues her way down the river, passing various earthworks and river obstructions constructed by the southern troops in the late war—passing numerous ships at anchor, receiving their cargoes from lighters, their heavy draft preventing their nearer approach to the city—passing Fort Pulaski and Tybee; and the setting sun finds the steamer once more breasting the waves of "the deep, deep sea." Scarcely half the night is gone, when the ship heads in for shore and, passing within close range of the guns of Fort Clinch, is soon moored at the Fernandina wharf—having run the distance of 137 miles from Savannah in a little over nine hours.

Fernandina, situated on Amelia Island, at or near the mouth of the St. Mary's River, is called, by courtesy, a city but is actually surpassed in size and beauty by the majority of northern villages and by many at the South. It is separated by but a few miles of water from the town of St. Mary's, Georgia, the St. Mary's River being the Jordan which rolls between. It is six miles south of Cumberland Island, where General [Nathanael] Greene of Revolutionary fame had a princely estate, and where "Light Horse Harry" [Lee] was buried and where his ashes still repose. The lands are peculiarly adapted to the best qualities of cotton, and recently one hundred thousand dollars have been offered for the property to a descendant of the family and been refused, so it is said.

Fernandina is an old town, originally founded by the Spaniards, and if all the tales of its commercial importance and prosperity while in their possession are true, or if even the half can be credited, then it is a pity for the sake of Fernandina and the rest of the world that the place ever passed from under their control. It is asserted by sea captains that sixty or seventy years ago as many as three hundred vessels were in port at one time. This would indicate an exporting and importing trade which certainly seems mythical in the midst of the silence which now broods over the waters, where no shipping appears except a revenue cutter lying in the stream and one or two lazy looking schooners moored at the wharves. But this may be only another sad instance in which the *fuit Ilium* of human history records the inevitable mutations of time.

Its citizens, however, by no means despair. They claim that the climate is the finest in the world and that up to January 8 there had been no frost there this winter, that banana trees had ripened their fruit, roses were in bloom, green peas were fit for the table, and the vines covered with blossoms; the tomato was ripening its second crop, and all the garden vegetables were in full and luxuriant growth, and the mercury was 83 degrees (eighty-three) in the shade. From these facts it is affirmed that unusual inducements are presented to fruit growers and market gardeners; that the lemon, orange, citron, plantain, banana, tamarind, date, fig, grapes, almond, strawberry, peach, pineapple, and in fact, nearly all the fruits, berries, nuts, and vegetables grow luxuriantly and produce abundantly. The strawberry ripens in March, the peach and grape in June, new potatoes can be shipped in April, and the garden vegetables at all seasons, and the profits of early shipments of these products would be immense and beyond competition.

Such are some of the inducements held out to immigrants. They are plausible, and climate, soil, and other unquestionable advantages considered are certainly within the range of the possible. But a faithful reporter is not to rely implicitly on any local and interested representations, by whomsoever made. Personal observation and living facts can be trusted, and, these being the judges, the foregoing El Dorado picture exists more in fancy than in fact; the frame and the canvas may be there, but the painter's brush is yet to come. The soil and the climate and the other adjuncts are there, but they are not as yet applied by human energy and skill to the development of such grand results as are described by land agents and other interested parties. It is said that the actual settler can realize a fortune in a few years even in the vegetables and fruits raised for the northern markets. But it is very certain that the present residents are not realizing nor attempting anything of the kind.

It is very certain that in Fernandina itself there is a scarcity of these very products which are to be raised for exportation, and that such vegetables as can be obtained there and are offered for sale in the stores are brought in crates and barrels from Charleston, in the very steamer which brought the passenger who is making these inquiries and listening to the flattering recital of the capabilities of the country. When a man in the West, with a hard ague on him shaking his bones until they almost make music and his wife and children keeping up a lively accompaniment, declares that the neighborhood is perfectly healthy, the visitor with all his politeness falls back upon his reserved rights and discredits the statement. A man traveling in such a country will look well to his "traveling companion," his blue mass and quinine and, if in search of a healthy location, will push on until he at least is at a safe remove from the shaker settlement.

So when the visitor is informed that fortunes can be made by raising vegetables, he naturally looks round for some signs of promise in model farms and well-cultivated gardens in which the old inhabitants are illustrating in miniature what might be accomplished by increased population, capital, and agricultural and horticultural skill. One such model farm with its fruits and vegetables at full maturity in midwinter, and shipping by every steamer its grateful products to the less favored northern cities, would do more for Fernandina than all the paper circulars will ever accomplish. Landreth's Philadelphia farm[3] as it is in August, once seen and realized at Fernandina in February, and the last doubt would give way before the beautiful reality—the demonstration in verdure, and flower, and blossom, and fruit.

JUHL

FLORIDA IN FEBRUARY   3

There is a general feeling of unrest among the people of the South, arising from the unsettled condition of the country, which prompts them to seek any change promising an improvement in their affairs.

---

3. David Landreth & Son, a Philadelphia seed firm.

But there is such a thing as "jumping from the frying pan into the fire," and this a prudent man will avoid. Broken as our people are in spirit and fortune, they are ready, like a vessel with a bad anchorage, to put to sea or seek other moorings at a moment's notice. And no greater wrong can be done them than by false information to encourage such emigration. Already during the few years which have succeeded the war, many excellent families have with great difficulty, expense, and risk, removed to Mexico, South America, Honduras, and other states and are either now there dissatisfied and unhappy, ruined, and unable to return, or have dragged their way back to their old homes, having lost in their experiment the last remains of their worldly estates. Those, then, who are looking to Florida and who may read these papers, can rely implicitly upon the honesty and fairness of the statements made.

The transit of the peninsula from the Atlantic to the Gulf is accomplished by the Florida Railroad extending from Fernandina to Cedar Key. A circular from this company inviting emigration is well calculated to deceive the unwary, although no such design may have been entertained. It unfortunately indulges in statements so palpably incorrect that an air of discredit is apt to be attached to the whole. "The Railroad Company have also a line of powerful steamers running direct between Fernandina and New York." Here the wish may be father to the thought; such an enterprise may have been and may still be contemplated and desired, but the fact is no such "line" exists, no such "powerful steamers" or steamers of any class are "running direct between Fernandina and New York," and there is no business or trade, and no immediate prospect of any such business or trade as would justify and support such a line. There are indeed eighteen feet of water on the bar, and the harbor is really one of the finest or safest on the southern coast. But the carrying trade is more than met by the inland and coasting steamers running to Savannah and Charleston and connecting these points with "lines of powerful steamers running to New York."

The time may come, and the sooner the better, when the productive capacities of middle Florida may be prepared to contribute enough to the commerce of the country to justify a direct steamship line to New York, but until that time arrives let it not be said that such a line exists, especially in a circular which is to be translated into German and circulated in Europe. A witness asserting what he is obliged to know is untrue will scarcely be credited in any other part of his testimony.

The same circular speaks of Fernandina as "an enterprising city," the harbor having "twenty miles of magnificent beach," and "thousands of bushels of superior oysters lie immediately in front of the city." The oysters are doubtless there, but there is an apparent want of enterprise to gather them, judging from the difficulty some of the passengers had in getting a mess. It is to be expected that all such descriptions given to induce and allure emigration should be rose colored, but even the policy of such reports is seriously to be doubted, for they must naturally create greater expectations than will be or can be realized, and nothing can paralyze the energies of a new settler more than to find that he has been duped. Hence in this, as in everything else, honesty is the best policy. There are men in Florida today who bitterly regret having ever gone there, because deceived, and it is doubtless equally true that there are multitudes elsewhere who would greatly improve their condition by removing to Florida with the facts all before them.

The country is flat. On the coast, on the rivers, in the interior, everywhere except in the west, it is a uniform flat country. A sea captain calls it a floating island, and everywhere within a few feet of the surface if you can't "strike ile" it is by no means difficult to strike water. And this surface water is neither palatable nor wholesome, a difficulty which might be remedied by boring or sinking wells to a proper depth, taking the precaution not to bore deep enough to reach the salt.

The soil at Fernandina appears rich enough to produce anything and never liable to require much artificial irrigation. It has had, since it was first settled by Europeans, all the natural advantages it now possesses, and yet the fact is undeniable that, so far from advancing everything about and around, it indicates an unmistakable decadence. Would the influx of a new population, with the energies which belong to more northern latitudes, change the scene and develop the agricultural and commercial and horticultural wealth of which it is said to be capable? Or, would such a new population, if it could be secured, yield in turn to the effects of climate and sink into the same lethargy in which all else around is involved?

A peculiar feature in the town of Fernandina is the uncertainty in which titles to real estate are involved. Complications growing out of the late war very seriously embarrass the question of ownership to nearly every house and lot in the place. Many of these were abandoned—occupied by strangers, sold for taxes, reclaimed, and the tax money refunded—and yet the titles are in each case still in dispute and among the several claimants; in the present confusion in which the country is kept by Congress, conventions, and courts, it may be a long time before the legal ownership can be safely determined. From all which it will appear that, like many other places in our once happy and prosperous South, the city of Fernandina needs "reconstruction" in more senses than one.

JUHL

FLORIDA IN FEBRUARY 4

The Florida Railroad runs from Fernandina to Cedar Key, a distance of 154 miles. For 80 miles from the Atlantic terminus there is an almost uninterrupted stretch of flat pine land, interspersed occasionally with small tracts of hummock and "swammock." The soil is light and underlaid at the depth of a foot or more with clay and sometimes contains considerable deposits of rich muck. These lands are said to be peculiarly favorable for potatoes, melons, fruits, and vegetables. A few miles from Fernandina the train crosses Amelia River on a very good drawbridge, and the first land on the main is the once magnificent estate of Judge O'Neill, of Florida, on which, before the war, sugar, cotton and tobacco were successfully and extensively cultivated. Since emancipation, these fine lands have not been planted, and they are now in the market. With a navigable stream, and the Atlantic coast so near, they certainly have great advantages; but whether free labor can ever be induced to work them successfully is a problem which remains to be solved.

There is very little along the line of this road to attract the eye of the traveler. The stations present a sameness and a tameness rather wearisome than otherwise. But beyond Gainesville and approaching the Gulf, the country becomes more undulating and the lands improve in quality and value. There is more of the rich hummock and less of the sandy pine land, and the soil is said to produce heavy crops of all kinds, including the sugar cane, orange, citron, banana and grapes. The Gulf terminus is at Cedar Key, a place of little or no pretensions, a kind of fishing village on trestle work, with a great show of saw mills, only one of which was in operation, the remainder being apparently abandoned. From this point also there is to be a line of powerful steamers to Mobile and other Gulf points, with this encouraging addition, however, that Mr. [D. L.] Yulee says the pioneer ship of the line, the *Mary*, is already at Mobile and will leave that port for Cedar Key on the 25th of this month. May she have a successful run, inaugurate a heavy business, and be followed by numerous consorts!

Practical men will naturally inquire where the business is to come from which is to support this arrangement. It is expected that the travel from all points on the Gulf, west of Cedar Key, will prefer the railroad transit of the peninsula via Fernandina to New York to the present long and somewhat dangerous voyage round the Florida Capes, or via Havana. This consideration may secure the passenger travel, especially in the winter months. But a heavy freight business is not to be expected, for that will naturally stick to the bottoms in which it is first shipped as long as there is a water route to its destination, rather than submit to the delay and expense of repeated transhipments. This road may in time also receive a considerable increase to its business by the settlement and improvement of the lands through which it passes.

With this object in view, it is now offering free grants of twenty, forty, and eighty acres of land to actual settlers, the conditions of gift requiring actual settlement and cultivation of the land for a period of two years. Colonies of ten families or more are promised additional favors. Immigrants are offered free passage over the road to examine the country and select for themselves; and, in the event of settlement, first freights will be carried for them at reduced rates. Lands selected adjoining the track are given in twenty-acre lots, at a distance of half a mile the quantity is doubled, and at a distance of two miles from the road, the land is given in eighty-acre grants. The population at present is sparse and but little of the land has been taken up, and hence there is at present a wide range for choice, extending from Fernandina to the Key and including every quality of soil. As a general thing, the western half of the road has the advantage in climate, water, and fertility of the lands.

The shellrock (coquina), limestone and marl, which constitute the submarine basis on which the different soils of Florida are superimposed, are considered the best foundation in the world for an agricultural country. The fertility of the hummock lands is proverbial. They are peculiar to Florida and are not wet and swampy, but possess a rich alluvial or semialluvial soil, composed of vegetable mould and loam and covered with a heavy growth of live oak, water oak, hickory, and other kindred woods. They are often found interspersed among the pine lands in bodies of several hundred acres, and on some of them are extensive wild orange groves, the degenerate descendants of the finer and sweeter kinds of orange, originally brought from Spain, and introduced with the fig, as mentioned by the Portuguese narrator of De Soto's discoveries. These are now in great demand, and in trees of three or four inches in diameter are transplanted by orange raisers and budded with the sweet orange. Some of these hummocks were doubtless formerly highly cultivated, as there are still to be found among them traces of early settlement of a population, which has long since disappeared; and in looking upon the rank luxuriance with which nature is reclaiming and reclothing her own, one can hardly realize that here in bygone times, the Spanish cavalier and his señorita danced to the music of the castanets.

The most of the pine lands may be rated poor, but there is an exception to this in a class of land to be found nowhere else: pine land, with a soil composed of a dark vegetable mould several inches deep and brown sandy loam, resting on a subsoil of clay, marl, or limestone, with which the surface soil itself is more or less mixed. This soil is nearly inexhaustible and produces immense crops, when properly cultivated and the seasons are favorable, of corn, cotton, and sugar cane. No one should undertake a move to Florida without first examining for himself the situation of the country and forming a proper estimate of all he will be required to renounce and to undergo in making a settlement there. For, with all the forethought and investigation possible, some degree of disappointment will enter into the experience.

JUHL

FLORIDA IN FEBRUARY 5

The *City Point*, leaving Fernandina, again puts to sea and, following the line of white, sandy coast, in a few hours crosses the bar of the river St. John's. The navigation here is intricate, and with a sailing vessel difficult, and in foggy or bad weather dangerous. The channel is tortuous and serpentine and runs within pistol shot of some very ugly looking breakers. Before entering the river, the steamer passes within a few hundred yards of a barren and exposed island of sand, against which the breakers seem to roll in vain, while on its low surface may be seen countless water fowl and regiments of white pelicans, drawn up as if in review to witness the passage of the boat. Numerous buoys mark the channel, and two stately beacon towers on the shore guide the mariner in his course. The long experience and tried skill of Captain Adkins and the powerful engines which M'Namara controls give even here a feeling of security to the passengers, which is alike flattering to the officers and the ship. There are thirteen feet of water on the St. John's bar at spring tides and, of course, much less at all other times.

Entering the river, the first landing is at Mayport, the quarantine station, and Lighthouse Island, a cluster of sand hills and fishermen's houses, whose inhabitants are in many important particulars not yet reconstructed, and if they live where and as they do, never will be, if they live forever. Any reader who wants to get clear of church collections, newspapers, and school bills, and to plunge at once into all the independence of a Robinson Crusoe life should go to Mayport. No ammunition need be wasted here; there are wild ducks and geese enough in sight to supply all the restaurants in Broadway, and deer and turkeys a little further up inshore to furnish ample employment and food to the native or visiting Nimrods, and fish enough in the waters around to feed a multitude.

A few miles further on is Yellow Bluff, a somewhat more civilized-looking settlement, boasting the usual exhibition of seines, boats, and reels to be seen at this season all along the river with the hardy crews engaged in the shad fisheries. An abundance of these fine fish are caught in the St. John's during the winter and until late in spring, so that if the people suffer for food, it must be owing to a degree of laziness which rivals that of the famished beggar who refused the corn because it was not shelled.

The passengers are now all on deck to look at the river; even the invalids have left their staterooms under the encouraging influences of smooth water and a balmy atmosphere. They are mostly Northerners, and but few of them belong to that large class of persons who earlier in the season crowd the boats bound south to escape the rigors of a colder clime. Our passengers are either simply pleasure travelers, allured by the reported freshness and beauty of these tropical wilds, or men looking after land with a view to permanent settlement or a winter home. Many Northerners of capital have already bought places in Florida, looking to future improvement and perhaps residence, and every encouragement is given by the resident population to such immigration.

The river excites their admiration, and it is really a magnificent sheet of water. And yet it is less of a river than a continuous lake, or a continuity of lakes, varying from two to eighteen miles in width, whose dark waters are open to steam navigation for two hundred miles, with but little depth, and very little current, and extending in its course from its supposed sources nearly due north, parallel with the coast and but a few miles from the Atlantic. Its banks are uniformly low and present no such scenery as the Hudson or the Connecticut nor is its bosom cheered with the activity of a ceaseless commerce. All this is yet to come. But ample compensation for the monotony of its surface and shores is found in the living verdure of its winter woods. On either side are the primitive forests of oaks and magnolias, the palm, and the pine, with vines trailing among their branches and jessamines in full bloom. The long southern moss hangs in heavy gray festoons from the trees, and birds of curious plumage and some of wonderful size, including the eagle, look on with calm indifference at the passing steamer.

Deer also are sometimes seen swimming the river, wide as it is, and on a previous trip of the *City Point*, Captain Adkins discovered two of them in midriver and, lowering a boat under the command of his first officer, Mr. John Flynn, succeeded in capturing them both alive. He afterwards sent them as specimens of Florida productions to New York City, and at the last accounts they were being domesticated in Central Park. The announcement of this exploit kept the passengers on the lookout, the idea of a deer drive, mounted on a steamer of eleven-hundred tons, rushing with panting breath through these wide and wonderful waters, was novel and exhilarating; but the coveted antlers did not appear. Above the surface, however, of the sluggish tide, there did appear the upper ironworks of two gunboats sunk by "rebel" torpedoes during the late war.

Twenty-five miles from the bar and fifty miles from Fernandina is Jacksonville on the west bank of the river. It is the most thriving, populous, and attractive town on the route. Northerners constitute a large proportion of its population, and many of the buildings indicate wealth, refinement, and taste. It occupies a sand ridge overlooking the river, is ornamented with shade trees, and has some few very pretty gardens with vegetables and tropical fruits, shrubbery, and flowers. And yet even here, where there seems to be more of life and energy than elsewhere in Florida and boasting a soil and climate capable of producing vegetables all winter for northern consumption, they do not raise enough for their own use, but depend on gardens hundreds of miles away! And the *City Point* landed at this place as a part of her freight crates filled with cabbages and other vegetables raised by Charleston gardeners and bales of hay grown in New England. On the same side of the river, and just above the town, the flag flies, and beneath it in a grove of beautiful oaks are the white tents of the boys in blue.

JUHL

Jacksonville presents many signs of progress. The business houses are larger, numerous, and well stocked with goods. It has a controlling white population; and, as in all northern communities, idleness and vagrancy are discouraged and the views of the citizens in this particular are said to be endorsed and enforced by the officer having the military command. There is also a shipyard with one or two vessels on the stocks nearly completed, whose models and finish do credit to the establishment. On and near the river the town looks well enough, but in the suburbs, back from the river, are numerous groups of shanties crowded together on an absolutely barren sandbed and forming a very unsightly adjunct to the place. This is Florida, where the sugar cane and the orange grow, and yet either of these products can be bought in Charleston as cheap and oftentimes cheaper, by retail, and there were no indications of wholesale transactions.

A few miles from Jacksonville, going up the river and yet going down south, is "Mandarin," the winter house of Harriet Beecher Stowe. It is on the eastern shore of the St. John's, comprises four acres and a cottage, and cost sixty-five hundred dollars. Slavery being dead, there not only seems to be "no more work for poor old Ned," but no further demand for such fanatical publications as those which gave Mrs. Stowe at one time the entree to English drawing rooms; and from "raising the wind" and raising a whirlwind by writing extravagant caricatures of southern society, she has turned her attention to the more peaceful, if less notable, occupation of raising oranges on the banks of the St. John's. The talk on the river is that her last year's crop all turned *black* from a remarkable sympathy with the owner's tastes and partialities, but the talk on the river is sometimes like the talk in the village which charity will repudiate and nail to the counter as dishonored coin. It is hoped, for the sake of her cherished theories and predilections, that none of the numerous predatory gangs of

Negroes now infesting the river and its tributaries will visit and despoil her southern estate.

The opposite shores of the St. John's present almost opposite climates, at least in one very important particular. On the western side there is sometimes frost sufficient to injure tender vegetation, but even at such times the eastern shore is exempt from a similar visitation. The inhabitants ascribe the difference to the influence exerted by so extensive a surface of almost tepid waters upon the passing currents of air which at such times are always from west to east. So influential a fact cannot of course be overlooked by horticulturists, and hence all the places selected and occupied by vegetable and fruit raisers are on the eastern shore.

On the other hand, the towns and watering places are all on the western bank, presumed, on this account, to possess a more agreeable and salubrious temperature. Such are Hibernia and Glen Cove Springs, the next two landings on the river, at which there are spacious hotels for the accommodation of guests; and at the last named place there is also a sulphur spring, whose waters are said to possess remarkable curative properties. That they are strongly impregnated with mineral, no one can doubt who applies the usual practical test; and, unless the visitor believes in their virtue and feels his need of their assistance, one such trial will be voted "enough."

The arrival of the Charleston steamer is at these points, the event of the week. Landlord and guests appear on the wharf, greetings and adieus are exchanged between friends meeting or separating, and the boat approaching and leaving is saluted with the waving of handkerchiefs and the kissing of hands. The scene is one which can scarcely be realized by those of our passengers, who, a few days ago, left the homes where ice and snow and freezing winds prevail, and where beauty buries itself in cloaks and furs. For the gay groups on the landing are standing in the shade of umbrellas, the summer styles of dress prevail, the ladies are even without bonnets, and jessamines adorn their hair, and their light muslin dresses flutter in the breeze. One of them holds a parrot (or parrakeet) of brilliant plumage and strangely imitative powers of articulation, and altogether it is a picture of tropical life, of sunshine and flowers. The very luggage is in keeping with the other surroundings, for not only does the parrot come on board with its mistress, but an open box filled with cockleburrs is passed along the gangway to feed the pretty but troublesome bird. Verily, our young baggage master, Mr. Benjamin Deal, a nephew of the captain and hailing from Sumter, has abundant opportunity at these various landings to display the assiduity and politeness for which he is distinguished.

Thus far very few signs of farm cultivation have been observed, the riversides presenting the same unbroken line of forest relieved by occasional clearings, and a few orange groves with their golden fruit glimmering amidst the green. The boat touches at Picolata to land mails and passengers for St. Augustine. It is a dreary-looking place, comprising an old shell of a house with six rooms and some three hundred acres of cleared land. The land may be very rich and valuable and a good hotel there might make money during the winter, but at present it looks flat, lifeless, and desolate. There are two stages running, or rather walking, from this place to St. Augustine, a distance of eighteen miles over a pine barren country crossing a ferry and reaching the oldest European settlement in America in five or six hours. For this protracted trial of his temper and patience the passenger pays four dollars; and, if the opposition line was withdrawn, he might be allowed to perform the same feat in twice the time and for double the money. But St. Augustine is worth seeing. It was first settled more than three centuries ago, and was, therefore, ahead of Plymouth and the Pilgrims. But no man in his senses will say it is ahead of them now. The grand old Spanish fort is there, and its orange groves and other fruits, and its Minorcan population with their strange jargon, and its houses of curious composite masonry, and it looks as if it had the age, without the energies, of the grand old ocean that rolls its billows against the shore.

JUHL

FLORIDA IN FEBRUARY   7

The belt of country between the Atlantic and the St. John's is too poor to invite investment or settlement; and, therefore, those who are seeking either will avoid this part of Florida. St. Augustine itself, aside from its antiquity and the curious features of the place, really possesses no attraction to the visitor, except its fine climate. This to invalids is, of course, the paramount consideration, and many of them are to be found there all through the winter, enduring the rough fare and high rates of hotel accommodations and a comparative isolation from the outer world for the renewed lease of life which its balmy air affords. To such it is probably the most desirable and attractive place of resort on the continent. But in every other respect it is behind the times a hundred years or more.

A northern gentlemen, the *King* of Chicago, who with his family spent the earlier part of this month in St. Augustine, remarked that after leaving Washington, coming south, he thought he could perceive at every stage of travel a gradual falling-off in the energies and business activity of the people; that the further south he came, the less of enterprise and effort was visible; that cars and horses and men moved slower and slower; but that he never witnessed the culmination of this principle (of climate inertia) until he reached St. Augustine. The torpid sluggishness and sleepiness of everything here, in his opinion, could only be described by saying that, when compared with it, the rest of the South exhibited a perfect rush of incontrollable go-a-head-a-tive-ness. In vindication of the natives, however, it may be remarked that the most energetic Northerner making his domicile here soon and imperceptibly lapses into the prevailing habits of the people, yielding, however reluctantly, to the inevitable influence of all warm or tropical climates in enervating and relaxing the energies of man.

In the course of even one year's residence, it is not improbable that our critical Chicago traveler would himself be able to rival any of the present inhabitants in an easily acquired indifference to labor or to continuous effort of any kind. The laws of climate are inflexible; and, however strong the resistance of the will, a gradual, even though involuntary, obedience will be rendered by backbone and muscle. The truth of this principle will be amply tested in Florida, for no part of the South is at present receiving more attention from northern capitalists and emigrants. They are to be met with everywhere, particularly on the St. John's; and, while many of them will only remain there during the winters, a sufficient number will become permanent residents to demonstrate how far and how long, in defiance of climate, they can retain and apply the energies and the vim of a colder latitude. If they can remain proof to those qualities of the air and climate which have thus far never failed to work insensibly and unfavorably on the tone and habit of the body, they will develop a beauty of verdure and a wealth of production which no other country can surpass.

Palatka is on the western shore of the St. John's, seventy-five miles south of Jacksonville, and the head of navigation for vessels drawing as much water as the *City Point* and her consort, the *Dictator*. It is a very pretty village and a place of some business importance. The houses are neat and embowered in evergreens laden with tropical fruits. In one garden, visited by invitation of the proprietor, there were citron, lemon, several varieties of the orange, and other fruit trees laden with beautiful fruit. In the suburbs of the place these gardens alternate with groves of magnificent white and water oaks whose intertwining limbs shut out the sun and form a dense shade peculiarly grateful in such a climate, even in midwinter. Barrels of oranges and bags of cottonseed for planting were here seen, ready for shipment down the river. This is Putnam County, and its delegate to the Tallahassee convention was at home and made his appearance on the wharf, awaiting a boat to bear him on his return to his work on the constitution. He was a genuine black, in full convention rig, carpetbag in hand, whose business consists in hammering at his constituents from the pulpit on Sundays and hammering at the constitution the rest of the week. He was favored with the following unsolicited and quite unlooked-for address:

You are going to the convention. Many of your people have been deceived by designing persons who have promised them lands and mules and other gifts—persons who have no lands themselves to give and no idea of laying violent hands upon the property of others for any such purpose. They have fooled the Negroes and have thereby injured them and the country. Some years ago, on the Combahee river in South Carolina, a gang of Negroes while working in a field were obliged to take shelter in a weather-house from a terrific thunder storm. Alarmed by the severity of the lightning, they fell on their knees and resorted to praying. Old Sambo, among others, repeated energetically at least a dozen times: "O Lord, massa God, save old Sambo dis time, and Sambo gib you piece of tobacco big as he leg." The storm passed off and with it the fears of the company; when confidence being restored, Sambo was thus taken to task by one of his fellow laborers: "Look here, Sambo, how you tell de Lord dat big lie when you been so scare? Where you gwine git piece of tobacco big as your leg?" Sambo, looking at him with ineffable contempt, replied: "Shut up, you cussed nigger, I only been *fool um*."

Now, in one of your speeches in Tallahassee, relate this incident, and ask the leaders if they have not fooled the colored people by promising what they knew they could not give—did not have to give—and had no idea or intention of giving, upsetting the country, undermining labor and unsettling the minds of the credulous freedmen. Do this; do it in your best camp-meeting style, and you'll bring down the house.

The Reverend Mr. Woods laughed heartily, said it was a true bill, and promised to do it.

It is a fact that through all the wide range of country embraced in these travels, wherever opportunity was offered of conversing with the freedmen, they were found to be impressed with the conviction that the conventions would give them land, and on this account very many of them were refusing remunerative engagements for the year, content to perform a day's work occasionally for subsistence, while waiting, with Micawber's faith, for "something to turn up."

JUHL

FLORIDA IN FEBRUARY   8

The St. John's, whose waters present a surface of miles in width from the bar to Palatka and even beyond, is nevertheless a very shallow river, with a tortuous channel and innumerable flats, requiring skillful pilotage and preventing any approach to the shore by large steamers except at the regular landings. Unlike the Mississippi, an accident here could not involve the sinking of the boat, as there is scarcely depth of water sufficient to cover the lower deck. From Palatka the further navigation south is performed by a number of light draft steamers, some of which are of a very grotesque appearance. The *Darlington*, a very respectable and comfortable high-pressure boat, commanded by Captain [Jacob] Brock, follows the channel of the St. John's as far south as Enterprise. For the first fifty miles the river presents the same general scenery with which the eye has already become familiar. Perhaps the verdure shows a deeper green, the grey moss hangs in longer festoons, the wild orange is more frequently seen radiant with its golden fruit, and the revolutions of the paddles not only drive the boat southward but seem also to run up the thermometer steadily to summer heat.

On this part of the river there are a number of settlers who have bought lands since the war and are now engaged in horticulture and fruit raising. They are men of some means. Their chief embarrassment is a want of labor which in this country seems almost impossible to obtain. One of these gentlemen, a Northerner, whose place is six miles south of Palatka where he has been spending the winter, offers forty dollars and board for a competent white man to manage the farm and offers high wages for four freedmen to work on the same. Even with these inducements he had not been able to obtain the desired "help." He, in common with many others, had made what is probably a grave mistake in selecting a location south of Palatka, not only incurring thereby the disadvantage of increased distance from market, but the still more serious item of expense in the reshipment of freight both ways. The Charleston boats go no farther than Palatka, and freight to or from that place and all intermediate landings is handled but once.

From all points south of Palatka there must be super-added to this such transportation as may be afforded by small boats and flats, with the loss in time and money which such extra water-carriage necessarily involves. It will appear at a glance that this is a very serious consideration in the matter of vegetables and fruit, the very class of products to which the attention of newcomers seems to be given. Beyond Palatka a steamboat monopoly may by its freight tariff actually establish an embargo at any time; north of Palatka such a monopoly need never be apprehended, as there are several lines of steamers on that part of the river now, and in such waters and such an age and the growing interest in the country, it seems scarcely possible that the time will ever come when there will be less competition for its freight and passenger business. On the other hand it is not to be forgotten that every mile of travel southward increases the warmth of the climate and, other things being equal, reduces the price of lands.

Fifty miles beyond Palatka the river expands its width to eighteen miles, which width it retains for some ten or twelve miles of its course. This is Lake George, and as the boat passes over its dark waters, the passenger might easily imagine he was again at sea. Like all the other waters of Florida it is remarkably shallow, and therefore in high winds it becomes quite rough, and its navigation is neither pleasant nor safe. It is a great obstruction to raftsmen, and often occasions them much trouble and vexatious delays. On its shores are immense quantities of the wild orange, and many persons are engaged selecting trees of the proper kind and size, topping them to the standard length, and packing them away in large flats with a liberal covering of gray moss. These flats are towed to Palatka and other points, where the trees find a ready market at from twenty-five to fifty cents each. They are planted ninety to the acre, and budded with the sweet orange, and without much further attention in a few years yield an abundance of delicious fruit. The graft often makes shoots six feet in length the first season and bears its first crop the third year, and when a few years older, each tree will bear annually at least fifteen hundred oranges. This is considered a fair average yield, but instances are named in which ten thousand oranges have been picked from a single tree.

How many hundred thousand of these wild stocks have been planted and budded the present season, it would be difficult to estimate, but certainly on the St. John's and its tributaries and in all the adjacent country, the orange culture is quite the rage. It requires less outlay of capital and labor, is less liable to failure, and promises to be more remunerative than almost any other crop. Cotton has to be worked and watched and stimulated from first to last and is subject to all the casualties of drought or excessive rains, defaulting freedmen or the raids of the caterpillar, and after all, when ready for market, a fall in the price may ruin the planter. But with the orange culture, you buy and fence the land and plant the trees, and there you are! You can go to sleep or go to Europe; you own an orangery, which in three years is to be ready to honor your drafts. There are all the varieties of the sweet, sour, bittersweet, mandarin, etc., but it is only the first named which is worth cultivating. And this business may be considered only in its incipiency, very little attention having been heretofore paid to it. For sweet oranges, by the dozen or thousand, can be bought cheaper today in Charleston than at Palatka, where they are picked from the trees.

On the river there are some few fine plantations with handsome dwellings and splendid groves of live oaks and magnolias, with orchards containing almost every variety of the tropical fruits. South of Lake George, the coconut, pineapple, and banana are found. Cotton culture may be considered abandoned, and a larger area of land is being planted in sugar cane than ever before. It can be cultivated successfully and profitably even in small patches, but to obtain the best results it should be planted on a large scale. The hummock lands and climate of Florida are admirably suited to its production, and the cane there is admitted to be of the finest quality. If the requisite capital, labor, and skill can be commanded, the soil and climate will insure success.

JUHL

FLORIDA IN FEBRUARY   9

Volusia, ten miles south of Lake George, is a place of little note and still less attraction, with chill and fever in water, earth, and air. A few miles off the river the country is more healthy and is being occupied by settlers principally from the Carolinas and Georgia. Among these may be mentioned Captain M——, who during the late war was quite distinguished as the commander of a company of daring scouts, whose deeds rival the achievements of any similar band in the old Revolution. He has eighty acres of very good land, which cost him under the preëmption grant, forty-two dollars. This includes titles and all expenses.

His dwelling is a new and comfortable pole-house, having two rooms with an open passage between, for which he paid the builders one hundred dollars—they furnished everything. The land is in open woods and is very easily cleared, and can be planted, as he is doing this year, by simply deadening the timber. Sugar cane, cotton, corn, sweet potatoes, groundnuts (peanuts) yield abundantly, and he expects to devote a few acres to oranges, the proper kind of stocks for grafting abounding all through that section. The woods and waters furnish an inexhaustible supply of the finest fish and game, the latter including deer, turkeys, bear, and an animal called a tiger, but which makes no pretensions to rival the Bengal in size or ferocity.

There is also an abundance of cattle running wild; tough, hardy, and inferior stock, having a range which is almost without limit, extending far into the everglades, and furnishing excellent pasturage all the year round. Numerous ponds or small lakes of excellent water are interspersed through all this section, with a bottom of the purest white sand, and water perfectly clear and transparent. Captain M—— has one of these within a few rods of his house; it is not only very convenient for purposes of the laundry, but he expects soon to have a yard full of ducks to sport in its waters.

The natives, indeed, tell him that there are numerous snapping turtles in these ponds which mercilessly snap off the feet of ducks or geese swimming on the surface and will thus prove fatal to his enterprise, but the gallant captain has not passed through a long war without profiting by its lessons, and he has determined to extend his fencing by a stockade into the pond enclosing in this way a sufficient water basin for his ducks, and from this he will proceed to fish out or otherwise destroy the turtles and trust to his stockade barrier to exclude the rest. He has quite a number of neighbors of the same stamp with himself, who have recently settled there, and they have no fear of depredations being committed on their stock, for it would be a decidedly hazardous experiment for any parties, white, black, or red, to interfere with that community.

Some obnoxious characters who were there on their first arrival have already "vamosed the ranche," and neither vagrant Negroes nor degraded whites will tarry long in that vicinity. The natives live in the most primitive style, and are generally without education, refinement, or high moral principle, and are perfect slaves to coffee, tobacco, and whiskey, to keep up a supply of which articles they are ready to incur almost any risk and to make any sacrifice. Although they make sugar, they do not use it in their coffee. They all exhibit an eagerness to sell out their improvements to newcomers, and when successful move on to another tract, where they proceed at once to build.

There are no schools and substantially no Sabbaths, although the day is, of course, remembered in such families as were accustomed elsewhere to observe it. Within the last few months a stray preacher of a somewhat amphibious type and questionable credentials passed through the settlement, but found little to induce him to "tarry a while in the wilderness." A dwelling here is literally a "lodge in some vast wilderness," presenting a "boundless contiguity of shade," and as such alone our soldier friends have sought it, and there they are willing to remain as exiles for the present from the homes and associations of former days rather than witness the humiliation through which their country is passing. They frankly admit that they regard it only as a refuge and retreat for the time. They are not overwell pleased with the country and have no idea of making it a permanent residence.

There is an abundance of unoccupied land in the neighborhood which can be had in eighty-acre tracts on the same terms as already stated. It embraces swamp, hummock, and pine land, which can be selected according to the preferences of the settler. Of sweet potatoes, fish, and game, an abundance can always be relied upon; the former grow and yield a marvelous return, with little or no cultivation. Corn cannot be kept, even if raised in quantities, for, owing to the warmth of the climate, the weevil will take it. Immigrants to Florida should provide themselves with all the implements, tools, and seeds they require, and also carry such a supply of provisions as their mode of transportation will allow. A small quantity of the leading medicines, such as calomel, blue mass, quinine, and salts should not be forgotten; they will be needed in almost any part of Florida, for the very air, which is considered a healing balm to diseased lungs, plays the fog with the liver. And the early fall is the proper season to make the move, as the winter is really the only time when the heavy work of clearing, fencing, and breaking up land can be comfortably done.

Volusia and the settlements described in this paper are in Orange County, and the foregoing description will generally apply to all of Florida in the latitude (29) of Fort King. With such a profusion of rich lands inviting settlement, it seems surprising that any persons should be found living in the absolutely barren pine sections. And yet there are such, actuated probably by a desire to avoid the chills and determined to depend for subsistence on occasional excursions after fish or game.

A specimen of the kind was furnished by a tall wiry man with carroty unkept hair, bareheaded, and barefooted, with pants reaching a little below the knees, and a shirt whose last washing day must have been beyond the memory of its wearer, without coat or vest, standing with a group of miniature repetitions of himself in front of a dilapidated cabin around which there was no sign of fence or living thing; and when a much amused Northerner addressing him said good-naturedly: "My friend, you seem to be quite poor about here," unabashed and with arms akimbo, he triumphantly replied: "Well, now, stranger, we're not so d——d poor as we might be—we don't *own* this yere land." The independence of the speaker was apparent more in the manner than in the words themselves, and if the wit contained in his reply was not considered of the first order, on the other hand it may safely be affirmed that it was not as poor as the land on which it was produced.

JUHL

FLORIDA IN FEBRUARY   10

A great many persons visiting Florida in the winter include in their travels a trip to the lake sources of the Oklawaha. The boat which offers for this excursion is taken at Palatka and is decidedly a nondescript, a curiosity in itself. Imagine an ordinary river flat, ten feet wide, and twenty-five or thirty feet long with a railroad boxcar placed fore and aft upon it, having a few feet of stovepipe projecting from the roof, and the Oklawaha steamer is before you. One division of the boxcar, arranged with berths or bunks and furnished with a small table and a few chairs, is assigned to the passengers. This they occupy for three or four days, except when they risk a precarious position outside, while the machine is traversing the two hundred miles of circuitous navigation to and among the lakes. The charge is twelve dollars, which is doubled if the passenger returns with the boat.

The round trip occupies ten days and, on account of the slowness of the steamer, the contracted accommodations, and the delays at the various landings, becomes tedious and wearisome. The boat follows the St. John's for twenty-five miles to the mouth of the Oklawaha, which it enters and traverses to the lakes. The waters narrow until there seems to be no passage, but the boxcar pushes through, and they shoal until progress appears impossible, but the little steamer draws only sixteen inches water and goes puffing onward. An overhanging limb takes the hat off an exposed passenger, and if he is not prompt in dodging the next one, his head may follow. And thus day after day, with waters varying from rods to miles in width, and scenes of tropical vegetation and undisturbed everglades, of grand old oaks and flowering vines, and fruits and majestic magnolias, the journey continues until Lakes Griffin and Harris and Dora and Eustis are severally visited, all beautiful sheets of water fringed with perpetual verdure and hidden away in these wilds of the peninsula.

Some wonderful natural curiosities and phenomena exist in this part of Florida. There is a mammoth spring of miles in extent whose pure translucent waters bubble up through sands of beautiful pearly whiteness. And there are small lakes or ponds having no visible outlet in which shad are caught during the season, in numbers, size, and quality comparing favorably with the fisheries on the rivers—a phenomenon which can only be explained by the supposition (which is a fact) that there are subterranean marine currents underlying this part of Florida and connecting these ponds with the Atlantic. And in some localities the earth occasionally gives way in small patches, sinks, and disappears, leaving a pond of water in its place. And a story is related of a wagoner who, in one of these unsubstantial neighborhoods, discovered that his wagon and team were going down, when he hastily abandoned them to their fate and only saved himself by a rapid retreat. This is gravely stated as a fact, and may or may not be true; it is not vouched for in these papers, although a report of this part of the country would not be complete which did not include some reference to these strange freaks of the land of flowers.

The Oklawaha floating boxcar, with its stovepipe attachment, is owned by a gentleman residing in Palatka, who first opened the navigation of these waters, and for so doing received from the legislature a large grant of the public lands. These he offers at fifty cents an acre, and they are well adapted for cotton, sugar, oranges, etc. There are very few Negroes in this section; the population, such as it is, belongs to the white race, and enjoys a hermit-like seclusion from the busy outside world. And notwithstanding the difficulty of access to the Oklawaha country and its remoteness from market, many northern men are investing in its lands, without having the most remote idea of ever living there. They say the purchase requires but little money, and they have a plethora of greenbacks, that it will be pleasant for them to speak of their Florida estate, with its incomparable verdure and tropical fruits, and that some of their children may in the future find it a desirable refuge from the rigors of a northern winter.

If the traveler, prospecting in the Gulf counties around Cedar Key, can rejoice in the assurance that he is at last "away down on Suwanee River," one of the Edens celebrated in Ethiopian song, he can indulge in the higher poetry of Indian memories as he wanders among the windings of the Oklawaha. For here, but a few years since, when the orange blossomed and filled the air with its fragrance, the Indian warrior woo'd his dusky mate. And over these placid lakes his light canoe shot like an arrow in the soft moonlight. And through these forests he pursued the deer and roamed at pleasure, unfettered and free.

And here Osceola gathered his tribe around him and held his court. Ah! little thought he then the pale face would hunt the red man even to the Everglades; that the eagle would be pinioned; that he, proud chieftain, would be torn from the hunting grounds of his youth, and his spirit, sinking under the shackles of the captive, would yield up the ghost in a casemate of Fort Moultrie. But the story is not yet finished, for many who aided in the conquest and expulsion of the Seminole, are themselves today conquered and captives—some in exile without a country, and others passing under the yoke; "Then," cries the inspired Koheleth, "I praised the dead which are already dead, more than the living which are yet alive."

A few months after the death of Osceola [1838], a steamer from Florida arrived in Charleston harbor with another detachment of Seminoles en route for the Far West. They were landed at Castle Pinckney, where they remained under guard while waiting transportation. The warriors were splendid specimens of Indian manhood, but appeared sullen and savage. Among the squaws was the venerable mother of the dead chieftain. She was profusely ornamented with silver trinkets and was an object of marked deference among the rest of the tribe. In return for some little presents, she unhooked from her bosom and gave to the writer one of the largest ornaments she wore.

In a few days they were gone on their long journey towards the setting sun. But the reminiscence comes up afresh amidst the scenes from which these people have been driven. True, their wigwams have disappeared, their council fires gone out, their war songs hushed, but all so recently that the shadow of their presence can still be felt. And it does not require a very vivid imagination to call up again the sad picture of their retreating forms, looking back with lingering regret upon their native woods and breaking into the exiles' lament, "we return no more, we return no more!"

In the depths of the Everglades there are still a few Seminoles, the only survivors in Florida of what was once a powerful tribe. They carefully avoid any interference with the property or pursuits of the white man. They are said to be slaveholders; and, although informed that the institution is abolished, they repudiate the doctrine and defy its enforcement. It is probable, however, that the few Negroes among them are only nominally held as slaves and have really become so far assimilated with the Indian in habit and manner of life that they desire no change and would oppose any if attempted. These Indians are few in number and are seldom seen by the white settlers, and their retreat in the remote Everglades is too distant and difficult of access to be visited, although it may not be without its attractions, for it is "down where the bluebells grow."

JUHL

Within the three hundred years since its first European invasion, Florida has passed through great changes in its population and government. It bloomed for the Indian and was long his beautiful and unconquered empire. It welcomed the Spaniard with its voluptuous breath, its virgin loveliness of verdure and flower, its prolific waters, convenient ports, and untold wealth of soil. But the Spaniard was a troublesome and dangerous neighbor to the adjoining states and, with the assistance of his Indian allies, could at any time threaten Georgia and even Carolina with his formidable hostile incursions. Hence the bayonet, the popular American argument, was brought into play, and thus, having accomplished its mission, was succeeded as usual by a treaty, which swept the Spaniard from the peninsula and gave up the country to the United States.

Then came the southern planter, with his rich agricultural experience, and his unlimited command of capital and reliable labor, and addressed himself to the cultivation of its splendid lands. And under his competent direction and judicious control, the timber was cleared and the hummocks converted into fields of luxuriant cane, cotton, and tobacco. This regime, which promised more for Florida than any preceding it in the development of its resources, had only been fairly inaugurated, when the late war came and swept it also away, paralyzing its energies and sapping the foundations of its agricultural system, and leaving its landowners without capital or labor. The disasters of last year completed the ruin of the plantation dynasty, for all the embarrassments which overwhelmed the planters elsewhere were multiplied and aggravated and intensified in Florida.

The seasons were most unpropitious; it is even said that out of 130 days in summer there were only 3 when no rain fell, and the warmth and moisture brought the caterpillar, and the cotton fields became a blank and a desolation under their fearful ravages. In the counties of

Marion and Alachua men who expected to make fifty thousand dollars are actually left without the means to give them bread for the year. General———, who planted for three hundred bales which would have been an ordinary crop with the land and force engaged, made but ten bales, and these reached a market under a fatal decline and had then to contribute to the national revenues under the beneficent Radical protection of American industry. In the face of such facts and the doubt and uncertainty arising from the political and social system now being enforced upon the country, there is no disposition to renew these experiments, and the cotton culture in Flordia has entered upon a decadence from which even the most sanguine can see no hope of immediate revival.

Under the reconstruction scheme, Florida has recently entered upon a new and anomalous experiment of government so-called. Registration gave a list of 28,000 voters of whom 12,000 are white. The vote in November resulted in 14,300 for a convention and 132 against, and it is said that even these figures were reached by a process which would not bear inspection. "At the same time delegates were chosen, of whom 27 were whites and 18 colored. Soon after they met (in January) a question arose as to the right of certain delegates to their seats, and a long and disgraceful wrangle ensued, the result being the division of the convention into two bodies, each bent upon getting up a constitution of its own." As this is the language of H. G., in the *Tribune*, the testimony must be admitted even in the Radical camp.

Great excitement prevailed in Tallahassee, mass meetings were held by the rival factions, each threatening to hang the other, when General Meade and staff appeared and persuaded them instead of pounding each other to pound away together on the constitution. From all this the white population stands aloof—even the large numbers of intelligent Northerners met with there expressing an indifference bordering on contempt for everything relating to the Radical rehabilitation of the state.

In Florida nature has lavished her treasures with a most prodigal hand and mingled beauty of flower and fruit and foliage in richest profusion everywhere: vast depositories of undeveloped and unutilized wealth appear on every hand; timber—invaluable for the ship-yard and the countless manufactures in wood of every variety and the choicest kinds and in quantities sufficient for ages to come; moss—which can be gathered by the thousand tons on the miles of lake and river shore with little labor or expense and which can be so easily cured and made a valuable article of commerce. The palm and palmetto—whose roots are said to make the best qualities of paper and whose leaves, when properly cured, would supersede in northern manufactories the same article now imported from the West Indies. Fruits—which with but little attention yield in a few years an almost fabulous return.

Lands—rich enough to satisfy the most avaricious owner, lands of every grade and price from a free grant to actual settlers to a transfer by purchase at from fifty cents upwards; including the savannas or meadowlands, invaluable for sugar cane, which in south Florida requires replanting only once in ten years; and including the prairie lands on the head waters of the St. John's, the Kissimmee and the Caloosahatchee Rivers on which there is a heavy growth of grass with occasional patches of timbered hummock where immense herds of cattle and deer are always to be found.

All this and more is there, and it only awaits the touch of a skilled and enterprising population to unfold and gather its rich products and pour them into the lap of commerce. It has already received very liberal installments of such an immigration, and it has room and a welcome for as many more. The theory of "climatic inertia," to which so much of tropical lethargy is ascribed, may impair its energies, retard its progress, and become a fatal bar to its complete development. Or it may, in defiance of all such laws of climate, become, indeed, under indomitable and faithful husbandry, the garden of the continent.

1868

March 3

JUHL

SUMTER, S. C., March 3

On last Saturday there was quite a large gathering of the colored voters of Sumter District in the courthouse at this place, and the most of the day was consumed by them in arranging the nominations for state and district officers. Of whatever else these people may tire, there is no indication that they will very soon tire of politics and elections. They have the entire track to themselves and can walk over the course under the direction of a few white Radicals who engineer all their movements. Among the speakers on this occasion was Mr. John T. Green, who was honored by the meeting with a nomination for a judgeship. Among the other nominations the following are reported: for governor—[T. J.] Robertson of Columbia; for Congress—[B. F.] Whittemore; for state senate—[T. J.] Coughlan; for sheriff—[J. H.] Ferriter; for clerk of the court—[G. W.] Reardon; for tax collector—[D. G.] Robertson of Mechanicsville (brother of the candidate for gubernatorial honors). None of these persons, except the first named, originally belonged to Sumter District; and, what is a matter of still greater surprise, among all the nominees reported and depending entirely on the freedman's vote, not a black man is named for any office.

The Negro may indeed be promised subordinate positions as deputies, delegates to the lower house, etc., but certainly in the arrangement as decided on in one of their own meetings, their inferiority and unfitness to rule seems to be insisted on by the very party which depends on their votes. To the lookers-on, there seems in all this a wide variance between the preaching and practice of the Radicals in restricting the colored voter to the lower privilege of elevating others to place and power.

225

1868

March 3

Last night a daring and successful burglary was committed by a gang of thieves who effected an entrance into the front window of Mr. J. E. Suares's store on Main Street and carried off goods to the value of eight hundred dollars or more. The entrance was effected by boring, and the whole transaction was evidently the work of accomplished hands. From the quantity of goods removed, there can be no doubt the rogues were in strong force and were well supplied with the means of transportation. Similar outrages have been chronicled in this community before, and the impunity with which they are perpetrated promises to insure us in time, if we have not already, a formidable array of graduated adepts in crime.

The season has been very unfavorable, too wet by far for farming operations; and, with the long list of offices which it seems are to be given the popular vote and the multiplicity of elections which must therefore be anticipated, there is reason to believe that during the entire year there will be—at least among the freedmen—far more attention devoted to politics than to the plough.

JUHL

SUMTER, S. C., April 10

On Tuesday the 7th inst., being the second day of our spring term, a somewhat novel case was tried and disposed of in the common pleas for this district. It appeared on the docket as *Robert M. Thompson, Escheator,* v. *the Real Estate of Isaac Haithcock*, deceased. The decedent was a free person of color who lived and died in the upper part of the district. He is represented to have been a man of good character, untiring industry, and an excellent manager of his private affairs. He must have been all of this, for as the fruits of his labor and economical habits he acquired by purchase a tract of one hundred acres of land on which he lived and thus became the owner of his wife, who was a slave. By this wife, while she was a slave, he had several children, and these, according to the law of the state, following the condition of the mother at the time of their birth, were also held as slaves and in the course of time were removed by their owners to a Mississippi plantation.

Isaac Haithcock and his wife both deceased, and the land was left in the hands of trustees and without an owner, the said Haithcock having died intestate. It, therefore, became liable to the law of escheat, and accordingly the proper officer instituted the usual initial steps for this purpose before Judge [Thomas W.] Glover in February, 1867. About the same time, Hampton Haithcock, a son of the decedent, born a slave thirty-five years ago, but now a freedman, returned to Sumter District after long years of absence, claimed the land, employed counsel, submitted a report of the facts to the bureau, and was instructed to hold the estate. He moved his family to the place and, being like his father a man of great industry, has already added much to its value in the way of improvements. Notice of inquest to be held having been served on the said Hampton Haithcock as terre-tenant by the escheator, the case came up at the time and in the form above stated. The escheator was represented by Mr. T. W. Dinkins and Mr. James S. G. Richardson, and the respondent (terre-tenant) by Mr. J. J. Fleming.

No issue was made as to the facts in the case, but the counsel for the escheator maintained that by the laws of inheritance in this state no slave could claim by descent, and that as the respondent was born a slave and was a slave at the time of his father's death, he could not be regarded as heir-at-law to the said decedent. In reply it was argued by the counsel for Haithcock that an attainder for treason in England might involve corruption of blood and forfeiture of estate and be extended even through several generations, and yet an act of Parliament was sufficiently potent to remove all such disabilities and restore the forfeited estates to the descendants, even though such descendants were born under attaint. That slavery might be regarded

227

as such an attainder under which the respondent was born, and by which he was debarred the right of inheritance, but by an act of Congress—equally potential with an act of Parliament, and also by an act of our own legislature—this attaint had been removed and the respondent as a free man and the recognized son of Isaac Haithcock had a right to the decedent's estate as his heir-at-law. The view of the case was enlarged upon and illustrated, and the jury urged as an act of justice to the living and the dead to give the respondent the land, as the tract in question, if resulting to the state as ultimate proprietor, would be but another drop to the ocean or another grain to the sands upon the ocean shore, while to the defendant it was everything—a home for his wife and children, which his father had acquired by years of toil.

The charge of the Judge (Moses) was . . . that if it [the jury] restored the Negro to his former or original status, it would be restoring or returning him to slavery (is slavery the normal condition of the Negro?) and that the law plainly excluded the respondent from the inheritance, and the land must escheat. The jury, under such instructions from the court, could not do otherwise than find for the plaintiff, but an application will be made to the legislature in behalf of the respondent and any other children of the decedent who may hereafter be found, for the passage of an act restoring to them the land now escheated by law.

By an act of the legislature all such escheated lands in this district are given to the Sumterville Academical Society, of which Judge Moses is a member, and it is due to his honor to state that in his charge to the jury he avowed that his sympathies were with the respondent and that as a member of the Society in whose favor the law requires a verdict, he would vote to renounce all claim to the land and leave it in the possession of Hampton Haithcock. But against this appears the formidable fact that the Society owes four thousand dollars which it is unable to pay, that a judgment has been obtained against it in equity for that amount, and that the creditors will scarcely allow any renunciation, but will avail themselves of the verdict to fasten on the land.

So that after all, the children of the decedent will be ousted from the estate, unless the legislature interposes and the courts subsequently refuse to interfere with such legislative action. The respondent expects to make such application at the next session of the legislature; and, as far as his counsel has conferred with the gentlemen of the Society, they will unanimously recommend that his petition be granted.

This is the first term in which we have been favored with colored jurors; one freedman served on the grand jury, three on (petit) jury no. 1, and two on jury no. 2. As far as ascertained, they caused no embarrassment whatever in making up the verdict, but harmonized with the more intelligent and better-informed white men on the panel.

On last Sunday afternoon the barn of Mr. J. G. Fort, six miles east of this town, and also the other out-buildings adjoining were burnt to the ground. The barn contained Mr. Fort's entire stock of provisions, including five hundred bushels of corn, fifty thousand pounds of fodder, all his rice, peas, seed potatoes, and some farm implements, all of which were destroyed. It was clearly the work of incendiaries, and amounts to a disaster, if not to ruin.

JUHL

SUMTER, S. C., April 29

A state of things has been developed in this section with a few days past which cannot be too promptly considered or too soon corrected. If the press is silent, the people must suffer on without an advocate under the most grievous wrongs until, forbearance ceasing to be a virtue, the present disorders culminate in the dread catastrophe.

We are becoming so familiar with the repeated recitals of burglaries, larcenies, barn burnings, cattle stealing, and other kindred depredations that little or no surprise or interest is expressed or taken in such announcements. The only effect of the oft-told tale is to deepen the feeling of insecurity which now attaches to all movable property in this country. Mr. [J. A.] Fullwood's barn was broken into a few nights ago, and a quantity of provisions and one horse carried away. Night before last Mr. [J. H.] Dingle's barn shared the same fate, although two men slept in one end of it as a guard, who were either not aroused by the entrance of the robbers or were intimidated and induced to lie *perdu* by their superior numbers.

And these examples might be multiplied. But a still more serious source of disquiet exists in our midst. It is an unquestionable fact that for some nights past the streets of this town have been patrolled by armed bands of Negroes, who have waylaid and followed (dogged) white citizens on their way to or from their houses or places of business, offensively peering into their faces and making other annoying demonstrations. A young gentleman who landed from the train in the night, while walking up Main Street to his home, was overhauled by one of these bands and escorted for some distance, some of the party exclaiming, "Take his carpetbag," and others, "Kill him." He is a comparative stranger here, a youth in his teens, knew none of the Negroes, and it is not likely that any of the band knew him. Any white man landing here at that time would no doubt have met the same reception. Some of our citizens who have been interrupted in this way by parties thus unlawfully interfering with the passage of the streets are able to identify some of those participating in these outrages.

As your correspondent aims to do justice to all parties, it must be added that the only cause which can be imagined for these unseemly demonstrations is certain fabulous rumors which have gained currency of late in this community with reference to the Ku Klux Klan. One or two manuscript notices have indeed been posted, all, of course, in hieroglyphics, but with the three K's sufficiently prominent to indicate the design.[4] And some anonymous letters are said to have been received by certain persons (no new thing, for such was often the case prior to the war). But, if all this amounts to anything more than what is believed to have been the injudicious acts of a few idle persons in quest of amusement, it is unknown to the writer.

If any Klan exists, it has certainly done nothing in its organized capacity, has molested no one, frightened nobody by its nightly parades, or in any manner disturbed the quiet of the people, white or black. And the country would have nothing to fear in the way of social disturbance if the conduct of the white population in this respect had been followed by the blacks. But it is a well-known fact that a secret oath-bound league keeps the freedmen under its poisonous instructions—a league which seems to combine all the alleged objectionable features of the imaginary Klan. And it is equally well known that in this section no attempt has ever been made to interfere with such league meetings. And if any attempt of the kind had been made by armed bands of white citizens waylaying, arresting, or otherwise molesting the freedmen while passing peaceably through the streets at night, would not the authorities have promptly interfered and checked by the heaviest penalties such unlawful acts?

The freedmen have everything. They (or the wire-pullers who lead them) control the ballot and every office. Our people have quietly looked on at the great changes which are forced upon the country, and but few even have taken the trouble to vote in view of the certain minority in which they stand. At the late election, a freedman was

4. On April 8, 1868, the editor of the *Sumter Watchman* reported that he found this note in his office with funds to pay for its publication: "Ku Klux Klan.—Hyena Cave, Bloody Month, New Moon, † 22 X, 9th Hour. *In Hoc Signo.* Hist, ye Brother Skeletons – Division No. 160. The Great Grand Cyclops † demands Attention. Assemble! There is Work To Be Done! 'To them which sat in the region and shadow of death light is sprung up.' Let Justice † now resume her throne – though Blood darkens the plain. By order of the Grand Giant ††† Pale Death, Sec'ry."

seen leading three white (?) men (of course they were of the pine-barren order) up to vote the Radical ticket. He did so unmolested. If a similar feat had been attempted by a white citizen with three colored voters for the Conservative side, would not a desperate effort have been made to take the voters from him? Other significant examples might be given in which they presume to do what would not be allowed on the other side. They had the convention, they have the governor and the legislature, and will have the district offices. Let them be content; let them be quiet. And, if they and their advisers have not the sense to see the folly and imprudence of these self-constituted armed patrols in a quiet and peaceable community, they should be instructed better by those in authority for the good of both races of the whole country. And the lesson should be given in time.

JUHL

SUMTER, S. C., May 1

It cannot be denied that previous to and even during the late war, this country was self-sustaining. The annual crop supplied the entire population with an abundance of provisions, and what was not raised at home was imported and paid for out of the proceeds of the cotton, turpentine, and other products raised for market. Since emancipation, however, every year has witnessed the same appeals for assistance in furnishing supplies of bread. The lands, extent of population, and facilities remain substantially unchanged. The immediate results of the war have passed away, and reasonable time has certainly been given for the agricultural interest to recover by ordinary recuperation its antebellum status. Why, then, is a beautiful country like this, which has always heretofore liberally supplied the wants of its inhabitants, no longer able to meet the necessities of its people without extraneous assistance?

Unpropitious seasons, embarrassments of the planters, demoralizing influence of bureau and Union leagues and carpetbag politicians, and the multiplicity of elections, agitating and disturbing the labor of the country, may all have had an influence in producing this result. But there is one fact, perhaps more material than any other, which is worthy of the gravest consideration. In the opinion of the most intelligent and observant planters in Sumter District our last year's provision crop was sufficient to have sustained the entire population for the current twelve months. And yet at this time corn is scarce and rules high, and it is said that there are very few Negroes in this section who have any of their last year's crop on hand.

When the crops were divided, they received their share, enough in some cases, it is said, to supply them with bread for two years. From their natural but unfortunate improvidence of character, they have disposed of their crops, and their corn has found its way to the stores, and thence been shipped to Wilmington and other places. Thousands of bushels have unquestionably disappeared in this way—actually sent out of the district to a distant market. Formerly all this was under the control of the planter, who with a careful calculation of the plantation demands reserved his supplies in ample measure for all his dependents.

But now, while he retains his share or so much of it as has not been stolen, which may be sufficient for his own wants and to feed his stock, that portion which under the old system would have been still in his barn for the maintenance of his working force has disappeared and is no longer available, and the laborers in his employ came to him early in the year with the complaint that they are destitute of provisions and he or the bureau must supply their demands. It is, perhaps, not an exaggerated estimate to say that at least one-half the provision crop of 1867 in this district has disappeared in the manner described or in the destruction of barns by incendiaries. This last is by no means an insignificant item. In two barns burnt within a few miles of this town, thirteen hundred barrels of corn besides other provisions were consumed, and in both cases the owners ascribe the disaster to disaffected freedmen. In these two instances alone (and there have been many others) enough corn was wantonly destroyed to have furnished one hundred full hands with bread for twelve months.

The corn bartered away at one dollar per bushel will have to be replaced with corn at probably two dollars per bushel, to be obtained (if not by bureau loans) by planters' advances, and deducted from the coming crop. This, unless timely checked and corrected in some way, must result in the continued impoverishment of the freedmen and embarrassment of the country—a country sufficiently productive to repay with rich returns the toil of the husbandman and which cannot be, and ought not to be, chargeable with any scarcity which is clearly the result of prodigality and want of thrift.

The crops may be abundant, but with such a wretched disregard of the ordinary rules of management on the part of those who constitute a large majority of the population, the spring and summer will always witness a scarcity of provisions in this country. The bureau may continue to be a convenient resource to these improvident ones in their time of need, and thus encourage and perpetuate a system of prodigality which is the bane of the country. This country is abundantly able to feed its population if they will work and take care of what they make.

But it cannot do this unless the practice is abandoned of shipping off large quantities of grain during the winter, rendering necessary the importation within a few months and throughout the summer at greatly enhanced prices of carloads of corn for distribution. The evil is one which the white population, the planters particularly, recognize and deprecate, but which they have no power to correct or control; it is one in which the character of the country is wrongfully damaged, for our lands are not so barren nor our seasons so invariably bad as this annual scarcity would indicate. And, aside from the additional bureau expenses to the government and the taxation increased there-

by, it is an evil in which the freedmen themselves must be the principal ultimate sufferers.

JUHL

SUMTER, S. C., May 30

The people in this country can afford now, if ever, to be jolly. They
have heretofore been considered a very staid people—moral, law-
abiding, quiet, and peaceable, not given to excess of rioting, nor
indulging in anything else particularly unseemly or indecorous. But,
voila! times change, and if grief kills, joy makes even the sedate frisky
and rollicksome. Hence it is to be expected that even the demure
inhabitants of middle Carolina will exhibit briskness, buoyancy, bril-
liancy, under the stimulating pressure of unusual good fortune. What
a joy it is to know that we live in "the best government"—a government which relieves the white population of all care or participation
in its management, fills all the offices by machinery, and regularly
compliments the taxpayers by emptying their pockets to feed its hungry host of followers.

What an honor to have the privilege of feeding and clothing the
many charming adventurers who, unable to get bread or to make
bread in their own states, are devoting themselves to the sublime and
self-sacrificing work of reconstructing the South! What a proud satisfaction it is to contemplate those even among our native born who
were once active and enthusiastic in the cause of secession, while
secession was the best market of the day, but who now present a
picture of penitence, even in dust and ashes, crying *peccavi* and content
to receive a small pittance in the way of an office, abandoning (as a
suitable and convincing penance) race, country, honor, and all.

And how happy the thought that the former slave who was only
useful in a subordinate sphere has thrown aside the plough and the
hoe and consented to devote his magnificent intellect and profound

acquirements to the arduous toils of the convention, the legislature, and the council chamber, nobly assuming the cares of state and asking us to do nothing but—to foot the bills. Everything is done for us, and we have no trouble at all, except in paying the bills—a very small matter when the country is so prosperous, money abundant, trade lively, property commanding fabulous prices, and the planters troubled with heavier crops and more stock than they are able to take care of. Oh happy, thrice happy people!

And then such a season—such delightful weather—such remarkable weather. Anybody would know, without reading the papers, that the country is reconstructed or something else. Surely, there was never such luck before. If Micawber had only lived to see this day his expectation would have been realized, for something has "turned up," as is evidenced by so much coming down. A diary of the weather might read thus: It rained on Monday all day and all night; then on Tuesday it began to rain and kept it up till the next day; Wednesday it rained and Wednesday night; on Thursday it set in to become rainy and rained till Friday, which gave us a splendid rain all day. It not only rained all last week, but the week before, and the week before that. During the preceding week there was a rain that lasted seven days and was the continuation of a rain storm that had been running, day and night, for the past three or six anterior months.

Such a combination of good times, good things, good prospects, and especially good government (a little dark it may be, but still, the darkest hour is just before day) seems like almost crowding and overcrowding the good things upon us. The effect is visible. The recent visit of Robinson's circus (a capital affair, by the way) drew but a small crowd. Some libeler assigned this to a scarcity of greenbacks, but not so. The true reason is the people have become independent of the circus. They are a circus unto themselves. They see somersaults enough, and ground and lofty tumbling, and have the Ethiopians in full blast on every hand, and have to pay for it all whether they like the performance or not. The riders perform at one time on two horses (the white and the black), the one they spur, the other they pat, but it is evident they are riding both horses to the ———, well, we'll not name him.

Is it not then a jolly time away down here in Dixie? Why even [H. L.] Darr & [N. G.] Osteen of the *News* are jolly—the former has been a practical printer for a third of a century—and has recently been presented with a silver goblet by some enthusiastic friends as a token of appreciation, and it is perfectly refreshing to see how jolly he and his more youthful but no less deserving partner have become.[5] And this has been intensified by a vote of thanks from the Bishopville Democratic Club; for, if the Ku Klux Klan are nowhere, the Democrats are coming to life, and their manners, sheening far, victorious seem to be. And why not? Train has hope for Ireland, and why should there not be hope for the South? True, ours is a harder case, a deeper humiliation, a more grinding oppression, a less appeasable despotism, but there are millions of white men on this same continent who may strike successfully for the right in November next. Even the rains must yield to the sunshine at last, and the wrongs which now eat into the souls of a gallant people cannot last forever. "The Campbells are coming. . . . "[6]

The spirit of this letter is not badly illustrated by a little incident transpiring here. Early in the spring one of our practical horticulturalists made considerable preparations for a crop of watermelons and took occasion to announce to his friends that when the fruit ripened they must call and enjoy a feast. The heavy rains set in flooding the country and proving peculiarly disastrous to the very crop on which

5. According to the *Sumter News* (June 2, 1868), the goblet was an anonymous gift to mark the newspaper's third year of publication.
6. Fleming refers to James B. Campbell of Charleston who was named U.S. senator in 1865, but was unable to take his seat because of Radical opposition. Now, Campbell was once more attempting to win a seat in the Senate.

his generous invitations were based. Meeting one of his invited guests a few days since, who punched him mercilessly on the melon question, he very coolly replied: "Well, it's not half so bad as you think for I have half the crop already secured; my land is well covered with the water, and all it lacks is the melons to make the crop complete." If there was a smile after such a report, it was no more than might have been looked for, especially when an excess of fortune's favors incline our own people to be jolly.

JUHL

SUMTER, S. C., June 5

A gentleman who owns a large plantation where formerly he made cotton by the hundred bales and whose dairy and poultry yard supplied his table liberally was seen a few days since purchasing eggs and butter at one of the stores in this town for his family in the country. The explanation given was, that the rogues around him left him not a chicken or an egg and had destroyed his cattle. He lives in a splendid mansion and has a magnificent landed estate, makes now about ten bales of cotton—one-half, at least, of which is appropriated by the freedmen—and has to buy in town even those little adjuncts to a good table which it is the province of the farm to furnish.

He is realizing, like many others in our stricken land, some of the pleasant experience (though from a different cause) of many a New York merchant who has moved his family to the country full of the fancied bliss of farm life and rural felicity, bestowing neither the time nor experience necessary to success in such a venture, and who has given up the experiment in disgust after discovering that the farm products of his own raising cost vastly more than when purchased at his city home. "The best laid schemes of mice and men, gang aft aglee" from a want of experience in the city merchant turned farmer, from the multitude of rogues infesting the vicinity of the southern farmer, preying *ad libitum* upon the fruits of his toil and care.

Another planter was in town offering corn for sale. This also excited some surprise, as it is well known that there is a scarcity of this cereal in the country and that the planters have been and will continue to be buyers. The gentleman referred to frankly admitted that his supply of corn was inadequate and that he had none to spare, but alleged that the barn-breakers were so bold and numerous that as a matter of self-defence he had concluded to sell all his provisions not immediately required and depend on buying from the stores as his necessities might demand. Locks and bolts are no protection; another way-mark indicating the progress of reconstruction.

A gentleman from Bishopville says the Negroes in his neighborhood have commenced a system of indiscriminate robbery, stealing from their own color as well as despoiling the whites; that where industrious and thrifty freedmen become the owners of stock, poultry, and hogs, their property is stolen by the vicious and vagrant rogues; and that hence, the better class of freedmen have recently avowed themselves as advocates of a law punishing larceny with death. Perhaps it is well that they are being taught by a severe experience that when liberty degenerates into license and defies the restraints of law, all classes of the community must suffer—the owner of one hog perhaps as keenly in proportion as the owner of a hundred.

The so-called election under the new constitution was held here on Tuesday and Wednesday of this week and seemed to excite little interest. The vote polled was a very small one, as the returns will show. The Conservatives stood aloof, and, of course, the Radical ticket, whether black, tan, or white, was elected. An incident, which is well substantiated, is illustrative of the manner in which the ballot is now employed. A semi-idiotic Negro man attempted to vote, but his name could not be found on the register, and he was rejected. This was on the last day of the election. He was persuaded to go to the registrar and have his name entered as a qualified voter. He did so, and was duly registered, and then voted on the same day.

The impression exists that after the time appointed for registration had passed the books were closed and could not legally be reopened for the accommodation of anyone. But aside from this—a physician who saw the aforesaid voter pronounced him an "idiot," and after his vote was cast he was asked for whom he had voted, and replied "for Raticul." "Who is he?" "Don't know who he is." "Where does he live?" "Dunno." He had, of course, voted a printed ticket with a list of names and offices of which he knows nothing; and, notwithstanding his palpable mental imbecility, his vote is as potential as any other placed in the box. Of such a constituency and such supporters the successful candidates may be duly proud.

Reports of the crops are various. Some planters say that, compared with last year, not more than half the area of land has been planted in cotton, and this will produce not more than half its last year's yield, as very little guano has been used this season. Their estimate, therefore, is one-fourth of last year's crop. All concur that the season has been particularly unfavorable for cotton and generally make favorable reports of the provision crop. This latter, in proportion to hands employed, is larger than usual. The fruits and berries promise an abundant yield and will probably constitute the summer diet of many who have contracted a distaste for the plough and the hoe. . . .

JUHL

SUMTER, S. C., June 13

A general interest is felt in the subject of immigration, and many landowners in this state are offering as much as one-tenth of their lands for the purpose of inducing and securing the right kind of population. And yet, very little seems to have been accomplished in this direction. During the month of May the commissioners of emigration for New York City sent out 34,000 passengers, and of this number nearly 8,000 were absorbed by New York State, over 2,000 each by Pennsylvania and Wisconsin, over 1,000 each by Iowa, Massachusetts, Michigan, Minnesota, Missouri, and Ohio, and of the southern states Virginia received less than 200, South Carolina only 29, Alabama 22, Texas 49, Tennessee 126, North Carolina 14, Georgia 11, Florida 5, Louisiana 109, and Mississippi 1. A free grant of forty or fifty acre farms to practical farmers of approved character from the North or great Northwest might be more successful than all the efforts hitherto directed across the Atlantic have been or are likely to be. . . .

. . . In this section the "clandestine" element cannot be conveniently ignored and is at a premium, especially with the knights of the carpetbag and other candidates for office. It has recently given us a body of "county" officers, most judiciously selected with a view to the public weal and the proprieties of the occasion. The three "county commissioners" are the present bureau agent and one ex-captain of the 30th Massachusetts Volunteers, at one time in garrison here, and one other person, originally from Massachusetts or some other little "Down East" settlement; so that this board, which, under the bogus constitution, supersedes all the old boards of crossroads, the poor, public buildings, etc., has not a southern white, black, or speckled on it.

The judge of probate was formerly for many years ordinary of this district, in which position he managed hopelessly to involve himself and several sets of sureties, as was duly chronicled sometime since in an equity case reported in the *Courier*. He has become a convert to radicalism and, if the machinery moves smoothly, will soon have another chance to manipulate the derelict estates of this new "county." The sheriff [a blacksmith] is the Vulcan of the party, who distinguished himself in the mongrel convention by two resolutions—

one against the freedom of the press, the other against the freedom of speech. The one excluding a reporter, the other fulminating all the fires of the forge against any unlucky wight who might incautiously use the words *Yankee* or *Negro*. It is confidently predicted that, if "the mills of the gods grind slow" as a general rule, such debtors as may hereafter fall into the hands of the sheriff will find Vulcan's mill a notable exception.

The clerk of the court also hails originally from abroad, but the school commissioner is a contribution from your city, in return doubtless for the generosity of Sumter in contributing one member of your legislative delegation—acts of reciprocal kindness which there is every reason to believe are not very highly appreciated at either end of the line. As an evidence of the liberality with which the "elect" treat themselves, it is noticed that very few of them are satisfied with one office: i.e., one finger in the pie. For example, the sheriff-elect is magistrate, registrar, delegate to the convention, state senator, etc., etc. The Sumter blacks, as well as the Sumter whites, are generously excused from the cares of office: the former, however, were allowed the high privilege of voting in the ticket and will have three members in the lower house, colored, but, in part at least, imported. . . .

JUHL

SUMTER, S. C., June 20

. . . A homicide occurred in Clarendon a few days since under the following circumstances: An industrious and well-behaved freedman, having a small farm under good culture and stock of his own, agreed to take charge of one of his white neighbor's cows and pasture it with his own, he undertaking to protect it. While the cow was in his pasture under this arrangement, he one day discovered three Negroes engaged in butchering the animal. He immediately went to his neighbor; and, informing him of the circumstances, they repaired to the pasture. When the Negroes saw them approaching, they walked off and disappeared in the woods.

The next day, while the freedman was ploughing in his field, one of the cow-killers came out of an adjoining thicket and requested him to accompany him to the woods, as there were parties there wishing to see him. Upon his refusal to do so, believing it to be a plan to murder him, the cow-killer said he would get his gun and come back and shoot him, and then disappeared. As soon as he was gone, the freedman went to his house, obtained his gun, and returned to his plough. He had not long resumed his work before he saw the cow-killer, gun in hand, come out of the woods; and, as the latter entered the field, the freedman fired and his enemy fell dead. The freedman at once proceeded to Manning and stating the facts, surrendered to the sheriff. The trial may elicit other circumstances, somewhat modifying this report, but those of the citizens who know the parties and the facts seem to justify full the act as one of self-defence.

There have been several fires during the week in this district; one at Mechanicsville, destroying a store room of Mr. F. H. Kennedy, with a large supply of provisions, groceries, etc.; another six miles east of Sumter, destroying Mr. A. Browne's kitchen and effects—all believed to have originated accidentally.[7]

JUHL

SUMTER, S. C., June 29

... In the larceny line, a marked improvement may be reported. In some places it is said that robberies have almost entirely ceased, not,

---

7. The *Sumter News* (June 27, 1868) contains a lengthy letter signed by twelve Negro citizens of Mechanicsville deploring incendiarism: "Friends, in this impoverished condition of the country, you cannot destroy any portion of the provisions or capital necessary to carry on the business of the country without injuring the *whole community in a greater or lesser extent.* . . . Whatever your grievances or wants may be, this is not the way to avenge the one or supply the other."

however, because the rogues have all been arrested or converted, but because they have swept the neighborhood of every movable worth carrying off, and there is nothing left to invite or reward a raid. In other places they have admirably contrived by one depredation to make amends for another, as when they have stolen plank or rails from fencing until the fields are left unprotected, they prevent any possible damage from cattle by killing all the stock in the neighborhood. Between Sumter and Charleston there are fields under cultivation this year which have no fencing whatever, and the growing crop has been disturbed by no four-footed animal, for the stock of the country has been swept from the range. . . .

The taxpayers in this country are unrepresented and voiceless in the federal, state, municipal, and county governments under which they live. They are, and will be still more, savagely taxed to support their rulers. They yield on the same principle that the traveler surrenders his purse to the robber who demands "your money or your life." But there is honor even among thieves, and the Italian brigand who forces a stipend from the peasantry in his district protects those from whom he thus derives his revenues and will allow no interference by others with their cattle or crops. And the regime which so fiercely fleeces the unrepresented taxpayers should at least afford them the like protection and prevent all other rogues, who go into the business on their own private account, from further despoiling its subjects. . . . "Too many cooks spoil the broth"; and, if the multitude of rogues so long operating unofficially are not speedily interdicted, the business will be ruined, the country be reduced to the last stages of poverty, and the horde of officeholders will make the very agreeable discovery that their share of the spoils will consist in picking the bones. Many affirm that the meat is already gone, and that even such bones that are left are becoming very dry.

JUHL

Sumter, S. C., July 14

Dullness reigns supreme in this portion of our "reconstructed" domain, and the very courthouse, which is usually considered the bustling and busy centre of this once proud corporation, stands wrapt in gloomy silence, frowning in all the majesty of outraged justice upon its present judicial and political surroundings. The portals of its halls and its varied offices are all closed, waiting the incoming administration; and, since the completion and occupancy of the new jail, it is no longer cheered even with the songs and breakdowns of the sable prisoners who whilom occupied its basement floors.[8]

A spasmodic attempt was indeed made on the late glorious Fourth to wake up its slumbering vicinage, when the Radicals took up a position in the rear of the temple and essayed with songs and eloquence and cheers to infuse new life into the party; when Mr. J. T. Green was the orator of the day and was conducted to the stand by School Commissioner J. N. Corbett and two colored members; and when Reverend (colored) Johnson read the immortal Declaration, prefacing said performance with the announcement: "If there are any Democrats here, their company is not wanted"; and when "old John Brown lies mouldering in his grave" was sung, the tune being raised by the school commissioner aforesaid; and when Massachusetts's Darlington senator, Whittemore, denounced Democracy with a voice whose thundering reverberations might well have reached the tympanum of the deaf, but failed to wake up sundry colored sleepers who appeared amazingly refreshed under it all; and when Registrar, Senator, Sheriff (and so forth) Coughlan favored the party with a few specimens of classic eloquence, which would have brought down the house, only there was no house to be brought down, for the attendance

8. On July 1, the *Sumter Watchman* reported that a new, two-story jail—fifty by forty feet and constructed of solid handhewn timbers—had been completed at a cost of approximately eighty-five hundred dollars.

was meagre, and no cheers or drumming could enlarge the crowd. And it is sad to relate that even in the midst of this grand demonstration a stalwart Negro member of the league was in front of the courthouse roundly cursing the secret order into which he had been entrapped and swearing he was done with it forever. And another, with a marshal's rosette as big as a cabbage leaf, was fast asleep on the stone steps of the ordinary's office, thus losing all his share.

And the said stone steps were pressed a few days after by the weary feet of the probate judge elect, who demanded the delivery of the keys. But to this the stubborn incumbent responded: "Nay, brother," and utterly refused to vacate the post until his successor entered into proper bonds, and in this course he has been sustained by instructions from Columbia. And the latest glimpse which this deponent has had of the scene of all these marvels, to wit, the courthouse aforesaid, was on Saturday last between the hours of 8 and 10 A.M., at which time the street appeared deserted, the temple of justice and all the offices thereto, incident or appertaining, were closed, the probate judge was seated *solus* on the front steps in profound rumination, and the bureau and Massachusetts county commissioners (their shoemaker colleague having gone to Columbia as a member of the House) were sitting on the rail enclosure of the square enjoying the scene—or at least I "guess" they were. These, with a couple of goats in the upper porch chewing the cud (ruminating) were, at the time, literally the only living things visible in, about, or around the venerable pile or the plaza attached.

The tax collector for this district reports more than half the taxpayers defaulters, and this is doubtless true throughout the state. The people have not the money to pay, and unless the dry weather is soon relieved by showers, the crop will be cut off, and in many places it is hopelessly damaged already. Where then is the immense amount necessary to support the ponderous and costly machinery of the new government to come from? The state may use her credit and borrow the money, and the sharp-witted "powers that be" will doubtless do this rather than continue to sigh over an empty treasury. But such loan, if successful, will involve additional debt, filling the pockets of the present incumbents it is true, but leaving their successors to a forced repudiation or a fearful experience in footing the bills.

In Darlington there is a Negro sheriff. If he was a native it would not be so bad, but even he is from abroad. The native freedmen begin to realize the fact that in the general distribution of the spoils their share seems likely to be confined to a moiety of bureau corn, the privilege of hearing buncombe speeches which they don't even understand, and the still greater privilege of voting a printed ticket, which they cannot read and which is duly filled with the names of their "true friends." A little more experience and their increasing indifference to politics will run into disgust. The Rev. Darlington Senator is said to have made five dollars a clip for marrying couples, some of whom had been living as man and wife ever since the parson first looked forth with baby innocence upon the beautiful scenery of the old Bay State. A prominent white Radical is authority for the statement.

JUHL

SUMTER, S. C., August 26

On last Saturday the courthouse at this place was well filled with freedmen from all parts of this district. They were addressed by three colored members of the Columbia assembly, and gentlemen who were present report the speeches to have been of a very incendiary character and calculated to do great mischief with an audience unable either to read or reason for themselves. Notwithstanding this, these colored solons are said to have been the guests, during at least a part of their visit, of one of our citizens who held a prominent office under the past dynasty and who finds it equally comfortable to hold prominent office under the present.

1868

August 26

This season has been the most sickly ever probably experienced in Sumter. Fevers of various types, in some cases very obstinate and malignant, have prevailed, and very few families have escaped. There have, however, been but few deaths among the white population, but among the blacks the mortality has been and continues to be heavy. A few more seasons would effectually deprive this place of its character for healthfulness, which has long been its boast.

Reports concur in making the provision crop rather better than usual. The recent heavy rains, continuing for nearly a week, have damaged the cotton, and this crop must fall below the usual average, as there is less land planted and certainly a lighter application of fertilizers than ever before.

As one of the results of "reconstruction," it may be mentioned that there is no qualified and acting sheriff, magistrate, constable, or court in all this county. The town is without a council, and the poorhouse, one mile distant, is filled with white paupers who are said to be actually suffering for bread. And Negroes, as they walk the streets, amuse themselves by drawing their pistols and firing at the trees.

JUHL

SUMTER, S. C., September 1

. . . On Saturday another meeting of the freedmen at our courthouse was addressed by three colored speakers, one of whom [Rev. Burwell James] was from Janney's Hall and told his hearers that the Radicals would sweep the country from "Dan to Omega"—an original piece of eloquence which he thrice repeated. Another speaker said that as the white men were forming colored Democratic clubs, they (the blacks) must go to work and form white Radical clubs, that the poor whites would jump at the bait, if told that they would all have land and homesteads given them. The colored legislator explained and advocated the social equality bill and said he had voted for it, to the great delight of his audience. The attendance was very meagre, but another meeting on next Saturday is to appoint delegates to the Radical 8th of September convention, which meets in Columbia to nominate carpetbag electors.

JUHL

SUMTER, S. C., September 16

Mosquitoes and malarial diseases, so unusual in this section, continue troublesome. The presence and numbers of the former render nettings almost essential to comfort, and the latter occasion an expenditure of money for calomel and quinine which is needed and could be much more agreeably used for table expenses. Both plagues are ascribed by physicians to the heavy and continuous rains in the spring and the neglect of drainage necessarily attendant upon the disorganized state of the country. And it is worthy of note that the suffering falls most heavily upon the very class in whose interest professedly all the usual sanitary regulations, with everything else like good government, have been swept away under the misnomer of "reconstruction."

The prevalent fever is intermittent, in nearly all cases preceded by a chill, and readily yielding to treatment. Quinine is the principal agent employed; and, strange to say, many of the Negroes and even some of the more ignorant whites have so strong a prejudice against this remedy that they will not use it. The dividing line between the races has been so assiduously drawn and deeply indented by bureau and league and unscrupulous office-seekers that the blacks no longer seem either to appreciate or follow any advice which may be given them by the respectable white population.

In many cases of sickness among them there is good authority for the statement that they decline with distrust the very medicines they require and resort for a cure to the most ridiculous practices, such as blowing in the mouth of a live frog or walking backwards to a tree and tying a string around it in a hard knot, either of which is said to be a sovereign remedy for chills and fever. Withdrawn, as they now are, from the patient nursing and prompt medical attention which the owner's interest and humanity alike formerly secured to them, and indulging in superstitions and practices which almost appear incredible, and often spending whole nights in crowded and ill-ventilated rooms, at meetings in which their religious fervor is expressed by the most violent contortions of body and a terrific exercise of the lungs, it occasions no surprise that in a sickly season they are the chief sufferers and contribute largely more than their proportion to the bills of mortality. For even those malarial attacks, which in the early stages yield readily to proper treatment, under charlatan or reckless management often assume a congestive type and become inevitably fatal.

There is no doubt that a careful census of the colored population would exhibit a remarkable falling off in the number of very young children compared with the statistics of the past. Painful rumors are indeed afloat of the prevalence of infanticide to an alarming extent, and some of these rumors assume the definite shape of horrible narratives, containing the most revolting details. But while it might be very difficult, with such a population, to trace out any of these rumors to the conviction of the offenders, there is enough of plausibility in such current reports to awaken at least the gravest suspicions.

One sows and another reaps. The corn, now hardening on the stalk, is already leaving the fields and taking the highway, either for town or the still more convenient country stores, under the care, not of the planter, but of the numberless sable operators who—on their way to political gatherings—find it agreeable to carry something to exchange for tobacco, ammunition, or whiskey. So that these circulating corn-bags are now almost as dreaded as the once harmless, but of late mischievous carpetbags. Nor are these transactions confined to the retail department. A few nights since, a farmer living but a short distance from town was aroused from his slumbers by the barking of his dog. Going to the door and discovering nothing to justify the alarm, he gave a whoop to encourage the dog and then retired to his room. In the morning he was very much amused by discovering in one of his fields near the house some eight or ten bushels of corn in several heaps which had been pulled, shucked, and piled up during the night by some persons unknown, who were evidently only prevented from carrying it off by the watchdog's alarm and the farmer's timely yell. The wagon which came for corn went off loaded with disappointed rogues, but very likely paid a more successful visit before morning to some other plantation.

Everything is dull here except politics. As this district has really had the honor (?) of furnishing the Radicals with a chief justice, a circuit judge, speaker of the house, reading clerk of the senate, messenger, etc., etc., it is fair to presume that some of these officials will still retain as partisans a few, at least, of their former friends, and hence the white vote will be divided, although the overwhelming preponderance will be Democratic.

JUHL

SUMTER, S. C., September 28

The harvest is plenteous. Wherever proper effort has been made, it may confidently be said that the lands in this section have yielded an abundant increase. The earlier crops of wheat, rye, and oats turned out well, although these small grains are not cultivated here on a very large scale. The cotton crop is a very fair one, considering the area planted and the reduced quantity of fertilizers employed. It is rapidly coming into this market, and the plant is still bearing, the weather being warm and no appearance of a very early frost. The crop of corn, peas, potatoes, and rice is certainly heavier than usual. The last named article has received more attention from the planters in the interior than before, and the yield is such that with a full allowance for home consumption, there will probably be a considerable margin for export.

The lowlands in middle Carolina, reclaimed from swamps or contiguous to the almost innumerable water courses which thread this section—as well as the pond lands and savannahs—produce this invaluable esculent in abundance. From 40 to 60 bushels per acre is not an uncommon yield, and a planter in the western part of the district near the Wateree reports 600 bushels gathered from six acres. There are well-substantiated instances in which a single acre furnished rice enough for a family of seven to last them for twelve months, used liberally. And these lands, unlike the low country tide swamps, can be cultivated with white labor throughout the entire season. One acre of ordinary sandy land has produced 100½ bushels corn by actual measurement, and the fodder (blades) paid for all the manures used in its production. With these facts, it will readily be inferred that all this country requires to make it rich and prosperous is a stable and good government and the right kind of population to furnish intelligent and thrifty husbandry.

Among the various styles of contracts with the freedmen none seem to work better than the following: The farmer furnishes plough animals and farm implements and keeps all under his own care and contract. He gives to each laborer a house and as much land as he can cultivate on his own account and firewood—all free. The employee works for the planter the first half of the week and works for himself the balance of the time. The laborer meets his own expenses and, while working his own crop, has the free use of the plough animals and all the required plantation tools. The laborers have no claim on the planter's crop, but have absolute control of their house, land, firewood, and the use—for three days every week—of all the plantation animals and tools for three day's labor every week in cultivating the employer's crop. And the employer has all the expense of feeding the stock and keeping up the establishment. Those who have tried this plan say it works to the satisfaction of both parties and gives to the laborer, who behaves himself, a permanent home and an interest in the place he cultivates and avoids the dissatisfaction often attending a division of the crop.

There are those who have and would keep what they have, and there are others whose chief end seems to be to take what they can. Between these two classes there is a sharp contest of wits, and the barns and fields constitute the arena. One of the most innocent and successful expedients against the rogues was recently adopted by a lady whose garden had been despoiled of cabbages on several successive nights. Watching an opportunity when several Negro women of the neighborhood were in full view, she walked into the garden and proceeded deliberately to sprinkle wheat flour from a small paper over the cabbage leaves. The Negroes saw and were conquered; they had no desire to steal poisoned cabbage; at least such is the lady's influence, for her vegetables have not since been disturbed.

The Negroes cannot see what is patent to every intelligent observer that their very existence as a race in this country depends on their good conduct, and that their worst enemies are those who incite them to acts of hostility against the whites. The carpetbaggers by their teachings may succeed in making this once useful population a source of disquiet, not only to the South, but to the whole country, and when their party ends have been accomplished, they will be the first mercilessly to insist on their removal out of the way. [Hinton] Helper was terrific in his denunciations of slavery and now brands the Negro a pestilent beast and insists on his being driven from the country. And [W. W.] Holden is reported to have recently admitted that he and his Radical friends were only using the Negro to establish the party in the control of the state; and, when this was accomplished, it was their intention to send off and colonize the blacks. President Johnson himself has said to a deputation of colored preachers that if the Negroes could not live peaceably in a state of freedom with the other race, they would have to be colonized somewhere to themselves. The American people have the art of pushing out of the way everything which offers an obstruction to progress and civilization and peace and prosperity. The numerous and powerful aboriginal tribes have melted away in obedience to this law. The Indian may have had the sympathy of many, but this did not avert his fate. And now the great Radical Negro advocate of the North (*New York Tribune*, September 23) in its letter from Omaha, says:

> I have hinted at an Indian war. What to do with the Indian is a question which you have freely discussed in your columns. The western men have but one answer—kill him. I have found only one man in all the western country—I speak of the country west of the Missouri—who holds a contrary opinion. That one man advocates kindness and conciliation; everybody else argues nothing but extermination by the quickest method. They see in the redskin only a false, treacherous, fiendish animal and denounce the author of "Lo, the poor Indian" as a malignant enemy of every settler upon the plains. They listen to your theory of kindness and admit that it would be more humane, more Christian, and perhaps more potent than the system they advocate, if you had now to begin dealing with the Indian people; but, to take the facts of today and deal with a race which now sees in every unprotected pale face a victim to be tortured and murdered, they declare nothing but vigorous war will do.

How long will it be before "the party of progress"—"the party of great moral ideas"—will come to the same conclusion with reference to the blacks? The latter will find their attempts at political rule and their ill-advised reliance on the ballot and the musket the sure highway to their own extermination. Their identification in feeling and interest with the white race of the South might avert the ruin which their Radical masters will otherwise inflict upon them so soon as from useful tools they become social and political pests. But, if they continue to trust the horde of adventurers, native and imported, white and black, who now lead and control their movements, their future history is fairly written in the Indian's past. "Lo! the poor Indian." Alas! poor cuff!

JUHL

1868

October 4

SUMTER, S. C., October 4

We live in a moving age and a distracted country. Numbers of the best citizens of the state have gone into voluntary exile and are now living in distant cities and some even in foreign countries, where they have sought refuge until these calamities be overpast. Many have emigrated from this section since the war and have sought new homes in Brazil, Honduras, Mexico, Texas, the Valley of Virginia, Mississippi, Florida, North Carolina, and other places; but, strange to relate, all these emigrants, with scarcely an exception, have come back again, damaged of course to the extent of the outlay and sacrifices involved in such expeditions, but greatly enriched in an experience whose sad chapters would make a gloomy volume for a rainy day. Others, who came here as refugees during the late "unpleasantness" and have remained here since are now on the wing for a flight to the coast, finding Sumter rather flat and unprofitable for longer residence. . . . These latter examples falsify the common saying that the vessel which enters this port comes to a permanent anchorage and will never be able to get to sea again. . . .

In this happy era when—as poetically described by a sable Jews' harper, "Buckra's in the cornfield, nigger playin' gentleman"—the white families are rapidly and successfully adapting themselves to the new order of things. Many of the most respectable households do not now employ a single servant and, with the aid of labor-saving appliances and various modern conveniences, manage their domestic affairs with more real satisfaction and comfort than when they num-

255

bered their servants by the dozen. Others adopt into their families some young white persons of humble circumstances as a "help," and this arrangement succeeds well and saves them from many annoyances which the other class of servants under present teachings are so apt to occasion. The new system promises well; it tends to develop mind and muscle in the rising generation, and teaches them habits of industry and self-reliance. When every "mauma" becomes a "lady" and every "daddy" a gentleman and every sable urchin a candidate for academic honors and political advancement, it is time for white people to go to work, and many of them are doing this with every advantage to themselves. Let those laugh who win.

JUHL

SUMTER, S. C., October 9

Yesterday Sumter indulged in the, at this time, fashionable entertainment of a Democratic mass meeting and barbecue. A large platform with an amphitheatre of seats was erected in the Academy grove and tables arranged in the open square for the dinner. The crowd in attendance was very large and seemed to be composed nearly equally of the two races.[9] The speakers who arrived on the train were escorted in carriages to the place of meeting, and the fine band of Lowande & Co.'s capital circus (now performing here to crowded houses) contributed much to the entertainment of the crowd during the procession and, in fact, throughout the interesting exercises of the day. Speeches were made by Gen. Wade Hampton, Judge [Alfred P.] Aldrich, Colonel [J. P.] Thomas of Columbia, Colonel [R. F.] Graham of Marion (Democratic elector), J. P. Richardson of Clarendon, Pleasant Goode (colored) of Columbia, and others. The best of order was observed, and no unpleasantness or difficulty of any kind has been reported.

9. The *Sumter News* (October 15, 1868) estimated that a crowd of some five thousand persons attended this meeting.

At night the red lanterns of the Seymour and Blair Club appeared in the windows of the courthouse, and a lively meeting was kept up there to a late hour.

Whatever differences may exist among the people, the true policy of both races is to preserve the peace, and it is certainly a matter for congratulation that so large and mixed an assemblage passed an entire day under the discussion of exciting political questions without disorder or disturbance of any kind. It seems evident that if any interruption of this state of things shall in future occur, it must be forced by the other side.

The weather is now cold—cold enough for fire and blankets and winter clothing—too cold by far for cotton, although no frost has yet appeared.

JUHL

SUMTER, S. C., October 31

. . . This town has become quite a cotton market, and by consequence a heavy distributor of all kinds of merchandise. The adjoining districts all contribute to its present business prosperity. This sometimes gives us strange visitors who play antics which meet with neither approval nor endorsement in our peaceable community. Yesterday a party of white men, said to be from Darlington, after selling their cotton here left town in their carts in rather exuberant spirits and, while passing through the suburbs, indulged in very noisy demonstrations and attacked several colored persons whom they met and managed to leave behind them quite an excitement. A colored deputy of the sheriff was sent after them to bring them back, but when he succeeded in overtaking them, they took his pistol from him and beat him very severely. On his return to headquarters with this report, a white and colored posse was dispatched after the offenders, who were in due time conducted back to town and will be, doubtless, held to answer for violating law and resisting process.

These are believed to be the facts in the case, and there is no desire to add much in the way of comment. The occurrence assumed more importance than would otherwise attach to it from the peculiarly inflammable character of our present surroundings. This community has maintained a character for peace; and, fully apprised of the condition of the population, it is not prepared to thank anyone who will walk into the magazine with a pipe in his mouth. Colored deputies may in some respects be very useful to the sheriff, but their employment in arresting white men cannot be expected to work well in a country like this—at least such is a current opinion. And the more disorderly the parties to be arrested, the more probable will be an unpleasant result. Hence, while one class of our people may be urged to practice forbearance, it would seem not unreasonable to expect the party in power to avoid all unnecessary sources of irritation by which existing difficulties may be needlessly complicated and the peace disturbed.

Of the approaching election little need be said, as the result is so distinctly foreshadowed that there is scarcely room for any other hope than that it may pass off peaceably and give repose to the country. The whites may be almost a unit for the constitutional party, but wherever, as in this section, the blacks are in the majority, the Radical ticket will very naturally prevail.

Mr. William L. Brunson, one of the oldest residents of this place, was buried today.

JUHL

WALHALLA, S. C., November 24

The German element in this community is sufficient to give its distinctive impress to the customs and habits of the people. Industrious they are by nature and necessity, economical in everything, and yet not averse to such relaxation from business and toil as a harmless frolic may afford. Entertainments are not unfrequently improvised for an evening's amusement, and to these any and all are admitted who plant down the inevitable quarter. For the proceeds are applied to some local charity, and in this way they seek to promote the cause of benevolence, while contributing an hour's agreeable pastime to all who attend. A well-lighted and comfortably furnished hall, with all the usual machinery of the stage, is used on these occasions and is almost invariably crowded. . . .

The presence of the white man seems fatal to the Indian; it either results in his expulsion from the hunting grounds of his fathers or brings him under influences before which he inevitably deteriorates and melts away. The living remains of the once celebrated Cherokees are closing up the history of their tribe, just beyond this area in the mountains of the Old North State. A large party of them visited Walhalla a few days since, the wretched scions of a once noble stock. They have lost the distinctive outlines which made the red man the hero of poetry and romance. Longfellow would search in vain among them for traces of Hiawatha. The bard would turn disgusted away from such a wretched crew. Diminutive in size, tame and dwarfish in appearance, with garments ragged and tattered, the Indian is already lost, and this is but the counterfeit presentment in the style of mulattoes of the lowest type.

And yet, like the freedmen, they have their money value, and as such are not forgotten. A shrewd little "Down Easter" passed through here last week as an agent to visit these Cherokees at their homes and make a census of the tribe. Money is due them under a treaty, and eight years' interest has swelled the amount, and with a proper exhibit the treasury can be tapped. Somebody sees money in it, and somebody will get money out of it, but how much of the funds will ever reach the hands of these pumpkin-faced Cherokees is another question— perhaps a blanket apiece and a bottle of whiskey—this and nothing more. If their great chief, Bushy Head, is a sharp fellow and reads the *Courier*, he is advised to "look sharp" and employ a lawyer.

The railroads from Charleston to this place are admirably managed and the trains run through with great regularity. The grand trunk of the line is, of course, the South Carolina. . . . [10]

JUHL

WALHALLA, S. C., November 25

Rev. Dr. J. A. Reidenbach of Brooklyn, New York, preached in the German Lutheran Church at this place on last Sabbath. He has spent several days investigating the claims of Walhalla to a share of emigration and its advantages as a home for a German population. After a tour through the Northeast he expects to sail from Baltimore on the first of December and will reside at Oppenweiler, Wurtenberg, as an agent of the society whose headquarters on this side of the Atlantic are in Baltimore. He will be able to speak intelligently, from personal observation, of the different localities now inviting emigrants and judiciously advise and direct these latter so they may escape many of the annoyances and snares which otherwise often await them.

Neither he nor other intelligent and influential Germans believe, however, that it is practicable to induce their countrymen to settle at the South or elsewhere in America as mere employees at stipulated wages. As a rule, it is vain to expect to substitute them as farm or plantation hands. They will not be satisfied as such, even if induced in some instances to undertake it. Let them have farms of their own, on reasonable terms, and in sufficient numbers in the same neighborhood to insure congenial society, and they will not only enrich and improve their own land, but add greatly to the value of the vicinage

10. The *Sumter News* (November 28, 1868) noted that the *Keowee Courier* had these words concerning Juhl's visit: "J. J. Fleming, Esq., of Sumter, the famous 'Juhl' of the *Charleston Courier* and 'F' of the *New York World* has been sojourning in our town for several days. Mr. Fleming contemplates settling in our midst at an early day. Walhalla will gladly welcome this refined gentleman and scholar." However, considering some of the statements made in these letters and his many ties to Sumter, this appears to have been merely wishful thinking on the part of the *Keowee Courier*.

and give to the country a solid, reliable, and useful population. The efforts of Rev. Mr. [T. S.] Boinest in Newberry have succeeded in collecting more of these emigrants in that county than can probably be found at any other point in the state, except Charleston. But there are many sections having great advantages over Newberry, especially in the matter of health. And one of these is unquestionably the new county of Oconee of which Walhalla is the capital.

Passing up the railway from the seaboard to this terminus everything presents a striking and agreeable contrast after passing Columbia. Hogs, poultry, and cattle are seen in large numbers, instead of the desolated landscape below, which have long since been divested of valuable adjuncts of the farm. There is also more land under culture, and near the middle of November the fields were still white with cotton. Reliable farmers stated that there were thousands of acres then in cotton from which not a single pound had been picked, and there was much complaint of the difficulty experienced in inducing the hands to gather the crop. One gentleman said that before the war his annual crop was two hundred bales, that this year he employed no Negroes and with his two sons worked his farm and had but ten acres in cotton, and that as the net result he had more money than his two hundred bales ever left in his hands.

Practical men also expressed the opinion that it would be to the interest of the railroad companies to transport guano and other fertilizers to the up-country free of charge and thus encourage their increased employment; for, every ton of guano would largely swell the crop which the railroads would be required to move in the fall and winter. With the aid of this fertilizer cotton is now successfully cultivated almost in the very shadows of the Blue Ridge, for it drives forward and matures the plant even before the early frosts of this mountain region. What may appear still more singular to many, but is nevertheless true, is the fact that rice also is successfully cultivated here and that good bottom lands produce from 100 to 125 bushels of this essential plant to the acre. The cereals, fruits, and root crops all do well, but the magnificent apples seen in Walhalla and which find their way to your city are brought here in wagons from the neighboring counties of North Carolina.

All this season of the year large droves of cattle pass through the town on their way to the depot, where they are shipped by rail to Charleston and Augusta. North Carolina and Tennessee hogs will also soon be making their appearance, and wagons—large and small—are constantly arriving laden with apples, dried fruit, corn, and the smaller grains, butter, hides, pink root, poultry, and farm products generally. Very little cotton is seen, but rags are collected in quantities by tin peddlers and shipped north via Charleston in bales like cotton. The trade and, in fact, nearly all ordinary business transactions are conducted on the barter principle, very little money being used to complete the transfer or traffic. In such a state of things it may readily be imagined that very little interest is felt in the fluctuations in gold, and nobody in this latitude cares much what may be the temper or the tricks of the Wall Street bulls and bears. The barter principle requires no McCulloch to vitalize it, is serene—if not radiant—even when gold tumbles, and laughs with real mountain heartiness at stock quotations, which elsewhere bring terror and ruin to the millionaires of the Exchange.

Biemann's Hotel, the Newberry College, the German Lutheran Church, and the courthouse (or site laid off for such) are the salient points of the town, and persons occupying this central precinct will have whatever Walhalla presents today and whatever Walhalla in the future may be. The Courthouse Square is entirely destitute of trees or buildings and is to have transferred to its naked surface some of the houses now standing at Old Pickens. The first load of shingles arrived this week and were deposited without ceremony or parade of any kind—quietly done, as everything else seems to be done here. But barren and desolate as Courthouse Square may now look, the lots laid off around it as sites for offices, dwellings, etc. were sold at public outcry recently and brought fabulous prices. If they had been known to contain large gold deposits, they could scarcely have been sold for as much. This speaks well for the faith of the bidders and the purchasers in the future greatness of Walhalla.

The *Keowee Courier*, an excellent weekly paper, is published here, and the *Charleston Courier* finds its way even to some of the dwellers in Walhalla.

JUHL

WALHALLA, S. C., November 26

The iron pathway which years ago started out from Charleston and which at the time encountered so many predictions of failure has forced its onward and upward progress over swamps and rivers, hillsides and valleys until its locomotives have reached in this direction the foot of the mountains, which they seem impatient to penetrate in quest of the wealth that lies beyond. Only six miles beyond this town, the road already graded and tunneled ready for the track-layers and the trains, is the far-famed Tunnel Hill or Stump House Mountain, which forms the great obstruction to be overcome by a tunnel 5,863 feet in length. To visit and examine this work and return can be easily and pleasantly accomplished in a morning's ride from Walhalla. The tunnel is three-fourths completed, the work having been carried on simultaneously from the eastern and western openings and also at four intermediate points by shafts descending from the mountain summit and sides, at depths varying from 180 to 287 feet.

The work has been by blasting and cutting the solid rock, and the broken rock removed from it has been used for outside embankments, which gives the approaches to the tunnel a roadbed of the most solid and durable character. The tunnel is very much in the same condition in which it was left eight years ago, and to lookers-on it appears so substantial and imperishable that—like the pyramids of Egypt—it might remain unchanged for eight hundred more.

Within a quarter of a mile of the eastern opening is the powder mill, which formerly supplied all the blasting powder required, and near this are the Issequena Falls leaping in solid and beautiful volume so that a person can stand unsprinkled beneath the cascade. A legend of an Indian maiden hiding beneath these falls and thus eluding her pursuers has given the name (her own) to this romantic spot. The view from the top of Tunnel Hill is a fine and extensive one, including the town of Walhalla and various rural settlements.

The grand iron highway will be 195 miles in length from Anderson to Knoxville. Of this distance, trains are running over 32 miles from Anderson to Walhalla and over 18 miles from Knoxville to Maryville coming this way. The sections to be completed are 31 miles from Walhalla to Clayton, Georgia; thence 28 miles to Franklin, North Carolina; thence 28 miles to Natahala, North Carolina; thence 38 miles to the Tennessee line; and thence 37 miles to Maryville.

It passes through a country every mile of which will contribute to the passenger and freight business of the road and, when completed, will tap the great valley of the Mississippi and bring Cincinnati into direct communication with "the City by the Sea." There will then be no longer a question as to the success of your direct steamship line with Europe. Compared with this, the projected air lines passing transversely through middle and upper Carolina sink into insignificance. The Blue Ridge Road must be built; and, however long delayed, it will be built. Long recognized as "the most magnificent and important public work projected in our country," it cannot be abandoned. The greatest difficulties have already been overcome, and with an earnest effort the mighty enterprise will become an accomplished fact, a monument to its projectors and a proud triumph of railway engineering.

The new era has introduced great changes into this corner of the state. Old Pickens is soon to be numbered among the things that were—*fuit Ilium*. It is thirteen miles from Walhalla, and "the town" is for sale and will soon pass under the hammer. The material of which its houses are composed will find its way in wagons to this place and be used in the construction of offices and domiciles for those learned in the law and accustomed to the profits. New Pickens is twenty-six miles from this courthouse and, whatever may be its future grandeur and importance, at present it is only a town marked out and defined by streets and boundaries as staked by the surveyor and duly represented on his plat; but its incorporated territory is yet bare and vacant with but a single house in the vicinage to tell where the town is to be. Will new Carthage surpass in law and legend the glory of the old?

From Walhalla to the Georgia line by way of the Tugala bridge is seventeen miles and by way of the Chatooga bridge it is only fourteen miles. The most picturesque sight in all this section is the Whitewater Falls, on a stream of the same name, in Oconee County and near the beautiful valley of Jocassee, which is only twenty-three miles from Walhalla. The Seneca and Keowee also flow through this county on their way to the Savannah of which they are tributaries.

As soon as work on the Blue Ridge Road is resumed and the trains continue on to points west of this, much of the trade which now comes to Walhalla will stop at the successive termini as the railway progresses; and, hence, much of the interest now attaching to Walhalla will be transfered to points beyond. Still, this place possesses some advantages which, with judicious management, may secure it a good degree of permanent prosperity. Salubrity of climate (though somewhat severe in winter), good pure water, and the prospect of good schools are not the least of its claims to favor. At present, provisions are higher than one would expect in a country where very little else is raised. Corn during the year is from eighty cents to one dollar a bushel and other things in proportion, while in the neighboring corner of North Carolina it varies in different counties from twenty-five to fifty cents.

The apples which are sold here at one dollar per bushel are very superior both in size and quality, but even inferior grades are not offered for less than seventy-five cents, while a day's journey over the mountains will place the same fruit before you at very low figures. This subject is not only one of interest to families residing or proposing to settle here, but is vitally important in its bearing on the future of the Walhalla literary institutions. Where these depend on students from a distance, arrangements must be made for boarding them at such rates as will offer inducements to bring them this way. For where the curriculum and reputation of the teachers are substantially the same, the preference will be given to the school presenting the lowest scale of expenses. And, to secure this here, the surrounding country must be able to furnish all farm products at much lower rates than at present prevail. The agricultural interest must be stimulated either by bringing a larger area under cultivation by an increased rural population or by increasing the productive powers of such lands as are now planted by a higher system of farm culture.

JUHL

SUMTER, S. C., December 7

... The season has been remarkably propitious for the cotton planters throughout the state, and the effect is visible in all the departments of trade. A frost—just sufficient to check the further useless growth of the plant, but not sufficient to destroy its power to mature and open the bolls already on the stalk—was followed by weeks of bright and beautiful weather with scarcely a sprinkle of rain to moisten the staple. Hence the crop realized is greater in quantity and finer in quality than could have been expected under any other circumstances. The market also has been favorable, steadily maintaining prices which amply repay the labor and cost of production.

Those who had cotton to sell have money to spend, and while the North has sent its millions of greenbacks to the South for cotton, the greenbacks have found their way back to the North again for goods of almost every conceivable description. For unhappily the rule seems to prevail as a necessary incident of a cotton region that raising cotton precludes the power or disposition to raise anything else. The very labor employed in its culture, whether animal or manual, is supported by food and provender brought from the North and West over thousands of miles of transportation, and almost everything else required by the people—either in the way of substantials or luxuries, from a bundle of toothpicks to a barrel of biscuits—comes from abroad.

The South may be slandered and hooted and downtrodden, but its importance to the North cannot be ignored, for it vitalizes their manufacturing and commercial interests and contributes no mean portion to their vast aggregate of trade. To say that the South ought to be and can be self-sustaining is to reiterate a declaration which was by no means new even fifty years ago. It has the power to manufacture or raise a multitude of articles which it now imports from other sections, and by so doing could retain much of the money now sent away, and greatly improve, embellish, and beautify its homes with such surplus capital. But argument is wasted on this subject; the principle is admitted, the fault confessed, but the practice remains unchanged from generation to generation, and the country grows older day by day without its landscapes evincing any of the ripening influences of taste, culture, and wealth, which mark and attend maturity in other lands. For many of the finest lands in the country, upon which the eye rests with pleasure from seed time to harvest, look desolate enough when the crop is removed. The growing crop constitutes their entire attraction, and when that is gone, nothing is left but a blank and dreary place.

JUHL

SUMTER, S. C., December 11

The Walhalla letters contained an incidental allusion to the town of New Pickens made upon the authority of gentlemen of the highest social and professional standing in that part of the state and who certainly had no desire to make a "bad impression" of that place. They may have referred to its condition when, only a few months ago, the site was selected and laid off for a town. In the *Courier* of the 9th inst., S. D. G. feels called upon to "show up the new town of Pickens in its proper light," and while enlarging upon what is "proposed" and what is "expected" and what "will be," finds the progress very gratifying for "a town that was in the woods on the first day of August."

The inference would be naturally drawn that between that date and the present there must have been a time when the town could boast of but "one house," and if it has already attained to the dignity of "eight houses," so much the better; and, if it can continue on the grand pathway of prosperity until it presents an array of eight hundred houses and those of the tallest kind, it will be entitled to look proudly back to the time when—like all other cities—it commenced with "one house" or no house at all, being, as S. D. G. says, "in the woods on the first of August."

The *amende honorable* thus tendered to this mountain village may be enhanced by the remark that it is in a part of the state to which a valuable white immigration is tending and which is noted for the hospitality, energy, and self-reliance of its inhabitants.

JUHL

1869

IT WOULD SEEM that by now the worst might be over. General business conditions in Sumter were improving, churches were being painted and fixed up, a new fire engine arrived, and various projects were afoot for the betterment of the community. Juhl took time off from the courtroom circuit for another trip to Florida. This jaunt produced six letters concerning life in that state—"On the Wing and on the Wave."

However, another tour, Fleming's travels with the Georgia Press Association, was the major event of the year. As the representative of the *Charleston Courier* he joined about fifty newsmen and thirty guests, including Georgia's Gov. Rufus Bullock and a score of political figures, in a luxurious, eight-day trip throughout northwestern Georgia and adjoining sections of Tennessee and Alabama. Leaving Atlanta on August 25, a stalwart engine (the "U.S. Grant") hauled gaily decked cars filled with champagne, the best of cigars and wines and fine food to Dalton, Rome, Chattanooga, Selma, and back to Atlanta again. Ostensibly the purpose of this tour was to acquaint the press— and, in turn, the reading public—with the great natural resources of this region and point out the many opportunities for investment. The whole undertaking was masterminded by Col. Edward Hulburt, carpetbag superintendent of the Western & Atlantic, a railroad owned by the state of Georgia. It would appear that the colonel was a sincere, efficient operator, but his decision to invite controversial political figures to make the trip raised many eyebrows.

Fleming's reports—seventeen letters in all—are crammed with intriguing details of rudimentary industrial life of the late 1860s, expressions of the high hopes of pre-New South spokesmen, and occasional references to humorous incidents which happened en route. His letters are much more revealing that those of his youthful companion, Henry W. Grady. Grady was brash, smart-alecky, and, above all, suspicious. Instead of telling readers of the *Atlanta Constitution* what he saw and heard, Grady was much more interested in proving the whole trip nothing but a giant scheme to corrupt the Georgia press corps. He finally deserted the group to accept a job with a Rome newspaper, but not before raising the cry that state officials tried to bribe him. It is quite apparent that this young man is not the same Henry Grady who, two decades later, would stir the whole nation.

Fleming, neither concerned with nor involved in Georgia politics, completed the trip and, when called upon to say a few words at a final banquet held in Atlanta's National Hotel, made these remarks:

> It has been . . . a memorable trip, and will be so regarded for years to come. To my mind, it marks a new era in the history of Georgia, and in the history of the southern states [Applause]. Volumes, sir, might be written, and doubtless will be written upon the experiences of the past eight days in Georgia, and they will reach the people of more northern climes, and show them that though conquered as we are believed to be, not only have we iron in our hills, but iron yet in our hearts [Applause].[1]

1. *Atlanta Constitution* (September 3, 1869).

SUMTER, S. C., January 23

The marks of improvement and prosperity are visible through all this middle country. The merchants are doing a good business, and the last year's crop of cotton seems to be by no means exhausted. A fall in the market checks for a time the movement of the balance on hand, but an advance in the price gives briskness to the trade, and trains of wagons and carts come rolling into town laded with the iron-bound bales. The business thoroughfares are suddenly invested with new life, and numbers of men, including a large proportion of freedmen, are seen with cotton samples in hand, passing from store to store receiving and noting various bids. The streets of this town are now lighted with large and lustrous lamps, and policemen with stars and other insignia of office patrol the place.

Last week and the week before were judicially devoted to the January term of the sessions for Sumter County. Judges [Lemuel] Boozer and [J. T.] Green having for a time exchanged circuits, the former presided here. Among the novel features of the occasion may be noted the mixed composition of the juries, the colored element largely preponderating. Several capital cases were tried before juries made up of eight colored and four white, and in one instance by a jury on which there were only two white men. Colored constables also figured as officers of the court, and the colored prisoner delivered by the colored jailor to a colored officer was brought by the latter into court. From all which, without other comment, it may safely be concluded that this part of the state, once known as the "Game Cock District," is thoroughly "reconstructed." . . .

The open square in front of the courthouse is now the daily scene of banquets crowded with joyous freedmen. The tables are spread, the fires kept burning, and hot coffee and refreshments supplied at all hours. Headless chickens are seen dancing about these roofless restaurants to the great delight of the lookers-on, whose "eye so bright, he shine by night, when de moon am gone away." During the two weeks of court the patrons of these eating establishments were largely reinforced by the friends and witnesses of the numerous prisoners to be tried, and a blind performer on the tight rope improved the occasion by performing for several days to rings of delighted spectators, all in the open air. The tintinnabulation kept up during their performances, with the shouts and laughter of the crowd, formed a most refreshing accompaniment to the eloquence which was resounding throughout the halls of justice, and doubtless made a juror wish he could escape the argument of counsel and join the merrymakers across the street.

JUHL

SUMTER, S. C., January 25

The village of Manning is nearly equidistant from Kingstree on the Northeastern Road and Sumter on the Wilmington and Manchester Railroad and can be reached in a drive of a few hours (about twenty miles) from either of those places. Its principal thoroughfare is adorned with rows of shade trees, its churches are furnished with spires, its stores are well supplied with goods, and many of its private residences give evidence of taste and cultivation. It has also a steam mill in successful operation, several workshops, and all the other usual adjuncts of a thriving village. The *Clarendon Press* represents it in the world of newspaperdom—a well-printed weekly, published by Lucas and David, young and hard working, practical printers.

Swamps of no mean dimensions lie around it, and yet the village is as healthy as if it reposed in the shadows of a mountain range. Its cosy location, remote from railways and their obnoxious accompaniments, has measurably secured its exemption from many of the annoyances to which other and more accessible communities have of late years been subjected. Its beautiful courthouse and jail and some other buildings were burnt by Potter, and some of the debris still remains to mark the desolations of that sudden and successful raid. But such disasters, however damaging at the time and still painful to recall, seem not to have deprived the citizens of recuperative energy, and a spirit of hopefulness and of active improvement is clearly developed on every hand.

The January term of the common pleas and general sessions for Clarendon County was held last week at Manning. Judge J. T. Green, the Sumter contribution to the circuit judiciary under the new regime, presided and rapidly and effectually dispatched the business of the court. In readiness of decision and affability to the bar, he makes the duties of the term pass pleasantly enough and has already received very flattering commendation wherever he has been in his new and responsible position. The jury boxes were occupied by white citizens, only two or three colored men having been drawn as jurors. The feeling between the races is said to be much better in this county than in other adjacent sections, and this is ascribed to the absence of those disturbing and incendiary agencies which are at work elsewhere. The roads and bridges are very much out of repair. Detached shanties, in the most primitive style of construction and occupied by freedmen and their families, appear at various points along the roads, generally in the woods, with no cleared land or other signs of cultivation in the immediate vicinity. At such places the picture presented is one of semibarbarian dreariness, reviving the recollections of Sunday School literature with its glassless huts of ignorance and poverty, the homes of Ashantees and Kroomen, the oftentime ungrateful objects of missionary benevolence.

The Clarendon trade is almost entirely with your city, which its nearest rail and river facilities favor. The once projected and nearly realized road from Gourdin's to Sumter via Manning would secure to Charleston a very large trade from the entire section included between the Camden branch and the Cheraw Railway. Will another crop of cotton give life and capital enough to our people to renew and complete this important undertaking? . . .

JUHL

SUMTER, S. C., March 1

A continuous railway leads from your city to the town of Cheraw on the Pee Dee River, and its management is worthy of all commendation both in the directory and on the trains. A smooth road, comfortable cars, gentlemanly conductors, and good time and enough to commend the Northeastern and Cheraw and Darlington Railways to the traveling public. . . .

Ten miles from where this line [Cheraw and Darlington] crosses the Wilmington and Manchester Railroad at Florence is what remains of the once thriving and still beautiful village of Darlington. Its citizens have had a rough experience within the last few years. The torch of the incendiary has done its work, and a substantial courthouse and jail have been destroyed, and the business heart of the village burnt out, and the ruins remain as the sole monuments. The most of the private residences, however, have escaped, and with their magnificent oaks remind the visitor that at least a part of the population are distinguished for a refined and cultivated taste.

The past two weeks have been devoted to the February term of the circuit court for Darlington County. The sessions business was sufficient to exclude all other. Besides the cases on the old docket, there were some sixty or seventy prisoners awaiting trial. The mass of these were freedmen, and many of the offences charged were of the most atrocious character. On the calendar appeared some eight cases of murder, and the victims were of the white race. In one case of peculiar aggravation, the defendants were colored men. . . .

The numerous prisoners held for trial had been brought under guard from the jails of Marion and Sumter where they had been confined for the want of a jail in Darlington. The guard was composed of colored men, armed with loaded muskets, and the sentinels were posted and relieved with military precision. Counsel and friends of the prisoners, approaching, were met by the cry for the sergeant of the guard. No rudeness or offensive conduct on the part of this *corps d'Afrique* appeared, as far as known to the writer, and not a prisoner succeeded in making his escape, although transported on the cars over two roads, marching over highways and public streets, and often attended by large and sympathizing crowds. The county has a colored sheriff; and, of the four magistrates, three are colored men. The same may be said of the deputies and constables waiting on the court. The jurors with two or three exceptions were exclusively white. The judge is from Winnsboro, was a member of the Charleston Reconstruction Convention, and senator from Fairfield under the new regime. He and the solicitor are both white, and neither show any inclination to furnish the violators of law with a bed of roses. . . .

The three villages of Florence, Timmonsville, and Darlington are in the same county and within ten miles of each other and all have rail facilities—and hence, the trade is very much divided among them and not very heavy at either place. Darlington needs a good courthouse. The hall at present occupied as such is cramped and badly ventilated and with its three inches of sawdust on the floor does not favorably impress the visitor. And it needs, and from present indications will need for a long time to come, a capacious jail—and the sooner these are built, the better. The village itself is beautiful and, when separated from the company and the transactions of the court, may be a very garden of flowers for the young and the beautiful—the *darling-ton*. But during term time so much of crime and corn juice come to the surface that the contingent paradise is converted into an actual anything-else.

JUHL

SUMTER, S. C., March 12

. . . We have an artist here—a young painter, whose only fortune is his genius—a genius which has already achieved enough in the ideal and the real to place upon a sure foundation his youthful fame and to give certain promise of distinguished future triumphs.

Mr. Albert Capers Guerry was born in Stateburg in Sumter District of a well-known family of that name. He is a nephew of the late Bishop [William] Capers. His gifts are remarkable and decidedly stamp him as a genius in the art of painting. He has also had the advantage of association with and instruction from Mr. J. B. Irving, Jr., of New York City, an artist of distinguished abilities and known to many of your readers through his father, Dr. John B. Irving, for many years the leading spirit of the Charleston literary and sporting clubs.

Mr. Guerry now resides and has his studio in this place. He has recently completed two paintings, which are sufficient to establish, beyond cavil, his claims as an artist. "The Village Dreamer" exhibits all the loveliness of landscape and attractiveness of romance, which a most beautiful ideal admits under the brilliant coloring and masterly touches of true genius. This painting has been very much admired and will soon be sent to New York City to be submitted to the inspection of connoisseurs in art, under the direction of Mr. J. B. Irving, Jr. The other painting, to which the artist is now giving the final touches, is a life-size portrait of Rev. Donald McQueen, the pastor of the Presbyterian Church in this town. It is a wonderful success, the living original seems transferred to the canvas. . . .

JUHL

SUMTER, S. C., March 23

. . . The labor of this country has, of course, been subjected of late years to many disturbing influences, and yet it does not appear that the annual crop is less in the aggregate than the old system produced on the same area. And the present system is perhaps more favorable to diversified crops and diversified industry, which are both desirable innovations on the old state of things. Small farms are rapidly multiplying, and capitalists from a distance are buying lands, either for speculation or settlement. Whatever the motive, it is evident that such investments indicate strong faith in the future prosperity of this section.

The spirit of improvement is also greatly on the increase. One of the best signs in this community of a state of convalescence from the disorders which for a while so greatly depressed the popular energies appears in the increased attentions now being paid to the adornments of the churches. The Methodist Church, whose able and popular pastor, Rev. H. M. Mood, is from your city and college, has been recently repainted and fitted up and furnished with a bell of excellent tone and ample power. The Baptists have ordered an organ and will also repaint their church. The Presbyterians have ordered an eight-hundred pound bell and contemplate important improvements in their house of worship. And the railroad interest is being revived and projections are spoken of from here to Columbia, also from this town to the Northeastern Railroad via Manning, also to Bishopville.

The courthouse is in the hands of a contractor for repair and promises soon to present a new appearance inside and out. Cotton factories are under consideration; and, if half the speculations and propositions now afloat are realized, a wonderful change will be affected in the condition and prospects of this section. The plough, the loom, and the anvil—the music of machinery—the hum of peaceful industry—the waking up of a people to the necessity and importance of labor, of diversified industry—will make this county independent, self-reliant, prosperous, and—in God's own time—politically free.

JUHL

Sumter, S. C., March 26

General D. H. Hill, being on a brief business visit to this town, yielded to the urgent solicitations of numerous friends and delivered a lecture last night on Stonewall Jackson. Notwithstanding the unfavorable weather, the Presbyterian Church, the largest in the place, was well filled, and for nearly two hours the audience listened with unflagging attention to the recital of numerous and characteristic incidents in the life of the departed chieftain.

The character of Jackson, as given by army correspondents, was pronounced a myth: the majority of anecdotes published about him were declared to be imaginary, and the real character of the man, as intimately known to the speaker for many long years of friendship and relationship, was unfolded in all its simplicity and eccentricity, its beauty and its grandeur. With the portrait thus graphically presented, there was a fund of anecdote and a flow of humor which gave increased zest to the entertainment.

General Hill is the editor of *The Land We Love*, an attractive southern magazine now published in the city of Baltimore—and at the close of his leacture he drew attention to this work and urged in a very forcible manner upon the audience the duty of sustaining a southern literature. The effort will doubtless add largely to the subscription list of his magazine and extend his reputation as a graceful writer and attractive lecturer.

Juhl

Sumter, S. C., April 5

On Saturday afternoon last, a large and promiscuous crowd assembled at the depot to witness the arrival and reception of the Eagle fire engine from Charleston. The firemen in their red uniforms were drawn up in line under the command of Captain [E. C.] Green and, as the train reached the depot, gave three hearty cheers for the Eagle and the committee who had negotiated for the purchase and brought up the machine. As soon as the engine and reel were taken from the cars, they were decorated with beautiful wreaths which had been made for the purpose by the Sisters of Mercy, and the men, taking hold of the ropes, started off with lively huzzas up Main Street. This principal thoroughfare presented a crowded appearance; and, the evening being pleasant and the business of the week closed, everyone seemed disposed to make the occasion a gala time. On reaching Liberty Street, the machine was placed in communication with one of the principal fire wells and was soon engaged sending streams of water high over three-story buildings, to the admiration and delight of the crowds looking on.

It is understood that the Sumter Fire Company intend giving their old engine to a colored fire company who, with a little experience in repairs, will have a machine which—with the muscle they can furnish—will do good service. And, with these two companies and their equipments under proper management and direction, the Sumter Fire Department may in a very short time be reported in every sense efficient and adequate to the demands of this corporation.

The weather is quite cool, and this morning there is a heavy frost which will no doubt have a damaging effect on vegetation.

JUHL

ON THE WING AND ON THE WAVE[2]   1

"The city by the sea" can point with pride to her magnificent steam marine. In addition to the many other steamers constantly leaving your wharves for northern and southern ports, and ports in Europe, and towns and landings in the interior by ocean and river routes, one line alone furnishes a cargo capacity and an amount of elegant passenger accommodations which the trade and travel of the country are

2. These letters appeared in various issues of the *Courier*, April 24-May 14.

obliged to appreciate. By this line the trader is conveyed in a few days from New York City to Palatka, Florida, or from the blooms and fruits and repose of the tropics to the rush and bedlam roar of the nation's metropolis. The splendid seagoing steam ships *Manhattan*, *Champion*, *James Adger*, and *Charleston* of which Messrs. James Adger & Co. are the Charleston agents make regular, safe, and expeditious voyages between New York and Charleston twice a week, connecting with the *Dictator* and *City Point* of the Florida line of which Messrs. J. D. Aiken & Co. are the agents.

These boats are not surpassed in our southern waters. They are officered by gentlemen of tried skill and experience. Their staterooms and tables afford the luxurious accommodations of a first-class hotel. They are not only safe boats, running with astonishing regularity in all seasons, but some idea may be formed of the manner in which they "walk the water" from the performance of the *Dictator* on a recent return trip from Florida with the writer on board; when, leaving the wharf at Savannah at fifteen minutes past nine A.M., her New York passengers were placed on board the *Champion* at the wharf in Charleston at forty-five minutes past three P.M., thus making the run in five and a half hours.

An excursion on any portion or all of this route presents every inducement to the pleasure traveler and to the invalid seeking recuperation and, in a very short time and at very little expense, gives to very many weary and exhausted sufferers a fresh lease of life and health. . . . But the invalids are comparatively few in number. The most of the passengers are traveling for pleasure or recreation or business or seeking investments for idle capital or prospecting with a view to settlement. And among them all there is not enough of the fading and the suffering to occasion any such draft upon human suffering as sensibly to impair the pleasure of the jaunt.

JUHL

On the wharf at Fernandina there were quantities of live turtle and drum fish just landed from fishing boats and offered for sale at prices which certainly seemed to place a delicious fish diet within the reach of all. Turtle, ranging from fifty to one hundred pounds, at $.10 a pound, and a drum of fifty weight for $1.50; shrimps at $.10 a quart, and a fine string of whiting at the same price, and all these can be caught here with a little effort or with a little money. Large shipments of turtle and fish are made to Savannah and Charleston by these steamers on their northward trips.

The railway which crosses the peninsula from Fernandina to Cedar Key is now said to be doing considerable business. On the Gulf it has a line of steamers running to Mobile, and the railroad wharf at Fernandina was crowded with cotton bales waiting shipment, although late in the season when it is believed the bulk of the crop must have already reached the market. There is also from this place a bi-monthly line of steamers to New York, but much of the freight intended for the latter city is forwarded via Savannah or Charleston; and, judging by recent observation, the travel northward gives the preference to the *Dictator* or *City Point* to Charleston and thence by the magnificent ships of the Adger line to New York.

While passing up the St. John's on this trip, the passengers witnessed the somewhat novel spectacle of a steamer of a thousand tons pausing in midriver to play the part of a dentist, in extracting a troublesome and dangerous snag. A huge sawyer had drifted into the channel and anchored its lower trunk firmly in the mud, while its upper section appeared above the surface at just the inclination to fatally perforate the hull of any passing vessel colliding against it. So dangerous a foe to the safe navigation of this noble river could not be left to do its work of destruction, and hence a small boat was lowered and a stern line run out and secured to the sawyer. And, with the small boat and the sawyer in tow, the signal was given, and the *Dictator* soon dragged the enemy from his muddy moorings into shallow water far from the channel route where the line was cast off, the yawl restored to the davits, and the obnoxious log left in a position where it can do no harm, and where it is likely to remain for years to come.

The two most notable and popular watering places on the St. John's are Hibernia and Green Cove Springs. The former belongs to the Fleming estate and is conducted by members of that family in a style which secures a full and fashionable company all the season. The latter also is a very attractive place and possesses a spring of remarkable appearance and great medicinal virtues. In depth and surface dimensions, it is large enough to float a good sized schooner. Its waters have a soapy appearance and yet are perfectly transilient. It bubbles and boils in some places with ceaseless activity, and early in the day (the time of this visit) vapors of sulphur were rising from the surface and sensibly affecting the olfactories of the visitors. . . .

Bathing in these waters is said to exert a wonderful influence in purifying and recuperating the human system, if not in renewing one's youth and investing with a fabled immortality, and for this purpose there is a cluster of small houses on the lower margin of the spring furnished with all the appendages required by the bather. A gentleman who had spent ten weeks (at fifteen dollars per week) at this place reported a vast improvement in his health as the result and gave the hotel a good name, except in the matter of coffee and bread. . . .

JUHL

ON THE WING AND ON THE WAVE   3

The rush of northern and European travelers to Florida since the war has given new life and vigor to many interests which otherwise would have remained sluggish and dead for years to come. The aggregate of the amounts thus added to the money circulation on the main line of travel it would be difficult to estimate, but the effect on places and people is palpable. The town of Jacksonville, for example, presents the most gratifying evidence of the vitalizing influence of such constant incursions of money-spending tourists. It has probably more than six thousand inhabitants, a market well stocked with fresh meats, vegetables, fish, and fruit, substantial blocks of stores heavily stocked with merchandise and goods of every description, private residences equaling in elegance and horticultural surroundings all that our own Palmetto capital used to be before the torch laid its beauty in ashes, streets well laid off and with their unbroken lines of beautiful shade trees forming a most inviting promenade, and a commerce which not only follows the St. John's to the everglades and the Oklawaha to Lake Griffin and communicates by steam and sail with all the ports on the coast, but even essays a direct interchange of commodities with the trans-Atlantic world.

For here were two French barques direct from the grand empire which the name and shade of Napoleon still govern, and the cargo they were discharging will soon be reared into a stately pile for the worshipers of the Catholic faith, the foundation of the cathedral being already laid and the basement of granite ready for the bricks which the Frenchmen brought and of which the structure is to be built. But little can be said in praise of the Protestant houses of worship at this place. They have no architectural beauty and are sadly in want of paint and repairs.

A spacious and elegant billiard saloon, furnished with seven tables to which seven more are soon to be added, its walls presenting a gallery of sporting and voluptuous paintings; ten pin alleys, restaurants, and barrooms; a canvas tent *à la circus* in which the velocipede is exhibited and pupils trained to master and manoeuvre the coquettish bicycle; and graceful yachts in which fishing, sailing, or excursion parties can glide at pleasure over the whole river—all these are there and handsomely supported, which indicates the character of at least a part of the population, whether resident or transient, making up the beautiful and thriving town of Jacksonville. Here, as throughout the entire region bordering the St. John's, the canoe, the skiff, the sailing or steam yacht seem to perform all the gondola does in Venice.

Animal power is only employed in field work or occasional transit overland. And fortunate it is that horses and mules can be so far dispensed with, for corn is high and will not keep through summer; and provender must be scarce, as the diminutive steamers navigating the extreme southern waters of the Oklawaha were freighted with northern and eastern hay. A friend owns an entire island in Lake Harris. He and his family reside there all the year. He planted successfully, his principal crop being the sugarcane. There are no neighbors, and a lady lives in his family as private teacher for his children. Of church privileges they have none, but he has applied to several denominations for missionary visits to his neighborhood and been promised compliance. The nearest points to which he can go for information from the outer world are two landings, each three miles distant and in opposite directions where a little steamer from Palatka touches once in ten days.

All his country and neighborhood intercourse is conducted by water, and he keeps a fine sailing boat which answers the purposes of wagon and team or coach and four. Fish and game are at hand in abundance whenever he wants them; and, while his family are debarred some of the pleasures of society, they are likewise freed from many of its annoyances. Luscious tropical fruits are around his dwelling and plucked fresh from the trees possess a flavor which is commonly lost in transportation. A trip to Jacksonville and return consumes some two weeks or more, and all imported articles accumulate costs before reaching his island empire. But he and his live comfortably and in seeming content, almost in the shadows of the Everglades and present by no means an exceptional picture of Florida life.

Juhl

Capt. L. M. Coxetter may be justly considered the animating spirit of the Charleston and Florida line. . . . Captain Coxetter has important interests in Florida and has already illustrated by actual experiment how much can be done at the South by a system of immigration properly directed and suitably encouraged. His colony, which commenced with a few families pitching their tents in the woods, has already expanded into a large community where German, Swiss, and American settlers have leveled the forests, reared comfortable houses, enclosed and cultivated the lands, and are gathering around them from year to year increased facilities for a prosperous future. It is located some ten or twelve miles from St. Augustine on the narrow belt of land which lies between the surf line of the Atlantic and the wide and placid waters of the St. John's, is distant but a few miles from Picolata, and is still nearer a landing on Six-Mile Creek, a bold stream which enters the river from the east, below (north of) Picolata.

Captain Coxetter has been giving lands to heads of actual families and one-half that amount to single men and, for the protection of the community as well as to guard his own interests, exercises a proper care in investigating the character of each new applicant for a location in the settlement. The houses thus far erected exhibit the national peculiarities and individual ingenuity of their respective owners, without much regard being paid to the strict rules and requirements of art. In some instances, a single substantially built room, the first and only house of the settler, has had one and another room added, as time and means allowed, until now the owner has ample space and accommodation for his family and guests, all on one floor and composing a not inelegant "cottage in the wilderness."

The founder of this colony is satisfied that the same system pursued on a larger scale by land proprietors in associated effort would soon fill up these southern states with a population which would correct and remove many of the evils now afflicting the land. He has also now on hand a still more important enterprise which, with his name and energy to push it, must succeed—but any further reference to which at this time would be premature and unadvisable, as well as unauthorized. The timber from his lands in Florida has yielded and is still yielding a large revenue; and, after giving away the portions of land now occupied by the colonists, the remaining is today valued at a vastly larger sum than was given for the entire original grant. Thus he has demonstrated the profitableness as well as feasibility of the plan, and the same result would follow if tried on a grander scale, unless defeated by the employment and intervention of an expensive bureau and army of salaried clerks and agents. . . .

JUHL

ON THE WING AND ON THE WAVE   5

The British steamer ship *Petersburg* was lying at the wharf in Savannah and was visited, and, by the courtesy of her commander, who seemed to take pleasure in showing this guest the ship, was examined from stem to stern. There was much in the interior arrangements of this vessel—in the immense carrying capacity, in the style and power of the engines, and in the model and rig of the ship—to repay the little trouble and time involved in such a visit. But enquiries elicited the unpleasant information that this vessel had already been lying at the Savannah wharf for two months, waiting for cargo; that as yet only one-third of a cargo had been engaged, and this at rates which could not possibly pay; that it might be a month or two more before she could leave for Europe, and then probably not fully loaded, even at unremunerative rates; that the ship was sinking money for her owners every day, and would not be likely to renew the experiment. . . .

And yet Savannah is a thriving and beautiful city with a rich back country to which well-managed railways extend; with the still further advantages of a river, navigable as high up as Augusta; with a commerce by no means insignificant, but which manifestly prefers sailing vessels to steamers in its shipments of cotton to foreign ports; with parks and squares in such profusion that the *rus in urbe* seems the inheritance of its citizens; and with a white population which thus far, even in these disjointed times, seem to have maintained successfully the right to manage their own affairs. . . .

The pier at which the *Dictator* moors is near the lower limits of the city with extensive gas works and a steam rice mill with its four stories of masonry in full view on one side and a vast area of Carolina rice on the other. Landing and mounting the high bluff, the plateau is reached on which the city is built. But let no tourist pause incautiously in the first half mile of hovels and habitations unless he wishes to see in real life a picture of some of the scenes which [George] Crabbe has described in the "Borough"; undivided lodgings for vagrants and idlers; dens in which the poor sailor is entrapped and fleeced; windows, through whose oiled paper and old glass the conquered sunshine's melancholy gloom enters and gives a dusty warmth to the wretched interior; floors chalk-marked for various games; greasy tables and rickety chairs; gin and snuff; pipes and pouches; cards and cribbage; and scattered specimens of unwashed fractured ware, the silent remains of many a revel, when in the wild carouse the frenzied inmates share. Nor is this description applicable here only, but wherever one travels in this civilized land, North, East, or West, as well as South, there are places which fill all the outlines and incidents of the picture.

. . . But there is no use in pausing even to moralize, for a little further on Savannah unfolds its beauties and charms the visitor with its refreshing contrasts. Here is the busy mart of the Empire State; here the homes of elegance, refinement, and wealth; here the spacious and shaded thoroughfares crowded with lovely promenaders in all the rich colors which modern fashions sanction and prescribe; here the costly temples in which the Sabbath congregates the population; here the monuments which commemorate an age when men loved liberty more than life and patriotism more than patronage or self.

The steamer, when southward, stops here from daylight until 3 P.M. and returning, remains from daylight until 9 A.M., time enough for an active passenger to take a view of the city and even to include a rapid drive to Bonaventure and other charming suburban retreats.

The rice lands on the river appear to be under the same lazy, small-patch culture of a year ago, and there was the same profusion of canoes and small boats manned by Negroes who derive a precarious subsistence from the oyster and fish business, gathering marsh or grass (cow feed) for the city market, or collecting drift wood for sale as fuel. Twelve months appear to have made no improvement in their condition; but, with the nonchalance and improvidence peculiar to the race, those who are most ragged seemed the most joyous and in leaky boats half filled with water floated along over the muddy tide with a boisterous merriment which clearly defied the cares and wants of the morrow.

JUHL

ON THE WING AND ON THE WAVE   6

. . . There are all the varieties of soil in Florida and all varieties of people. Settlements of vagrant blacks were reported and described, but not visited. Camping in the wild lands otherwise unoccupied they are said to live like savages, and many in time become as great a nuisance as an equal number of Seminoles. They already exhibit the effects of such a separation from civilized communities and are under the control of the most absurd superstitions. This, however, should occasion no surprise, for others in the higher walks of life have been apt pupils in the school "where superstition weaves her airy dreams. . . . "

To persons in the interior of the Carolinas, no more pleasant excursion offers than this Florida trip. The boats are easily reached at Charleston by the Tuesday or Friday train on the South Carolina or Northeastern Roads. Emigrants from these states are constantly going thitherward and settling in companies where they maintain the undisturbed control of their own neighborhood affairs. The "Land of the Flowers" will always have its attractions and has become an annual resort for travelers of all nations.

But close not this notebook without one more mere mention. The last day on board—the purser's lunch—was ever-fragrant and juicy pineapple, served up more artistically, sliced and sugarcoated with delicious entremets. Thanks to Mr. Cavedo—and to the *Dictator* and her noble commander, blue skies, and pleasant seas for ave.

JUHL

SUMTER, S. C., May 23

This is, of course, "the *best* government,"—it would be disloyal, if not impious, to dispute it. Is not that government the best in which the people are the most heavily taxed and the most unfairly represented? The enormous tax on tobacco must have been imposed by a body in which the producers, manufacturers, and even the great body of consumers of the weed were not allowed a free hearing. And the many restrictions imposed on the tobacco trade and the costly machinery required by this special tax clearly indicate a belief on the part of Congress that the very exorbitant tariff itself would popularize the business of smuggling and make a fraud on the revenue in this instance, if not a virtue, at least not much of a crime. Hence, revenue officers all over the country inspecting tobacco and seizing and detaining it on the slightest pretence of a noncompliance with the law. Hence, an army of government detectives hovering around the manufactories, peering into box cars and railway stations, overhauling and searching country wagons, and interested by the statutory share of the spoil in forcing an unfavorable construction on any omission or other defect in the packages seized. The present law is so complicated that it will require some time for its details to be understood and accurately complied with, and in many cases mistakes and omissions may occur even after the requirements of the law are understood. And yet every advantage is being taken of the ignorance of the manufacturer and shipper by those representing the revenue department. . . .

The tobacco seized at a single point in this state (Columbia) and now detained under the circumstances described above is said to be valued at over twelve thousand dollars. How much is collecting at other points under similar detention may be conjectured. . . .

However oppressive the laws and however odious the lawmakers, the good citizen recognizes even as a Christian duty the obligation to "render unto Caesar the things that are Caesar's." But nothing that is entitled to respect forbids an honest protest against the ruinous misrule now cursing the land with taxes so exorbitant and so managed as to paralyze trade, discourage production, check the industrial energies of the people, reward peculation, and at the same time defeat the end for which they were imposed. The lawmakers who have done this—call them Radical or what you will—have violated the doctrines of a sound political economy, inflicted a serious and damaging blow on the commerce of the country, and are utterly unfit to control the affairs of a great and intelligent people.

JUHL

SUMTER, S. C., May 29

The state universities are suffering under the stunning blows of a party legislation which tramples in the dust the cherished sentiments of a people who appear to be too far nauseated to oppose any present resistance to measures which they never can approve. In the University of Alabama, it is said, there are but eight students and at Chapel Hill (N.C.) but two. And the same causes which have occasioned this ominous decadence, in schools well known to have been of the highest grade and largely patronized under a former regime, are at work in South Carolina on a still more extravagant and uncompromsing a scale and, of course, must be followed by the same results.

The state college at Columbia has been by recent legislation thoroughly radicalized. The trustees and faculty are debarred by statute from making any discrimination in the admission of students on account of race, color, or creed. One student is to be received from each county, free of tuition fees, and such beneficiaries are to be appointed by the governor on the nomination of the county delegations in the legislature. The class from which such nominations will chiefly be made can readily be determined from the color which prevails in the legislature itself, as well as from the certain refusal of the respectable white population either to seek or to accept such appointments from such a source.

Sumter, for example, has three colored and one white in the lower house and by a recent election has secured a colored senator, and a glance at the legislative rolls will show that this is by no means the only county in the state which is similarly honored. And it is reasonable therefore to infer that any appointments made and accepted under this arrangement, at the instance of the county delegations, will place at the university only students who belong to the class of persons now controlling the institution and the state, and that *ipso facto* all others will keep away. This is the logical conclusion, and it can hardly be doubted that precisely this result was expected and desired by those who gave the coup de grace to the college by an act which they knew would inevitably exclude from its halls the very class from whom its entire financial support would be derived.

But are they not playing the part of the dog in the manger and, while driving off the only class who have heretofore attended the institution, are they not themselves unfitted for its benefits and incapable of enjoying the fruits? It is well known that when the college was popular and well conducted, its catalogue seldom contained the names of two hundred students in attendance—so small even then was the number of persons in the state (exclusive of those preferring other colleges) who could exhibit the attainments necessary to secure admission and command the means to meet the expenses of a four year course. What then must be its chances now, when the very class which is alone likely to furnish students qualified in scholarship and pecuniary means for a university course cannot be expected to patronize it, and those who are alone practically invited to its halls are not prepared either in mind or money for a residence there.

Its curriculum may, indeed, like everything else be lowered to meet the necessities of the occasion. But certainly there is good reason to believe that in its present hands it will either be a university without students or an old field school under the name of a university. With Webster's spelling book as the heaviest labor of the freshman class, and Parley's geography as the closing study of the senior year, a diploma would certainly be worth cherishing as an unimpeachable certificate of scholarship.

There is no possible objection here intended to the education of the colored race. Nor is there any desire to deny the black man a privilege for which he is qualified, or to refuse him the means to qualify himself for any privilege to which he can reasonably aspire. But he has just emerged from bondage and knows nothing of letters. And it will be long before any educational scheme adopted for his benefit will really require access for him to either a collegiate or university course. At present it might be thought that an expensive common school system, established for his benefit at the expense of the white people of the state in addition to the very numerous schools for colored children now supported by benevolent societies and individuals, was enough.

The university might have been left on its old foundation with no wrong, injustice, or damage to the black race, and with no discredit to the mongrel legislature. And, whenever the time comes that the colored race required a college, a college might have been voted without dissent. Without any party bias, without any local or sectional prejudice, without even any prejudice of race, it may safely be affirmed—and the wise man of any country or color will admit it—that it is best for both races that they should be separated in their schools, and any attempt to force the two together must be abortive, and indicates a malicious and vengeful purpose to mortify and irritate the white population. This is the calm verdict of an unbiased judgment which is sustained by the experience of the past and will be abundantly endorsed in the annals yet to be illustrated and written in the future.

But "it is an ill wind that blows nobody good." The obnoxious legislation which cripples the institution which it ought to foster will rapidly tend to build up other colleges outside of such control. The Georgia University at Athens, which the white preponderance in that state protects, and all schools not controlled by Radical legislatures or councils, even in South Carolina, will receive an increased patronage. Among others, the colleges at Due West, Greenville, and Spartanburg will receive the benefit, and at the last named place, Wofford College under the presidency of Dr. [Albert M.] Shipp, with its able corps of instructors, is being largely patronized.

JUHL

NOTES FROM THE UPPER PEE DEE[3]

The train leaves Florence for Cheraw. The afternoon is a beautiful one, with perhaps a trifle more of summer in it than is altogether

3. This letter appeared in the *Courier* July 10.

agreeable. The cars are well arranged, the road is smooth, and the speed amply sufficient to raise a breeze which fans the brow and refreshes the traveler. When Society Hill is reached, the sun has not yet gone down, although hidden now behind the luxuriant foliage which lines the road and clothes in rich emerald the ever varying landscape. Here an excursion train is met—a train filled with the teachers, pupils, and friends of various Sunday Schools along the line, chartered for the day's frolic to Cheraw and now on its return with its five hundred passengers to be soon landed at the stations below.

The scene is animated, noisy, gala, and generally joyous; the hundreds of young folks seem buoyant and rollicksome, like birds with tireless wings, ready for fresh fields and ventures now, but others of maturer years are there who confess to weariness and long for the calm repose of home. The whistle blows—the mail train proceeds on its upward way, while the excursion party whirl away homewards, rolling clouds of smoke from the engine into the dense verdure of the woods and gladdening the eye with the bright colors which appear in the windows as the long chain of cars recede from sight. They are gone, and there is no use in tarrying longer at the now-deserted depot, for this is at the foot of the hill whose summit contains the settlement with its churches, parsonages, and planters' homes.

The village is located on an eminence a mile or so south of the Pee Dee River—a site selected, doubtless, with a view to health by those who built their residences near each other for reasons which are suggested by the name—Society Hill. It contains at present several stores, two fine churches (Baptist and Episcopal); a small office in which presides a colored magistrate hailing from somewhere else; a respectable drum and its colored owner and performer who seems to delight in reminding the citizens of garrison times; a freedmen's school with the usual complement and kind of teachers; a colored constable who wears a sword when on duty; and it may contain still other curiosities equally notable. . . .

The largest church in this place is the Baptist, known as the Welsh Neck Church, and giving its name to one of the most respectable associations in the state. Its present pastor is Rev. W. D. Rice, a gentleman of quiet manners, unobstrusive piety, and decided pulpit ability, formerly and for a number of years the highly esteemed and successful minister of the Baptist Church in Sumter. His Sunday School is in a very flourishing condition; and, Dr. S. H. Pressley, its superintendent, evidently understands how to interest the young and to keep up the interest of this invaluable auxiliary to the church. . . .

A ramble in the adjoining cemetery was not without its appropriate meditations and pleasant thoughts. Here sleep the dead of the long ago, as well as those of yesterday—the congregation of the dead hard by the assembly of living worshipers—the beloved ancestral ashes to which faithful memory still clings. One inscription records the name of Martha, wife of Capt. Daniel Sparks of the Revolution, aged ninety-one. Another recalls the names of Dr. John K. M'Iver and wife, who seem to have been two of the pillars of this church nearly half a century ago and who now rest from their labors, life's fitful fever o'er, and sleep side by side in a repose which no rude alarm can shake. Another marks the place where earth has taken back to her fond bosom the children of T. P. and E. D. Lide—"of such is the kingdom of heaven." A simple monument thus tells its whole tale of loss and grief: "Our little Betty, aged three years." Others tell of Capt. J. K. M'Iver, Company F, 8th South Carolina Volunteers; Capt. J. Calhoun Sparks, Hampton Legion, killed at Catlett Station, Virginia, January 6, 1864; Charles W. Coker, killed at Malvern Hill, July 1, 1862. Here are the names of the Pressleys, Greggs, McIntoshes, McCullochs, Clarks, etc. And one little nameless grave where some darling child was buried, whose friends have also doubtless passed away, and no kindly hand remains to plant the vine or replace the headstone caved in; and, overgrown with grass as it is, a small blackberry bush has grown up in the cavity and was covered with berries which two beautiful birds were eating. Thus sleep the dead. What heed they how their tombs be decked or all neglected stand?

The distance from Society Hill to Bennettsville is thirteen miles, crossing the Pee Dee on a very substantial bridge, something over a mile from the former place. A pleasant ride with a friend afforded a view of this bridge and of enough of the surrounding country to form some idea of the crops. The lands seem admirably adapted to cotton and provisions and are in a good state of cultivation, with every indication of an abundant harvest. Some gentlemen are also paying attention to grape culture, chief among whom may be named Major Lucas (formerly commanding Lucas's Battalion), one of whose vines has produced twenty gallons of wine with an inferior mill, and the quantity would have been doubled by the use of improved machinery. The grape is the scuppernong and the wine excellent and commands a good price and ready sale.

On Cedar Creek which runs into the Pee Dee near the bridge, there are some mills which are said to be doing a good business, and the appearance of the people and the country generally indicates a rapid recuperation from the prostration and paralysis which immediately succeeded the late war.

JUHL

Atlanta, Ga., August 24

The Georgia Press state convention convened at the City Hall at eleven o'clock this morning and was permanently organized with the following officers: president, Colonel [Joseph] Clisby, of the *Macon Telegraph*; vice-presidents, J. H. Christy, of the *Athens Watchman*, Gen. A. R. Wright, of the *Augusta Chronicle and Sentinel*, and H. H. Jones, of the *Cuthbert Appeal;* secretaries, A. R. Watson, *Atlanta Era*, and C. H.

Willingham, *Lagrange Reporter*. The convention is a large and influential one and attracts much attention. Nearly all the papers in the state are represented in it, and among its members are some of the ablest men in the commonwealth. The representative of the *Charleston Courier* was unanimously welcomed to a seat and has been most kindly received in every way. Committees have been appointed to report on a variety of matters of interest to the profession at the next meeting of the body which will be at Macon in November during the Georgia State Fair. The convention has been inundated with invitations and tenders of hospitalities, and this afternoon will accept the invitation tendered by the mayor and council of the city to ride round, through, and over this Chicago of the South. Tonight there will be another session for an interchange of views, and tomorrow morning at half-past seven o'clock a special train will set off for Chattanooga with these press representatives on an excursion whose incidents and developments will probably furnish much interesting matter to be served up in due time for the benefit of your readers and the rest of mankind.

JUHL

GEORGIA PRESS EXCURSION[4]   1

Be it remembered that in the year of grace 1869, and on the 25th day of August, an excursion party started from the city of Atlanta, in the state of Georgia, to visit sundry places and to advance certain interests, which will be more fully set forth and described hereinafter in these veracious chronicles. On the morning of that day and at the railway centre of the said city, there appeared a train of cars, transcending in magnificence all other trains then or ever before seen in that latitude or perhaps in any other, rich in exterior polish and adornments and still more captivating in the interior arrangements.

There was the locomotive, a new engine, superbly finished and of

4. These letters were published in the *Courier*, September 9–29.

unsurpassed power and speed, beautifully decorated and surmounted with flags; and a long line of new cars, most elaborately finished and fixed up for this special occasion, containing a barber shop with him of the tonsorial art and ready for duty, with all the applicances of his profession at hand; the baggage room with its master to take charge of and check the baggage of the guests; the kitchen car with those in attendance who certainly understood their business; the restaurant and barroom, most bountifully supplied with wines and liqueurs, cigars and lemons, and a presiding genius well skilled in the mixture of fancy drinks; a long car, admirably furnished with small card tables and seats, which was used by whist parties, letter writers, and in general as a dining saloon; and then followed the passenger cars proper including several sleeping coaches and affording ample accommodations for all who had been invited.

The guests represented, in whole or in part, the four estates of the realm—the great commonwealth of Georgia—on a tour of observation and exploration, and to some extent on a frolic. The executive was there in the person of Governor [Rufus B.] Bullock, a man of fine personal appearance and address. Both branches of the legislature contributed numerous members to the party. The judiciary also had a place in the picture, Judges Harrall [D. B. Harrell], [I. L.] Harris, [J. R.] Parrott, etc., accompanying the excursion through the entire trip. Several other state functionaries of the existing regime, Comptroller General [Madison] Bell, Sec. R. P. Lester, and others, with some northern capitalists, scientific men, etc., might with the others already named, be considered as forming one division of the party; the other consisting of the gentlemen of the press, the largest element, with its own distinctive traits and its peculiar adhesiveness which hitherto has made it a unit on almost all the great questions which of late years have come before the people of Georgia. So much for the personnel of the expedition.

The scene at the start was one which would have furnished a capital subject for the pencil or brush of an artist. Atlanta is a great city and proved on this occasion its ability to furnish a crowd, and a very mixed and variegated crowd, too, to do the looking, and the waving, and the hurrahing, and the punching of ribs, and mashing of toes, and impromptu swearing, and laughing, and yelling, and joke-cracking and everything else thereunto incident and appertaining. Anyone looking on was bound to feel that it was a gay time—"a high old time," and that still more of the same sort was sure to be developed in the course of the fast-coming future events. Everyone seemed in a good humor, and mirth, and frolic, and fun were the order of the day.

Grave men and great men laid aside their cares, and waving an adieu to the business toils and anxieties of life, pitched in promiscuously to see and enjoy whatever might turn up in this august jaunt. In their then mood even little things created a world of merriment; and, hence, when a huge three-hundred weight legislator was discovered with a raw sweet potato projecting from his pocket, the attention of the party was called to the fact and he was gravely asked, amidst the roars of the crowd, whether it was from fear that his wants would not be supplied on the road that he had thus brought his rations all the way from home! The sun rolls up above the house tops of Atlanta—just such a sun as greeted Napoleon at Austerlitz—and greets today the Napoleon of the rail, Colonel [Edward] Hulbert, of the Western and Atlantic Railroad, the master spirit, who successfully invoked and arranged this magnificent excursion. There are tall men and short men, fat men and lean men, white men and colored men (in the crowd, but not of the party), learned men and men decidedly unlearned, but conspicuous among, if not above, them all, is the majestic, calm, bronzed figure of the self-made man, whose genius has already made its impression on the railway and mining interests of the South, and who, with an energy and an ambition which ordinarily command success, still aims at greater things in the future. . . .

And now, the hour has come, and with the ringing of bells, the waving of flags, and the huzzas of the crowd, the train, at first slowly, and then faster and still faster moves away.

JUHL

GEORGIA PRESS EXCURSION   2

With John Ellsworth as engineer, and John Holtzclaw as conductor—let them have the credit, for it was a memorable occasion the like of which may not occur again in their history, and they well discharged their responsible trusts—the train leaves Atlanta and swiftly and smoothly passes up the Western and Atlantic Road towards Chattanooga. The wide and rapid-flowing Chattahoochee is crossed at an elevation from the bed of the river of perhaps one hundred feet, the train creeping slowly and cautiously over the yawning abyss below and then dashing away again as if relieved of a burden, winding among hills and meadows, and farmhouses and fields of waving grain, and hilltops crowned with earth-works, and hillsides turned into vast graveyards where the dead of both armies in thousands repose, with the cedar and the vine and the wild flowers growing fresh and beautiful above them, and the grazing cattle and flocks of sheep giving a pastoral character to the landscape and an air of rural quiet to the scene, as though no hostile cannon had ever shaken these hills or human blood had crimsoned the earth. On the left is Kennesaw Mountain around whose base the road winds, giving a fine view of its peak and sloping sides, rendered memorable in the history of our great struggle as the place where the Bishop General Polk fell.

And then comes the Hightower River crossed on a substantial bridge. At this point the scenery is most beautiful. The rails here for a long distance describe almost a perfect semi-circle, within which and considerably below the roadbed, lies the valley with its meadow lands and cultivated fields, through which the stream pursues its serpentine course, and beyond all this—and as a background to the picture—are the ridges and spurs of mountains covered with the richest verdure. Here also we examined the engine and machinery engaged in grinding the rock, breaking it up rapidly into small pieces which are carried off in carloads for ballasting the road. In this way Colonel Hulbert expects soon to have his roadbed as firm and solid as the granite itself, making it one of the most substantial and smoothest railways on the continent.

At Cartersville a crowd of citizens with a band of music gave the party a public reception and invited all to accept the hospitalities of this pleasant village. The venerable Mark A. Cooper delivered a handsome address of welcome, and Governor Bullock responded for himself, and Colonel Clisby for the press. The officers of the Cartersville and Van Wert Railroad had collected specimens of mineral ore from this (Polk) County, which were classified and arranged in a room at the depot and these were examined by many of the party with a great deal of interest. They certainly demonstrate beyond cavil that the region from which they were taken is wonderfully rich in mineral deposits which for value and variety can scarcely be surpassed within an equal area of surface anywhere on the globe. Slate for roofing, for furniture, for building, and other purposes; marble of all varieties from white to black; iron ore in exhaustless beds; grindstones, whetstones, and hones; mineral paints, plumbago, fire clay, gold quartz, all in near proximity with stone coal. Specimens of iron ore from Etowah nearby were exhibited, the pig iron made from which mines had been sent to England and tested for iron and steel, and the files and cutlery, including razors made from it, were shown in the original packages. Here is the line of the great mineral formation of the South—the transition from the primary to the secondary formation, a treasure house of incalculable wealth which only awaits the hand of skilled industry and the application of the required capital to pour forth its riches upon the commerce of the world.

Of native iron ore there were exhibited seventy specimens from a tract eight miles square, embracing all the hematites, the sesquioxide, the limonite or hydrous sesquioxide, specular, olivine and rhombohedral iron ore, black oxide with fossils in profusion, the samples varying from 70 to 90 percent of pure iron. There were some thirty specimens from the Etowah mines of such extraordinary richness that they appeared to equal the pig iron of commerce. The collection contained numerous specimens of manganese, copper, and gold quartz found on the same tract and slate of all sizes and qualities from two feet by seven feet to seven inches by fourteen inches for curbing, roofing, flagging, and mantels.

There were forty-four different specimens of marble, some of them exceedingly beautiful, susceptible of the highest polish, and considered equal to the best statuary. Of rock for grindstones, fifteen kinds from very fine to very coarse. Also oil or Arkansas stone and razor hone, Tripoli, used for polishing silver and brass, and millstone closely approximating the French burr. Fancy building rock, which though soft when quarried, hardens by exposure and is susceptible of a polish which must give it great value when adopted by builders, and it can be sawed or chiselled into any shape and can be varnished into shades of walnut, oak, poplar, maple, cedar, and mahogany. The supply is said to be inexhaustible. There were specimens of fire clay, Powhatan pipe clay (heretofore believed to be confined to Virginia), dye rock, plumbago, red and yellow ochre, etc., etc. All the foregoing are said to abound in the section through which the survey of the Van Wert Railroad passes and within twenty miles or less of Cartersville. The specimens on exhibition were examined by the editorial fraternity, and by a number of scientific gentlemen and practical miners, and were admitted to be of the first quality in the order and classes to which they belong.

JUHL

Nor far from Cartersville and in the same county, there is a section of the Etowah River three miles in length, running through this rich mineral region, which presents five falls, each of fifteen feet, affording immense water power with topographical advantages rendering its application and control easy, effective, and comparatively inexpensive. The soil is fertile and produces with good seasons not only abundant crops of the cereals, but a heavy yield of cotton. And it is claimed that capital and skilled labor could in this locality raise the cotton, remove it directly, as picked, to the mills where it could be ginned and manufactured profitably into yarns, thread, sheetings, and other goods; that no raw cotton need be baled for market, but that the entire crop could be manufactured right where it is raised; and that the material for the buildings and machinery required can be procured on or out of the same land, clay for bricks, marble and rock, iron, copper, and gold, slate, etc.

This may not all be done in a moment, but the facts are such, and the confidence of practical men in the undeniable feasibility and advantages of such development of the natural resources of this section is so great that it can scarcely be doubted that such a consummation will be realized in the—by no means distant—future.

Let this be done there, and it will be done elsewhere. No such achievement, which utilizes what is now dormant and gives to the light of day and to the wings of commerce millions of wealth locked up for ages in the eternal hills, can be confined and restricted to one locality. Georgia will feel its impetus from mountain to seaboard. Charleston will feel it as the fresh and rising gale which is once more to fill her canvas. And especially will it vitalize the great railway interests extending now from the "City by the Sea" to North Georgia, Alabama, and Tennessee.

Before proceeding further, it may be well to give the elevation above sea level of the following places: Savannah, 32 feet; Augusta, 147; the railway track at Stone Mountain below Atlanta, 1,055 feet; Atlanta (railway track), 1,050 feet, and the rain falling on Judge Collyer's [John Collier] house in that city runs off one side of the roof and finds its way to the Atlantic Ocean, and on the other taking an opposite course empties finally into the Gulf of Mexico. The railroad bridge crossing the Etowah near Cartersville, 771 feet; the summit of Kennesaw Mountain, a few miles distant, 1,828 feet; the track at Dalton, 773 feet; at Tunnel Hill, 1,859 feet, and at Chattanooga, 666 feet above sea level, and a freshet in the Tennessee overflows it, so that in some instances the water has run through the cars at the depot. Track at Rome, 610 feet; Union Point, on the Georgia Railroad, 674 feet; Social Circle, on the same road, 890 feet; Macon, 297 feet.

A comparison of these figures will show the heavy grades required on all the roads above Augusta, and to this fact must be added the no less material embarrassment of abrupt and sharp curves at almost every point following each other in rapid succession and, where the trains are numerous, making the risk of collision very great in case of slightest variation from the timetables. The precautions taken are such, and the general management of these lines is so excellent, that accidents rarely occur, which seems almost incredible in view of the fact that very often when running at a high rate of speed, the engineer cannot see the track in open daylight one hundred yards ahead on account of the cliffs which fill the hollow of the curves and form precipitous walls of rock within a few feet of the track.

Marietta, remembered by many as one of the most beautiful towns in upper Georgia, presents no important mineral attractions, and hence the time given to that station of the route was only sufficient to enable the party to realize to some extent the effects of the late unpleasantness on this once enviable community. The place is now considered the mere shadow of its former self, and yet enough of loveliness survives in its suburbs and environs to make it attractive to the eye and lead to the hope of its early restoration to all, and more than all, its antebellum comeliness and prosperity. It occupies an admirable site surrounded by a picturesque and healthy district and has been always noted for the refinement of its principal residents, its excellent social order, and its good schools.

Situated immediately on the Western and Atlantic Railroad, ten miles above Cartersville, and one and a half miles from Kingston, are the Howard lime and cement quarries, owned by Rev. C. W. Howard, formerly and for a number of years the popular pastor of the Huguenot Church in Charleston. It was pleasant to meet this gentleman, and it seemed pleasant to him to revive up the delightful memories of the olden time and to recall the honored faces and dear associations of the brave old city. Mr. Howard held a command in the late struggle and in one of the battles near Atlanta was shot through the neck and narrowly escaped with his life. He has quite recovered from the effects of that wound and, although in somewhat feeble health, joined the party on Colonel Hulbert's invitation and went the rounds of the excursion. His quarries have been worked since 1845. They supplied the lime for the Augusta factory buildings and for all the earlier buildings in Atlanta. They are now worked by Mr. [George H.] Waring, a son-in-law of the proprietor. The rock is of blue lower silurian formation and is entirely destitute of fossil. Each stratum differs in its constituents from the one above and below it, and each has evidently been deposited at separate subsidences of the waters. (*Vide* Noah's journal of the flood.)

The perpendicular face of the quarry is about sixty feet, as far in as it has been explored. It is of unknown depth—a backbone of limestone rock, one mile in length and half a mile in width. One stratum whose color is nearly black affords the beautiful white lime known as the bird-eye lime from small dark spots in it resembling the eye of a bird. Another stratum which is less pure affords a building lime, the bond of which when made into mortar is exceedingly tenacious. Two other strata, differing in structure, make an excellent hydraulic cement, the only cement rock south of Louisville, Kentucky, which has yet been discovered. A large portion of the tunnel and other railroad constructions in Tennessee were made from this cement, which has received the highest endorsement from masons and civil engineers.

The machinery for making this part of the works productive and profitable was destroyed by Sherman, but will soon be replaced and be at work again. The lime-kilns now turn out between two and three hundred bushels of lime daily. Twenty laborers are at present employed in the quarry, besides woodcutters, coopers, etc. The lime sells at the kiln at thirty cents a bushel, without the packages, and the demand is greater than the present force can supply. Atlanta is the chief market. The somewhat unusual phenomenon is presented in portions of this quarry of strata of the limestone rock converging from east to west and uniting in roof-shaped conformations. Mr. Waring will soon add two other kilns to these works, and it is evident that, however valuable under their present management they may be, the production of lime here could be almost indefinitely increased by a liberal outlay of capital and the property receive a corresponding increase in value and become still more profitable to all concerned. Lime and cement are by no means unimportant articles of commerce, and whatever and whoever increases their supply makes a welcome and valuable contribution to the wealth of the country and the comfort of mankind.

JUHL

GEORGIA PRESS EXCURSION   4

The train crosses the Oostanaula River and reaches the battleground of Resaca, one of the notable conflicts of the late sectional war. On the summit of a hill not far from the track the earthworks are still standing which were thrown up and gallantly defended by the southern troops at the time when Gen. Joe Johnston on his retreat from Dalton arrived at this point and, after some hard fighting with the overwhelming numbers of Sherman's army, succeeded by his masterly address in crossing the river and baffling his antagonist. The dead of both armies in great numbers are here buried and, some distance from the river and in full view from the cars, a large tract of ground is enclosed with a neat white paling, and over the main entrance is inscribed in large letters "Confederate Cemetery." Within that sacred enclosure hundreds of brave men who perished on those hills in a hopeless struggle have been tenderly laid away by loving hands, and the tears which fall and the flowers which are laid upon their graves attest how dear to their friends will ever be the memory of these martyrs to the "Lost Cause."

The next point is Dalton, badly damaged, but being now rebuilt. On the edge of the town is a hill which was occupied and fortified during the war by some Negro troops, who were attacked and driven out of their breastworks with great slaughter by ["Fighting Joe"] Wheeler's cavalry. This is another railroad centre where several lines of railway connect; and, aside from this, it appears to be at present a place of no great importance and certainly of but few attractions.

A few miles north of Dalton the train passes at the Willow Dale Spring whose cool and refreshing waters gush forth from a handsomely finished granite basin within a few yards of the road. A light and fancy structure has been erected over the spring, and a number of thrifty young willow trees bend gracefully over it, furnishing a green canopy in beautiful contrast with the snow-white springhouse and its paling enclosure. It sends forth a copious volume of water at all seasons, grateful to the taste and cold enough to be agreeable even to those accustomed to the ice water on the trains. It is located in a romantic dale, as its name imports, and has all the high and picturesque surroundings necessary to complete the attractiveness of the scenery, being just such a spot as gave Thomson one of his charming lines: "Where mountains rise, umbrageous dales descend."

The train has been crossing rivers and passing round and among mountains, but now reaches a point which admits of no further evasion, no engineering artifice to secure further progress without a temporary adieu to daylight, and abruptly comes up to the lofty and frowning front of the Allegheny, which blocks the way westward. A small opening at the base of the mountain, barely wide enough and high enough to admit the cars, is the east end of the tunnel into which the track enters and is lost to view in the darkness.

Through this gloomy passage the train has to make its way, but the wires which have all along kept us company now take leave of the rail, as if afraid to risk the subterranean depths, and off they go up the mountainside from crag to crag and rock to rock, higher and higher still, as if intent on leaving earth and seeking congenial cloudland, where the forked flashes bear the messages of Jove, until beyond and over the dizzy heights they are lost to view, from where the looker-on stands beside the iron horse, which pants and trembles and gathers up his courage and his strength for the passage of the tunnel. And now slowly, cautiously, noiselessly, smoothly, stealthily, the long train creeps into the cavernous chamber, and in a moment there is a solemn transition from the glorious sunlight of an August afternoon to a darkness deeper than that of midnight.

The hand is brought up before the face and close to the eye, but it can't be seen. Nothing is visible and nothing is audible, for a dead silence seems to reign throughout this darksome narrow pass. No snorting, whistling, or puffing of the engine is here; no escape even of a steam or smoke seems to be allowed, lest the giant of the mountains should be aroused from the slumber of centuries and, turning in his bed, should smother the intruder under the pressure of his huge frame. The car timbers creak slightly and it sounds ominous in the awful stillness—is it the mountain or the train? Ha! my boys, one little break overhead and the superincumbent mass comes down, and then a long farewell to Georgia's governor and a thousand-year adios to some of the heaviest men who ever tried "the applause of listening senates to command," and a goodly number of vacancies on the Georgia bench, and a huge business for obituary writers in chronicling the virtues of so many Georgia majors and colonels, and fifty or more newspapers in mourning dress for the loss of so many leaders of the editorial corps.

Have not the engineers said that one point in the tunnel is a trifle unsafe and are not arrangements now making to give to that point additional support? But the darkness of Erebus is only for a quarter of a mile and, however slowly traversed, is soon over, and the iron horse rushes joyously into the sunlight and fresh air again; and the wires, having climbed over the summit, come leaping down from crag to crag, resuming companionship with the now flying train, and together they go through the valleys, over the creeks and the rivulets, passing the cabins of the Tennessee cotter, and making a wide circuit, with Lookout Mountain towering grandly on the left, pass the National Cemetery with its thousands of dead and the national flag floating high over them, pass the military post with its array of blue jackets and red bunting, and then run into a low level flat, and stop at Chattanooga. The party lands upon the platform, into a crowd of mosquitoes and child beggars and, before leaving, will doubtless know something more of this city on the Tennessee.

JUHL

GEORGIA PRESS EXCURSION   5

The whole country through which the 138 miles of railway passes from Atlanta to Chattanooga in ordinary seasons produces fine crops, especially of the cereals. But the long, continued hot and dry weather of this summer has been not only damaging, but literally disastrous.

The appearance of the fields presents an exact picture of upper Carolina in 1845. Thousands of acres of corn which ought to produce, from the quality of the land, fifty or more bushels to the acre will scarcely yield a peck of nubbins. And this is general, not confined to spots or neighborhoods, but extending far and wide, as intelligent gentlemen from various localities reported and observation from the cars confirmed.

The people in the towns and villages and the better class of farmers appear healthy and well preserved. But there is another class of a lower type than even the sand-lappers of the low-country pine barrens. The visitor naturally expects to find a hardy and vigorous race in these elevated regions, and yet, right among the mountains and in the midst of scenery which ought to inspire and exalt the mind and in an atmosphere pure and bracing and in every way favorable to physical development, there are many of the most pitiable specimens of squalid poverty to be found on the continent. Civilization, wealth, refinement, progress harnessed up to the iron horse pass within fifty yards of the door of these wretched cabins where human nature shrinks away in saffron skin and emaciated form.

The log hut is scarcely high enough for a man of ordinary stature to stand erect within its well-smoked walls. The crevices between the poles, once filled with clay, are now open here and there for the wintry blasts and drifting snows to sweep through. The low entrance requires a profound obeisance, not of politeness, but of necessity from him who would gain access to the hut. One room is all this mountain home can boast, having at one end the fireplace with its clay chimney and at the other such pallets for sleeping as promise no luxurious repose. And in this one room, the whole family, whether of six or sixteen, burrow or bundle in summer and winter and thus live and thus die.

No fencing in the immediate vicinity—no domestic animals are visible, unless, indeed, the half-starved cur, who looks sad and mournful as if repining at the fate which dooms him to such companionship.

Looking on such a scene one tries in vain to invest it with the associations of a Rip Van Winkle and his dog Shnider ["Wolf"], the Catskills, and the Hudson of the long ago.

Chattanooga was seen from Cameron Hill, a lofty and solitary spur at the lower end of the city commanding a view as extensive and in some respects better than that from Lookout Mountain. The Tennessee River is visible for a long distance above and below the city, winding its way among the hills, flowing silently around the base of the hill on whose summit we stand, rolling onward to the giant Lookout whose granite foundations turn its course, and thence sweeping away among vine-clad and forest-crowned banks until lost to view in the mountain azure in the distance. The city occupies a flat in the bend of the river and looks from this point as if it owed its existence to a shower of boxcars falling on the plain. The houses are low, generally of one story and in the boxcar style. Of the few churches in the place, not one can boast a steeple, and the spire, which lends so much beauty to other landscapes wherever civilization has grouped its homes—whether in villages or towns—has no place in this picture.

There are two or three handsome residences in the cottage style, but they are exceptional. The river is unreliable for navigation and was so low at the time of this visit that steamers drawing but a few inches of water were unable to proceed with the party to certain ironworks on its shores, and this part of the excursion had to be abandoned. A bridge once spanned the river from the foot of Main Street, but nothing remains of it now except the abutments, and its place is supplied by two ferry boats: one, a nondescript steamer with a paddle wheel on one side only, which dashes into the water spasmodically while the one-horse engine encourages its efforts with an asthmatic accompaniment; and the other, an ordinary flat manoeuvred and controlled in its crossing by a rope attached to a point higher up the river and supported by a line of floats.

The stores are numerous and well supplied with goods, and the business of the place may be considerable in winter, but at this season there is very little to indicate a heavy trade at any time or in any department. As seen from Lookout Mountain, the city presents by no means an attractive appearance. Not only is there the absence of architectural taste in its houses and public buildings, as already mentioned, but there is an almost total dearth of trees, shrubbery, and gardens, which necessarily gives the place a blank and impoverished appearance. On the night of the 25th of August, the air was intensely hot and close; some of our party occupied the sleeping cars, but could not escape the mosquitoes; others obtained rooms in the town, from which they were driven before midnight by bed bugs; others were sharp enough to repair in carriages five miles to the hotel on Lookout Mountain, where they found excellent entertainment, and slept refreshingly under a pair of blankets. And, reader, if a midsummer night should ever find you in Chattanooga, flee to the mountain for refreshment and repose.

On the opposite side of the river and facing the town, there is a semicircle of beautiful hills affording admirable sites for villas, which with the requisite means and taste might be made to rival some of the most charming scenes on the Hudson. Whether such locations would be healthy and whether the water is good, the writer is not prepared to say. At present, these and all other sites which an eye for the picturesque would select for building in and around Chattanooga are unmarked by a single farmhouse and appear never to have been disturbed except by the spade of the soldier.

JUHL

GEORGIA PRESS EXCURSION   6

There was a quasi-public reception, or a public reception so-called, at Chattanooga which was certainly a novel affair of the kind—

semiserious, semicomic, with a dash of the burlesque, and a considerable admixture of the buncombe, the droll, and the humorous. It was improvised some time after dark, when very many of the party had wandered off in the search of lodgings, and some had already taken their first nap in the berths in the cars. Such, however, as were seated in front of the railroad hotel were caught and incontinently pressed into service and made the recipients of the honors.

A small band of music suddenly appeared on the piazza of the hotel and saluted the night with their lively strains. This was succeeded by a short address of welcome from his Honor Mayor Sparks [A. G. Sharp]. More music and a rousing address from Mr. [V. A.] Gaskill of the Atlanta press who informed the Chattanooga crowd that they ought to belong to Georgia and he was ready to take their city into that state and give them a share in her glorious future. Some Tennessean made a speech in reply, repudiating the idea of any such transfer and objecting hotly to any such alliance. Mayor Hulsey of Atlanta patted Chattanooga on the head and called it one of the most prosperous cities of the South. Mr. [Peter] Zinn of Cincinnati unrolled the ten millions which his city had voted to connect the two places by railway.

Mr. James, another Tennessean, compared the Chattanooga of today and of the future with what it was when only known as an Indian trading post at Ross' Landing and announced that in a few years the merchants of Chattanooga would "receive and unload at their wharves the fruits of the tropics direct from the islands of the Caribbean Sea and deliver them to you in Georgia." There were others called for, and a cry for "Dixie," which the band gave with a will and which was received with acclamations by the crowd; and, then, in response to repeated calls, the versatile and irrepressible F. S. Fitch, of the *Griffin Star* got off one of his best speeches, designating the local politics of Chattanooga, which had been working hard to get into the meeting, and coolly telling his audience that he had come there to take Chattanooga, and he was going to do it; that he was willing to buy it, although from what he had seen of it he believed he would be badly stuck in the bargain; that he would have the papers ready in the morning and had the money in his pocket to pay for it, and if any man doubted this let him go into the hotel and wait till he came there, and he'd show it to him.

This *Star* representative and performer of the evening told the crowd that the excursion party had set out to examine the mines and iron works and help develop the country; that most of the editors who had undertaken this business couldn't tell the difference between a vegetable and a mineral; that there were only two great men among them, the one was himself, and the other modesty forbade him to mention; and that the reason so few of them were present was because they had taken too much soda water and gone to bed. All this was interspersed with roars of laughter and the wildest applause from the audience and was hugely enjoyed by the majority of the press delegates, who were lying in their berths or in neighboring houses, resting from the fatigues and heat of the day and with open windows could witness and hear and from time to time join in the calls for music and for speakers.

The crowd, no doubt, believed the humorous speaker was "drunk as a coot" and therefore gave him a latitude which in any other would have been offensive; but the fact is that Fitch is a great pacificator and a decided genius and on this occasion did some magnificent acting which even Jo. Jefferson could not surpass, and brought the meeting to a pleasant conclusion, the crowd retiring evidently delighted with the evening's entertainment.

With the kindest feelings for Chattanooga and with all proper respect and unaffected good wishes for its citizens (may they live long and prosper in every way!), this report aims to give the facts and incidents of the excursion and the impressions of the writer, fairly and without bias; and on no other ground could it have or does it claim any value with the reader. There is one feature which may be considered peculiar to this place; in no other southern community, probably, are there so many youthful beggars of the white race and of both sexes. They throng the platform on the arrival and departure of trains and importune the passengers for alms. They meet and follow the stranger on the streets: "Only five cents . . . only ten cents to buy some bread." It is but a small amount and hurts no one to give it, and even to multiply these gifts in response to an hundred such appeals would not greatly deplete the purses of many to whom such appeals are made.

But who are these children? Talk of Chattanooga and its future! Are not these its young and rising generation, and what is their future? Will not their future be, to a considerable extent, the future of the place? They are growing up in idleness, ignorance, vagrancy, and vice. The country looks abroad for labor and for emigrants. Would not its strength, prosperity, and development be promoted by a little more attention to its home population? These very little hands now held out for charity are numerous enough in Chattanooga to make and keep up the music of flourishing factories, to make bread and clothing for themselves and others also, and to support the schools which might be connected therewith for their instruction at least during portions of the year. What a golden chance for the capitalists to interweave the offices and rewards of the philanthropist with the more popular incentive of a money-making investment. Is there none such in Chattanooga, is there no rich man elsewhere who will go there and win immortality here and hereafter by giving employment and a guardian's care to the hundreds of these little white pariahs?

Some of these children to whom money was given were soon after seen with handfuls of candy which was greedily devoured when they resumed their importunities; and among them were a number of young and good-looking girls, evidently entered on their teens, who, bareheaded and barefooted, with nothing on but a short, loose frock

reaching to the knee, asked for "but ten cents to buy some bread."
Eheu! Les miserables!

JUHL

GEORGIA PRESS EXCURSION   7

The cool and refreshing night to the sleepers at the mountain house and the hot and oppressive night to the sufferers in Chattanooga at length lifts its curtains, and the sun glimmers on the crests of the hills, and the train is again in motion, taking the road leading to Nashville.

The Vulcan Mills, situated within a few rods of the Tennessee River and under the very shadow of Lookout Mountain, invite inspection, and the invitation is accepted. It is worthy of note as the only establishment at work in the Chattanooga vicinage, in or out of the corporate limits, in which capital employs machinery and skilled artisans in a way and to an extent which evidently means business. These works were established in 1861, were destroyed by [William S.] Rosecrans, but have been rebuilt since the war, and are now doing a heavy business, making merchant bar iron for bridges, shafts for cotton factories, and wrought iron work generally of every kind and style. It is essentially and exclusively a rolling mill and makes no castings. It has 135 hands employed and claims to be the only establishment south of the Ohio River having machinery as ponderous, a hammer as powerful, and such material and capacities for rolling iron.

The train moves on beneath the huge overhanging rocks of Lookout Mountain. On the right is the Tennessee, sweeping down against the rocks at our feet and, baffled in its attempts at a passage, turning off sullenly in search of some other avenue of escape. On the left is the grand old monarch of the hills where the Indian built his signal fires in the years long gone and whose towering peak served as a beacon to the pioneers of the West and is now rendered doubly historic by the suffering and valor of which it was the only unmoved witness during the dark years of a still recent struggle.

Look out of the car windows and look up, and high overhead hundreds of tons of rock impend in complete projection over the roadway and over the passing train. Cracks and fissures are in those enormous masses, and the cars move slowly and noiselessly beneath them, for the slightest jar to earth or air would seem sufficient to bring them down. And here, too, is the entrance of a cave, which is said to penetrate the mountain for the distance of a mile and which contains near its mouth a very cold spring of water and a remarkable draft or blast of cold air, constantly blowing and painfully chilling with its icy breath the visitor who stands but for a moment in its immediate current. But, the train rolls on into the open country, and Lookout Mountain looms up grandly against the clear blue sky—unchanged amidst the countless changes which the world has witnessed since it first reared its crest into the heavens—stern symbol of the truth, virtue, and patriotism which time proves incorruptible and eternity will surely reward.

The scenery presented in this day's travel is as beautiful as that which greets the Switzer's eye—an ever-changing landscape of mountain and valley with grazing herds and rippling streams. And in just such surroundings are the Etna Coal Mines in Marion County, where our noonday meal is taken and where several hours are most agreeably spent. These are the only coal mines of the many which have been opened in this section which have survived the discouragements and drawbacks of the past. Owned by a New York company, they are successfully worked at this time under the management of Mr. [Milo] Pratt, a man of large experience in the business and of most indomitable energy.

The pits are located in Raccoon Mountain, eight hundred feet above the railway level and one and three-quarter miles from the base of the mountain where the coal is dumped into cars for shipment. It traverses this distance over a succession of inclined railway planes in coal-bunkers mounted on low wheels and drawn by ropes, the stationary steam engine furnishing the motive power. On one of these stretches the grade is very steep, and the rickety rails are supported by a trestle of alarming height and still more alarming tremulousness—and some of the party who in the ascent were carried over slowly enough, on their return were shot over the chasm at a speed which took the blood from their cheeks and landed them below looking more like the dead than the living. It was a rash venture which none of the company would like to repeat and which some of them certainly will not soon forget. Others, warned in time, made the descent on foot, preferring to be exhausted by fatigue rather than provoke the paralysis of fright.

The mountain containing these coal beds is three miles long and a half mile wide; and the miners are now working three seams of coal varying from two and a half to four feet in thickness covered by a stratum of slate. The coal is bituminous and of excellent quality, is sifted and sized for market, and the residuum is burned into coke, for which there is considerable demand at remunerating prices. The one hundred workmen employed are nearly all Englishmen, and they and their families form quite a little community, isolated from and independent of all other society. They work eight hours a day in the mines, receive good wages, and enjoy almost uninterrupted health.

The owners have invested already two hundred and fifty thousand dollars in these works and for a long time failed to realize expenses, but are now doing a very fair business with a prospect of increased profits. They can now deliver three hundred tons a day if the demand requires it. The high freights formerly charged by the railroads amounted almost to a prohibitory tariff on this article, and made coal mining in this country a losing business. But, induced by the example and persuasions of Colonel Hulbert of the state road, the different lines have so far reduced their charges that the coal from this point can now be thrown on distant markets without involving the miner and shipper in absolute ruin.

A few years since, Mr. Pratt visited Augusta and made a conditional engagement to deliver a quantity of coal in that city for which he was to receive twelve thousand dollars. He then negotiated with the railroad companies for its transportation, he agreeing to furnish his own cars and to do all the loading and unloading, and offered them seven thousand dollars (seven-twelfths of all he was to receive) for such service, and they refused to pass his cars over the road for that amount.

Of course, the coal did not reach Augusta, but remained for the time locked up in the mountains. But a change has taken place in the administration of railway interests in Georgia, and men of larger views and a more comprehensive and liberal policy have taken the control, and the coal and iron are beginning to move to market. And when the way to market is thrown open, capital at once steps in and digs and delves and unearths the hidden treasures which otherwise might remain for ages a vast body of buried and undeveloped wealth within a few feet of an impoverished population occupying the surface. The iron rail is the key to the iron mine and the coal mine and the quarry, and he who holds it can lock or unlock the affluent hills, opulent as they are now known to be in deposits of more value to mankind than the gold or the pearls of the Orient.

JUHL

GEORGIA PRESS EXCURSION   8

The train, switched off from the Nashville track, has been run into the beautiful dell occupied by the white cottages of the Etna miners, and reposes among the willows and vines which line and overshadow the brook. The party, engaged in their explorations, wander among the surrounding hills. The invasion of such a train and such a company points to a reconstruction higher, better, and more salutary by far than any which political empires and graceless adventurers can impart. And everywhere in this fair land, which teems with inexhaustible resources waiting development, there is an earnest welcome for any man, hailing from any quarter or any clime, who comes with muscle and brain or capital and skill to aid in the practical and substantial rehabilitation of the South. Numbers of northern and European companies have already entered upon this work in the states visited during this excursion, and their machinery and artisans are making an impression upon the country which will serve as the best incentive to others to follow their example. There is room enough—work, material, and pay enough—for a thousand furnaces, quarries, and collieries where now there is one, and no greater service can be rendered by the press to the commercial and business interests of the whole country than by ventilating, impressing, and utilizing such information.

The interior of the Etna Mine is like all other coal mines and needs no particular description. The mine has been worked scientifically, the veins pursued by the usual method, leaving alternate solid sections as supports to the roof, and the miners are now working at least sixteen hundred feet from daylight. Furnished with a diminutive lamp attached to the front of their caps and armed with pick and shovel, they rapidly fill the coal bunkers, which are hauled off by mules over tramways to the foot of the inclined plane near the entrance. There the cars are attached to a rope and hauled out by a stationary steam engine, which also controls and regulates their descent of the mountain.

Some of the visitors who had never seen the interior of a coal pit undertook to explore these mines; a few persevered and experienced the somewhat appalling sensations of a novice in a darkness which cannot be described in narrow passages, barely wide enough for the tramways, whose walls indeed contain shallow recesses into which a man can press himself and avoid being crushed by the passing bunkers, which recesses, however well known to the miners, it is a bare chance if the stranger reaches at the proper time. Here and there in the deep gloom a light glimmers where some stooping miner moves through the sepulchral vaults, more like a hideous mountain ghoul than human form, and while you look there comes the cry "beware! the mule, the bunker." If this be not a picture of Hades or Tartarus, it certainly is rather too deep in earth for any man who loves the clear blue sky and pictures and dreams of heaven.

Some of the party, after entering the mine, paid liberally to be piloted out again—in one instance a ten dollar bill was given for such service, and the editor who purchased his deliverance from the horrors of the pit at this price, in describing his experience afterwards, said that he offered all the money he had with him to get out, and if it had been ten times as much he would have readily given it rather than to have remained any longer in the mine. In this case, as in some others, the *facile descensus* is fully realized, as well as the difficulty of a return; and some of the explorers found their way back to the open air in a plight which fully indicated the rough treatment to which they had been subjected—damaged clothing and shocking bad hats being on free exhibition.

The Etna Mines are furnished with everything which such a business requires—cars, chutes, screens, furnaces for coke, etc. The fine coal which is converted into coke is kept burning until it ceases to blaze when a stream of water is turned on the furnace, the fire extinguished, and the coke removed. The value of this article may be estimated from the fact that ten pounds of coke will melt to fusion one hundred pounds of iron. The water used is conducted to the furnace by a hose which is supplied by a force pump worked by an overshot water wheel driven by the stream of a noble spring.

After the adventures and fatigues of the day, the guests were quite willing to resume their places in the cars and, while recounting their hairbreadth scapes, to engage in the still more agreeable discussion of a capital fish dinner which was provided on board and to which ample justice was done. And the train moves off again; and, when the morning comes, the weary travelers joyfully take refuge at the choice hotel in Rome, Georgia. There are few places in the state possessing as many advantages and attractions as this. It may have seven hills, or seventy times seven, but its beauty is not in the hills. It may have the Oostanaula and Etowah defining its limits and giving a charm to the landscape as they glide into one and form the bolder and more useful Coosa—but its attraction is not in these rivers. It may have its elegant spires, its handsome churches, its model cottages and still more imposing mansions with gardens and shrubbery and trees of richest foliage, but these all combined do not make Rome more than a picture, such as the traveler finds in many a village or town in other lands. The charm is in the people of the place—refined, given to hospitality, cordial, generous, and full of energy and business vim, which makes the town a live town with a wide-awake, stirring look, and progression and improvement stamped on everything. From Myrtle Hill, where the Confederate cemetery is located, the town looks as lovely as an artist's dream. It has recuperated wonderfully since the war, and in every desirable way it may be said to be "still marching on." In foundries, workshops and factories, in railroads and business connection, it is running a race with Atlanta, and as a competitor is certainly by no means to be despised. Among other evidence of progress, it has extensive water works, nearly completed, which will supply the city with water and adorn with fountains its principal streets.

JUHL

The hospitalities of Rome were extended to the excursion party with a liberal hand and in a style not soon to be forgotten. Carriages conveyed the guests to all the points of interest, and a magnificent dinner was served up at the Choice Hotel, at which the mayor, the genial and indefatigable [Zachariah] Hargrove, presided, supported by Governor Bullock and Colonel Hulbert, and short speeches were made by these gentlemen, by Mayor Hulsey of Atlanta, and by members of the press, enlivened by the popping of corks and music by the band. After which the party proceeded in carriages to the landing and embarked in the steamer *Etowah* for a trip down the Coosa.

It was a lovely afternoon, and a pleasant breeze on the river gave promise of an agreeable time on the water to men now tired with so much "riding on the rail." A survey of the boat—its staterooms, accommodations, and supplies—was eminently satisfactory. And even to the landlubbers afflicted with a hydrophobic distaste to being afloat, a feeling of serenity was imparted by a survey of the river. In case of fire or striking a snag or getting immovably aground, a few yards swim would land you on the banks, if, indeed, you could find water deep enough to swim in. But it was evident in many places that if you reached the water—whether by being lifted and let down by a boiler explosion, or accidentally slipping off the guards, or voluntarily jumping overboard—if you had sense and strength enough to stand up, you would be well out of it. Verily the veteran and hardy navigators of the Coosa encounter all the perils of "a life on the raging canawl." Imagine the contrast of the descent of the narrow and shallow waters of the Coosa on the little steamer *Etowah* and the decks of the *Champion*, proudly riding the huge billows off Hatteras only a few weeks before.

Seated in the pilot house, we get the breeze and the best view of each bend in the river and of the ever changing and really charming scenery and can fully appreciate the admirable performance of the boat in the passage of successive rapids now clearly defined by the unusually low stage of the river. Our *vis à vis*, Col. W. S. Cothran, president of the Coosa Navigation Company, a railroad president also, gives us the history of the enterprise by which these waters have been rendered useful in the transportation of freight and passengers.

In 1845 a certain Captain Lafferty came from some place in the West and built a light draught steamboat at Greensport, Alabama, the lower terminus of the navigable waters of the Coosa, in which he ascended the stream to Rome, Georgia, and continued to run his boat between the two places during the winters of '45, '46, and '47. In 1848 W. S. Cothran, who had been engaged in steamboating on the Savannah River, came and with Captain [J. P.] Gould bought out the pioneer navigator Lafferty and built another boat, the *Coosa*, which was put on the line. In 1849 they built another steamer, the *Alabama*, which, drawing thirty inches, proved a failure. They sunk fifteen thousand dollars in the business before making a dollar.

In 1851 all the other parties sold their interests to Colonel Cothran, who became sole owner, and sent Captain Gould to Pittsburgh, Pennsylvania, who brought out some boat-builders from the Ohio River with whom a contract was made for boats of fourteen inches draught, with the additional stipulation of one hundred dollars extra for every inch under fourteen and a forfeit of the same amount for every inch over. The *Georgia* was the result of this effort and ran on the river during the winter and spring until 1855. Colonel [Cunningham M.] Pennington of Rome then went out West and somewhere along the Cumberland River picked up Captain [Francis Marion] Coulter and brought him to Rome and engaged him in boat building, then the *Pennington* was launched, and the great triumph realized of a boat drawing but nine and a half inches when wooded up and in running order. This boat could navigate the river at all seasons and did run the river from July to July when the line, for the first time, commenced making money. (Captain Coulter is present and with evident satisfaction endorses the statement.)

In 1858 the increasing business rendered an additional boat necessary, and the *Alfarata* was built and did good service. In 1864 this boat was chased by the Yankees and escaped by running the shoals below Greensport and was, on the return of "peace" (?), brought back and resumed her place on the river. The distance by the river from Rome to Greensport is 176 miles, and these little stern-wheelers make the trips there and return in three days. They carry the mail and run with such regularity that they have never failed to make mail schedule time but once since the war. The navigation is attended with some novel features. On the downward trip the boat with the excursion party would sometimes grate harshly on the rocky or sandy beds of the rapids, but *n'importe*, the flying wheel and flying water would carry her over all right, nobody hurt, nobody scared, for the banks were quite near and the bottom still nearer, and no danger of sinking, and these boats seem to run as well on the sand as on the water. And at these same places, on the return up the river, hawsers were run out forward and made fast to trees one or two hundred yards up the river, and with the crew at the capstan and one hundred and ten pounds of steam in the boilers, over and up the rapids she'd go. As the barber said to his customer whose beard resisted the dullness of the razor: "It's bound to come off if the razor don't break." So say these plucky navigators of the Coosa rapids: "The boat's bound to go over unless the boiler bursts and the hawsers break."

And it takes but a short time to accomplish the feat—a feat which seems to the uninitiated utterly impracticable, with a pebbly, rocky bed under the bow of the boat and only a few inches of water running like a mill race against it—and when it is done and the steamer with its crowded decks has once more gained the deeper, smoother waters above and the dozen stalwart half-naked blacks who have been wading out with the hawsers return with them on board, the feeling of the passenger is all which the Frenchman means when he says *c'est magnifique.*

JUHL

GEORGIA PRESS EXCURSION 10

When Mr. Cothran first commenced the navigation of the Coosa, the country was but sparsely settled and almost in a wild state. The people would come to the banks and sometimes remain camped for a day or two, waiting to see the sight of a veritable steamboat—the men barefooted, with dog and gun and the cap of coonskin with tail appendant. In 1848 the largest planter raised nine bales of cotton as a crop, but the boats now carry from four to five thousand bales during a season. Pollard's Bend alone contributes some six hundred bales. Of the Pollard family, it is said, there are two hundred voters, and out of sixty-seven of this prolific stock who emigrated at one time, only one could read and write.

After twenty years of struggle the navigation of the river has become a successful and paying business, and it has done much towards the development of the country through which the Coosa passes, increasing the value of lands from six to sixty dollars an acre. It is a very pleasant route for the traveler, as the table and sleeping accommodations are excellent, the scenery by no means uninteresting or monotonous, and the motion smooth and rapid wherever the water will allow. It presents also a very good picture of southern life in the olden time, the colored boat-hands being prompt, active, civil, and obedient, and evidently petted by the owner and officers of the boat. Some of these darkies improvised a performance on the lower forward deck in which various acrobatic and comic feats were presented and for which they were well rewarded by the lookers-on. Wooding up at night always furnished a lively scene, the hands jumping ashore with blazing lightwood torches which flashed amid the drapery of the bank and with the dark moving forms of the wood carriers gave a weird picture not without its attraction.

The first night on board also furnished the sublime spectacle of a terrific thunderstorm among the mountains, near enough to be seen in all its magnificence, but passing just below, the captain "tying up" the boat in order to avoid running into it and not resuming the voyage until the moon rose. In the early morning an incident occurred which served to illustrate the perils of the deep and the dangers attending even the Coosa navigation. A head was seen floating in the river—a bare head, for the hat was floating away on an independent excursion, and by its departure developed the fact that its owner "had no hair on the top of his head in the place where the hair ought to grow." The martin (*musteta Americana*) is believed to be found only in the region extending from northern New York to Puget's Sound, but here was evidently a *martin* in the water, away down South in the Coosa River. Taken on board, however, it proved to be of the genus editorial, one of the most quiet and sedate of the party, who had somehow managed to slip off the boat and was rewarded with a plunge bath which did him no harm. [This was J. H. Martin of the *Columbus Enquirer*.]

Eighty miles distant from Rome by the course of the river are the Round Mountain Iron Works in Cherokee County, Alabama. This mountain was visited and the ore examined. There is no doubt as to the value of the ore or the extent of the iron beds here located. The mine was successfully worked some years ago, but the works were destroyed successively by Straight [Abel D. Streight] in '63, and by [Francis P.] Blair in '65, and are still in ruins, the owner not having the capital to resume operations. Round Mountain is an outlying spur of the Red Mountain range which is thirty-five miles in length. It is within a half a mile of the river and with two furnaces before the war turned out from ten to fifteen tons of pig iron a day, which at the river bank commanded fifteen dollars a ton. The ore is the red hematite, averaging 60 percent of pure iron. Some of the specimens gathered on the mountain contained fossils of various kinds and sizes, seashell and fish in well-preserved outlines. Sandstone to line furnaces is also here in abundance, and limestone, fire clay, and everything else which the business requires.

The Cornwall Mines and Works were also visited. They are situated on the Chattooga River, three miles from the Coosa, and the longest three miles a distressed party ever traversed in coal wagons drawn by four mules each. The day intensely hot—the wagons crowded—the road rough—the scenery blank—the limbs rude enough to knock hats off and to scratch the wearers whenever the said wearers were not quick enough in heeding the constantly repeated alarm: "Look out! mind your heads." But the party had committed itself to the task of exploring and examining the mineral resources of the country, and they went through the performance. But on some faces even then could be seen the fierce editorials gathering which have since burst forth like flashes from a cloud of pent-up wrath. Elegant and luxurious cars and a nice steamer with iced liquors and fragrant cigars might do—but coal pits and coal cars and fiery furnaces adding their heat to a fiery sun, verily this was villainous and clearly proved a diabolical conspiracy against the Georgia press. Perhaps it did. Perhaps it did not. But with this the writer, living north of the Savannah River, had nothing to do. And as he had nothing to do with the champagne and the drinking, so he had nothing to do with the politics, or the feuds, or the personal likes and dislikes of the party, but is satisfied that neither politics nor men can make the country we visited other than a beautiful country and one abounding in the grandest deposits of mineral wealth.

The Messrs. Noble of Rome (Englishmen) seem to be the leading men of the iron interest of this vicinity.[5] They own and manage the

5. James and Samuel Noble would soon (1883) found the city of Anniston (Annie's Town), Alabama.

Cornwall Iron Works and also a large foundry at Rome, where all kinds of castings are made and engines (stationary, locomotive, steam fire engines, etc.,) built. Here is seen the machinery for breaking into small pieces the iron ore. It is then stocked and filled in with fine coal which when fired, burns the sulphur and other gases out of the ore and prepares it for the furnaces where it is melted and run into pig iron. All these processes were shown and explained to the party, the jets of stars flashing out from the furnace as the stream of liquid metal ran forth into the moulds forming a brilliant pyrotechnic display.

JUHL

GEORGIA PRESS EXCURSION   11

It was in Cedar Bluff, Alabama, that the party landed to visit the Cornwall Mines and Iron Works. There is a small village a few hundred yards from the river with dilapidated houses and sickly looking inhabitants, which makes one feel that this section gained but little by the expulsion of the Indians. This was the camp selected by General Jackson (Old Hickory) when with his Tennessee militia he carried on his campaigns against the Cherokees and Creeks. And near here he fought the battle of Turkeytown with the warriors of the two tribes. The same landscape and heavens are here, but the red man is gone, and the indomitable victor of the redcoats and the redskins is gone also, and the scene we now look upon is flat and lifeless. But some of the natives are seen in bed, well shaken with the chills, and before the day is over, the visiting journalists are well shaken in the coal wagons, so that there is some life about the place after all.

The wealth of this section is undoubtedly in its metals. The pig iron from the Cornwall Works is said to command ten dollars more per ton than the Pennsylvania mines, even in the northern markets, and to cost ten dollars less per ton in its production. It is affirmed that the ore of Pennsylvania yields but 30 or 40 percent of pure iron, whereas the ore from all of these mines yields from 60 to 90 percent. And these statements are made by men who have worked the Pennsylvania mines, abandoned them, invested their capital here, and are now working these. They also say that where charcoal is used in the furnaces the iron is far superior to any which is fused by coke or mineral coal fires, that here they have an abundance of such fuel which is seldom found or to be had in an iron region elsewhere. Thousands of cords of wood and huge charcoal kilns with miles of growing timber all around furnished ocular demonstration of one of these statements.

And a personal examination of the mines now being worked and of rich metallic mountain ridges not yet touched by the pick leaves no room for doubt as to the exhaustless quantities of the ore. And, as to the percent of pure iron in these immense beds, there is the evidence of iron miners and scientific men, whose analyses, in crucible or furnace, attest its richness. And all who have used the pig iron from this and other works visited during the excursion, whether in forge, rolling mill, or foundry, when it is made into heavy work, such as rails, shafting, merchant bar, wheels, axles, etc., certify to its great superiority over any other produced elsewhere, for durability, toughness, and all the qualities which give value to this metal.

After a thorough inspection of the Cornwall Works, the charcoal wagons are again brought into requisition. As many of the press gang crowded into each as would fill a street car and the line of march is resumed, fording the Chattooga and following a very tortuous road for the scene of the barbecue. The jolting ought to give an appetite; but, if it fails to do this, it at least provokes a vast deal of merriment which is in no wise diminished by the anathemas of those who are evidently looking back with regret to the carriages of Atlanta and Rome. The mules and the drivers heed nothing of this, but carry the live cargo forward and land the learned and distinguished guests in a wild ravine, where a bountiful and admirably prepared barbecue, and a generous spring of pure cold water, and the deep shade of the foliage which canopied the dell enabled the weary Bohemians to enjoy the *recubans sub legmines* as perhaps they never did before.

A cabin on the rise of the hill was occupied by a large family living in the plainest style of country life and yet apparently well supplied with the necessaries of life. Poultry, pigs, and cattle were in the yard, and an unpretentious dairy proved its ability to furnish buttermilk in response to an application properly supported by greenbacks. The old farmer said he was born in South Carolina, and that nearly all the old people in that section were from the Palmetto State. He and many others like him were met with who had emigrated years ago from Carolina, but have never lost their veneration for the home and memories of their early days. And their experience would not be calculated to induce others to follow their example. The disruption of social ties, of educational, religious, and local associations, has not been indemnified by any improvement in their worldly prospects or condition. The sons of Jacob and the daughters of Judah yearned after Jerusalem, whenever they wandered in a strange land, however fair that land might be. And today hundreds of exiles in other states and other lands look back to Carolina with a longing once more to stand upon their native heather. The mother may forget her child, but can they ever forget Glencairn?

But the roasted meats and other sweets are at length disposed of and, once more to the coal wagons, my friends, once more! Five miles, now, of the ups and downs of coal wagon experience, and the tired mules and tired men hail with joy the shining river. Verily the Coosa hath grown in value and is greeted with a welcome, cordial and deep as ever weary soldier or pilgrim gives to Rhine or Nile. And the *Etowah* becomes a floating palace, which some rashly swear they'll never quit until they get back to Rome. Ablutions and toilets and a good supper and a fragrant cigar and a pleasant seat on the open decks in the evening breeze, and the equanimity of the party is restored. And hence, when the editors hold at night a grand council and the meeting is duly organized and it is expected that a resolution to break up at Rome and go home will be offered and unanimously adopted, after a due quantum of speech-making the meeting resolves to go to the whole figure and to do all the developing which the case will admit of. And Colonel Hulbert makes a practical railroad and coal and iron speech, and the eloquent Howard makes an instructive and flowery address, with a brave dash of southern fire in it, and the meeting adjourns. The whist tables are again surrounded, and the conversation circles again formed, and the party is again as comfortable as though no coal wagons had ever jostled it into a meditated flight for home.

JUHL

GEORGIA PRESS EXCURSION   12

A beautiful Sabbath morning witnesses the return of the party to Rome, Georgia. The stores are closed, the streets quiet, and the church bells make a music suggestive of better things than earthly feastings and revelry profane. At the Episcopal Church the services were conducted by the rector, Rev. Wm. Williams, and Rev. R. W. B. Elliott, son of the late bishop of Georgia. The latter preached the sermon on "patient continuance"—a subject not without interest in its spiritual sense and which in another sense would have been very apropos to the press party at this juncture, but unfortunately there were not more than half a dozen of them present to hear it. The church music was very good, but the officiating clergymen went through the service in a style somewhat beyond anything in the high church order which this deponent has ever witnessed in that denomination. Perhaps this, however, was in obedience to the adage (not canon) which requires us "when in Rome, to do as Rome does."

In the afternoon, the opposite extreme was presented at the Baptist Church where a Dunkard from Ohio held forth, by permission of the pastor. A stranger and belonging to a strange sect, he at least succeeded in satisfying the congregation of his profound ignorance; and, if his effort provoked the mirth of some, it scarcely could have edified any. He was sharp enough to advertise the audience that he was examining the country with a view to settlement; but, with this object in view, he should have called a halt in East Tennessee, for surely there is no opening for such a brother in any of the precincts of civilized Rome. Reverend Mr. [Luther R.] Gwaltney, the pastor (said to be a popular and able minister), was present and had the full benefit of the Dunkard's drivelings, but it was a lost afternoon to some if not all in that assembly, and the propriety of such permissive desecrations of the pulpit and the Sabbath is at least questionable. The Dunkards or Turkers are Seventh Day Baptists, originating in 1724, and found in some parts of Pennsylvania and some of the western states. They derive their name from the German *tunken*, "to dip"; they wear a peculiar dress when *en regle*, cut neither hair nor beard, the men and women live in separate habitations, they allow marriages, but regard celibacy as a virtue, and book learning almost a crime—and of this last offence, few if any of the sect could ever be convicted by an honest jury. There are small communities of them in East Tennessee, but they live in obscure neighborhoods and seldom appear on the surface.

Rome is well supplied with churches of different denominations, and its population seems impressed with a commendable regard for the Sabbath and the sanctuary. Its streets are well-shaded and some of the trees, such as the silver-leaved maple, are very beautiful. The ladies, God bless them! such as were visible, were comely enough to compare favorably with their Georgian (Circassian) sisters of the East and looked as pretty as the picture on a ten cent fractional of the new issue, only a little more so. And Bill Arp [Charles H. Smith] was there—a member of the city council—good enough on the retreat from Rome—good enough now in a quiet useful life—but in the press party, quite overshadowed in his own line by the dear, good Fitch. . . .

The country around Rome commends itself for agricultural purposes. It also has an abundance of water power for manufactures and mills and is rich in minerals. Mr. [Daniel R.] Mitchell has in his private cabinet numerous specimens of copper, alum, gold-bearing quartz, hematite and acicular (fibrous, needle-shaped) iron ores, slate, plumbago, coal, whetstone, oilstone, fuller's earth, porcelain, etc., all of which he says were collected within a few miles of Rome and were taken promiscuously from places where they exist in immense beds. As the writer did not examine these deposits, he can only report the character of the specimens submitted to his inspection. They were very rich.

JUHL

GEORGIA PRESS EXCURSION   13

A new and continuous rail extends from Rome to Selma, Alabama. The road is in fine order, this distance two hundred miles, and the whole line is now to be traversed and retraced by the excursion train. Sixteen miles of rapid running and the party land at Cave Spring with its beautiful little village, large bubbling spring, and clear rippling stream meandering through the settlement and crossed by fancy bridges. The water is impregnated with lime and not unpleasant to the taste, although some protested against drinking it unmixed; but, as they found the same objection to all the water along the route, no importance was attached to their verdict in this instance.

The spring is at the base of a very high hill in whose precipitous sides there are two small openings to a very considerable cave. One of these it would be death to enter, as the first step would be into the darkness and depths profound of a frightful abyss. The other is provided for some distance with a stairway; and, preceded by guide with a lamp, the descent is by no means dangerous. There is nothing to repay the fatigues attending its exploration, as the only objects worth looking at when far in its dark, damp chambers are the pale and half-frightened faces of the company, watching the solitary lamp which threatens every moment to leave the party in darkness. And, if there is any place on earth, or more correctly, in the earth where a light is appreciated, it is in a cave or a coal mine half a mile from sunshine.

From these ground-mole performances in a noisome cavern, it is pleasant to return once more to the balmy breeze and pebbly stream which gladdens the villagers of Cave Spring. Here an enlightened legislation has provided for the amelioration of human misfortune by the establishment of an institution for the education of the deaf and dumb. Its motto suggests and explains its object and system: *vicaria languae manus*. There are fifty pupils, who are instructed under the most improved deaf-mute methods, and some of the inmates are usefully employed during a part of the day in making shoes and other articles. The institution is almost entirely dependent now on the public treasury, as the pay pupils of a former day have by the sad reverses of the war been added to the list of beneficiaries. In a place of no business importance and having but three or four small country stores, it might occasion serious misgivings as to the health of the country to find two drugstores in full blast. But this trifling circumstance is explained by a local regulation forbidding the sale of liquors in the limits prescribed, except by apothecaries vending the same as medicine. This law is passed and presto, two drugstores spring up where one could not have been supported before—and the drugstore becomes in Cave Spring dialect a synonym for a licensed grocery. Again we say: *Eheu! Les miserables!*

Five miles further the train allows time to examine the rich iron beds belonging to the Cornwall Company of Rome. The ore is the brown hematite and for miles appears in vast beds, in some places gathered in heaps and in others rising in huge boulders. The average quality is reported at 60 percent, but in some places reaching as high as 72 percent of pure iron. The Messrs. Noble will soon have furnaces at work on this tract also. Decidedly the richest specimens in this vicinity were from the lands of A. S. King of Cave Spring, which were rich also in fossils and crystalline combinations and for some of these 90 percent was claimed. All this is now lying dormant for the want of capital; and, although these lands are considered good for grain or cotton, their real value is assuredly in the mineral wealth which they contain, which will be demonstrated in another generation, if not in this.

Calhoun County was next visited, and the iron works located three miles from Oxford and taking their name from that place. Here the ore is the black hematite, and contains about 65 percent of iron. These works were rated before the war at twenty-four tons a day, but their fires were effectually extinguished by [James H.] Wilson, the marauder, and have never since been rekindled. The substantial masonry of the furnaces rise up over the somewhat dreary surrounding waste like the ruins of Thebes or the imperishable monuments of the dead nations which greet the traveler as he floats on the Nile. But may we not hope that here the comparison ceases, and that while the river of Egypt has flowed for ages past obelisk and sphinx and pyramid and those proud remains of the pharaohs are still unchanged as pictures of desolation amidst the drifting sands of the desert, that our southern ruins will all soon be repaired, and a new industry and a new energy once more enliven and beautify and bless our land.

Pennsylvania is a great and wealthy commonwealth, and her iron interests may be regarded as the chief foundation and source of her wealth. . . . Men who have lived there and are familiar with all this—practical men who can tell at a glance the quality of ore and the inducements to work it—say that all that Pennsylvania has derived in this way can be more than realized in the great mineral belt extending from north Alabama through Georgia and into the western parts of the two Carolinas. And they say more: that while Pennsylvania has iron and coal, and Missouri has iron and lead, and New England has marble and granite, that all of these can be found in the belt referred to and which is now being examined by the notable excursion. With such testimony . . . the prediction seems in no way extravagant that in a few years the iron crop of Georgia will be worth more than her cotton crop and that mining and manufactures in the Carolinas and Alabama may become the paramount interests in those states.

Juhl

Georgia Press Excursion   14

On the route to Selma the party was reinforced by a delegation of Alabama editors; and at one of the stations a few professional gamblers managed to smuggle themselves on board and, occupying the card room, soon inveigled a member of the press who had taken too much soda water for his own good into a game which cost the said member enough to have paid for a few acres of the mineral lands over which we were passing. The real character of the intruders was soon discovered, the train stopped, and the well-dressed gentry tumbled into the road. Some of the party were in favor of "losing" them right there, but they escaped with their plunder, and were, no doubt, picked up by the next regular train.

The Shelby Iron Works in Shelby County, Alabama, was the objective point of this part of the trip and the lower terminus of the excursion. Arriving there too late in the evening for an examination before the morrow, it was concluded to run the train through at night to Selma where it could turn and not be compelled, as it otherwise would be, to run backwards for 150 miles to Rome. Getting a hint of this arrangement, it was the good fortune of the writer to get off at

Shelby Springs, 12 miles below the works and remain there until the return of the train. The party went on to Selma, reached there in time for a midnight supper, and the next day returned to the springs to dinner.

The Shelby Springs, under the admirable management of Mr. E. S. Gossett, are crowded with some of the best society of the state and have only one objection—their limited accommodations. On this account alone the proprietor had to refuse others of the party who would have paid almost any price to have tarried there for the night. There are five springs whose mineral properties are decidedly pungent to the taste and possessed of great reputed medicinal virtues—three of sulphur, one chalybeate, and one limestone. The company was as agreeable, refined, and charming as one could expect to find even in the select society of a southern watering place. Music, dancing, croquet, the moonlight walk, the light flirtation, the silvery laugh of bewitching fairies with hearts as light as gossamer dresses, and eyes as blue as their own summer skies—ah! this is Alabama ("here will we rest").

Talk of iron, coal, lime, slate, developing the country? Let the rest of the party keep at that business for the nonce; but, as to someone else, "if the Court knows her own mind and she thinks she do," this is the place to talk poetry, and plunge into romance, and revel among the flowers, and to drink in the deep and long-to-be-remembered draughts of the beautiful and of sulphur water. Better drinking this than excursion champagne or excursion whiskey, and far more agreeable than the hundreds of horrid mineral specimens which we have been called on to taste, in proof that they were rich in alum or some other abomination! Rich in alum? Rich in living, glowing, fragrant beauty are the fair. There!

Among the pleasant acquaintances formed at this place, Chancellor [Samuel Will] John of the Alabama equity bench under the old regime holds a prominent place, and from him a variety of useful information was obtained. Well acquainted as he is with the resources of the state, he entertains no doubt of the vast increase of its wealth and importance by the mining and manufacturing interests which must in time be established. There are wool factories, shoe factories, lime kilns, iron works, and rolling mills all over this section now, and such investments are becoming daily more popular and more remunerative. The Irondale Works, which were destroyed during the war, have been built and are in successful operation in Jefferson County. The Round Mountain, with its rich fossiliferous deposits of iron, is considered a mint in itself. The Roupes Valley coal mines are of great value. They are owned by Mr. [David] Thomas of Lehigh County, Pennsylvania, who has gone to Europe for the purpose of investigating the Bessemer process of converting the iron ore into steel rails instead of iron pigs. The pure steel bar is said to be not sufficiently elastic, and the iron bar is too soft and wears too fast, and the Bessemer process is to use bituminous coal in securing a medium. In the most of coal there is too much sulphur for this purpose, but this is not the case with coal found near Roupes Valley, which is the edge of the Warrior coal fields and not far from immense beds of brown hematite.

During the war a great many experiments were made at the arsenal and naval foundry at Selma from which a store of useful, practical information was derived. It was found that the iron produced by coke fires was as good (if not better) for some purposes as that, in the smelting of which, charcoal was used as the fuel for the furnaces. The iron beds of brown and black hematite are all over the country traversed by the Selma and Rome Railway and, at the lowest estimate as to richness, will yield double the amount of iron which can be obtained from the Pennsylvania ore, and are of vastly superior qualities. At the close of the war northern men collected all the old Confederate cannon made of this iron, cut them up by machinery, and shipped the metal to Boston. This fact alone is demonstrative. There are large rolling mills at Briarfield in Bibb County and lime quarries and kilns at work within four miles of Shelby Springs, where some two hundred barrels of lime are the daily product, and the lime is said to be the best which goes into the market.

The Cahaba River also runs through immense coal fields before emptying into the Alabama River. And the Coosa meanders through a section abounding in coal and iron both—the Coosa, which is navigable only by a wonderful class of amphibious steamers from Rome to Greensport and thence to Wetumpka, presents unlimited water power in a succession of falls—the charming, winding, tortuous Coosa with every bend except that styled the Grecian—a bend suggests a "bender"—and this reminds that on and through this trip some found it easier to navigate the river than 'twas to "navigate" at any other point whatever. *Ergo* and then, for iron or for coals, or most accommodating shoals, and for easy navigation, *viva la Coosa!*[6]

JUHL

GEORGIA PRESS EXCURSION   15

Selma is becoming a great railway centre. It has the two hundred miles of rail to Rome (and thence to Dalton) which is not now paying, but will increase its business and receipts as the very rich mineral country through which it passes becomes developed. It also has the Selma and Meridian line to Vicksburg, which is said to be miserably managed. The rails are laid for half the distance on the route to Montgomery, and the contract requires this road to be completed by February next. Another line is to connect Selma with Pensacola, and the directors held their meeting at Selma during this visit and seem sanguine of success. General [Nathan Bedford] Forrest is also approaching with the Memphis and Selma Railway, laying down the rails at the rate of a mile a day. The receipts of cotton at Selma before

6. The "Grecian Bend" to which Fleming refers was a posture fashionable among women of this era. Its most distinguishing feature was the body bent back sharply from the hips.

the war were eighty thousand bales annually. Last year they amounted to thirty-six thousand, and this year it is expected the same number will be reached. There is another railway in course of construction to Columbus, Mississippi, passing through a rich cotton belt, which, when completed, will add at least thirty thousand bales to the Selma receipts.

Before leaving this part of the state, there are some items connected with it which should properly be included in this report. The marble beds, perfectly stratified and of every variety, are worthy attention. There is the pure white statuary marble, and the black and white, the blue and white, the gray, and the pure blue, and beds of fancy bird's eye and beautifully variegated. One cannot stand in the presence and contemplation of such immense beds of dormant treasure without looking forward to the day when busy hands will put the mass in motion and utilize it in beautifying the landscapes of Alabama with marble halls and marble temples, in which its people shall dwell and worship, while railways and shipping shall bear it also to other climes as a rich contribution to the commerce of the world.

The sandstone itself is of remarkable quality. The pillars of the new hotel at Selma are made of this material, and a Scotch mason who worked on them says that this sandstone which was quarried near Monte Valle is as fine as any in Scotland or the world. Near Talladega on our route there is a bed of lithographic stone which has never been worked, but Professor [Michael] Tuomey, who examined it, reports it to be very fine and of superior quality, and specimens of it were sent to the Paris Exposition and pronounced by lithographers superior even to the calcareous slate found near Munich and used in their art. . . .

As a pleasant digression from so many practical facts, you have but to look from the train as it glides over this splendid road to find amusement in the passing scenes. This long line of cars, with its unusual exhibition of flags and glitter and gloss, and its hilarious, not

343

to say distinguished, company, certainly created something of a sensation and woke up the country while it was running down this road. And now on the return, everybody along the line seems to be on the *qui vive*, and at the sound of its coming the natives rush for the best places to enjoy the view.

In the doors and windows and on the doorsteps and fences, on horseback and in carriages and wagons, and in crowds at the stations, and in denser crowds at the villages, "everybody and his wife" appeared in every variety of costume and in every style of feature and figure, and with every expression of countenance. The general expression was that of pleasant excitement exhibited in smiles, varied occasionally by a look of wonder or a sour and distempered grin. Who was that *sui generis* who at one of these places pushed his way energetically through the crowd and, standing in his shirtsleeves, with his hat thrown well back on his ugly head and his long gaunt arms akimbo, sent a half-pint of tobacco juice on the platform, and hotly inquired, "What the darnation is all this muss about?" An unearthly blow from the engine and the moving of the train shut out the reply, if any was given.

And then there is a saw mill and a huge heap of sawdust within a few yards of the track, and on the top of the heap a group of rustic maidens in holiday attire, and some of them have thrown themselves into romantic attitudes as if reclining for their picture, and the song and the music come fresh to memory, "on yonder rock reclining"—but substitute "sawdust heap" for "rock," and you not only spoil the measure and the rhythm, but ye sacred sisters nine! Where goes the romance and the poetry? And yet there be those who dare to say, "There's nothing in a name" and "a rose by any other name would smell as sweet." Barbarians! at whose feet did you study physics?

And then there comes a queer-looking conical hill—rising steadily from the track into a sharp apex, its sides covered with growing corn, the stalks dwarfing gradually until near the summit they almost dwindle to nothing—and on the summit stands a whole family group, the smaller children perching in their parents' arms gazing on the wonderful train. A moment's view, and 'tis gone forever—but it has left its memory with that humble group—not of the great men, or the would-be great men, or the so-called great men who filled the cars, for of these they doubtless neither think nor care—but for many a day and night in their thoughts and dreams will come the visions of the gay colors fluttering over the engine, and the glitter and the glare of that resplendent train, and of the bright gay world from which it came, and to which it has gone back. Alas! that the press excursion which had such good intent should thus become a disturbing influence among the humble, peaceful hamlets of north Alabama—greater than any which monster comet ever wrought by invading the sacred precincts of Saturn's rings or dashing recklessly among the satellites of Jupiter.

JUHL

GEORGIA PRESS EXCURSION   16

The Shelby Iron Works were the last visited, and they are by far the most extensive and complete of all those named in this protracted itinerary. They occupy the entire slope of a vast hill and present a very imposing appearance to an observer taking a front view from the opposite heights. At the base of the hill are the substantial and capacious furnaces, long rows of workshops, a brickyard with machinery for smoothly compressing the fireclay to line the furnaces, and quantities of pig iron which numerous hands were engaged in transferring to platform cars for shipment.

Ascending the hill next above and immediately beyond these, are the machine shops and powerful engines. One of these is a magnificent piece of machinery, driving a powerful air-drum steadily night and day without intermission since it was first put in motion seven months ago. Another ascent, and there are thousands of cords of wood and a long row of houses, the most improved, expeditious, and economical kilns for burning charcoal. And, when the summit of the hill is reached, there are the workmen with pick and shovel delving the ore, and from this point by a railway of easy grade it is passed down and through the furnaces and moulds to the cars for transportation. These works are owned and carried on by a New York and Connecticut company who have spent two hundred and ten thousand dollars here and are conducting the business on a grand scale. They have one hundred workmen employed in the charcoal business alone and at least as many more in the other departments, besides the most costly and improved machinery for every required purpose. They have their own flour mill and other establishments for making everything needed and own six miles of track connecting the works with the Selma Road and a locomotive and rolling stock of their own also. The ore is the fibrous brown hematite, rich, abundant, and dug from the surface; and their iron is in high repute and commands forty dollars a ton at the works.

It is refreshing to contemplate such a magnificent exhibition of enterprise and determined practical industry as is here presented, showing, as it does, a regenerated South, not in dreams or promises and prophesies, but in a living reality, at least in this vicinity, where the music of ponderous machinery is heard day and night, and the smoke from furnaces and kilns clouds the canopy. Well may Shelby County be proud of these works, and well may it be proud also of the delightful retreat it affords in the Shelby Springs, which, with a little outlay of capital, might easily be made the Saratoga of the South. And well may other sections catch the same spirit of progress, and other men of capital follow the example here given and turn their greenbacks into gold, not by Wall Street stock operations nor by uncertain speculations in cotton, but by investing in southern lands and working southern mines and bringing forth the treasures of the hills which, in exhaustless store, wait but the bidding of intelligent, persevering industry. What has been done already, although but a beginning, is enough to inspire and justify the hope of a great and wonderful future. One decade more, and Aladdin's lamp could not call forth a greater transformation than this country will present between its *then* and its *now*.

This report covers a considerable extent of travel, extending westward well towards the "father of waters" and southward almost to the Gulf of Mexico, and in height climbing some of the loftiest mountains, and in depth exploring some of the deepest mines and caves. Still far, very far, from our Carolina skies and landscapes, there is pleasure in the thought that the programme has been carried out, the work accomplished, and we are now homeward bound. Is it this thought which makes the air feel fresher and the heart lighter—or is it really an unusually pleasant sweet evening and an unusually lovely country upon which we look, as the train glides swiftly along the rails? The glow of sunset gives its rich purple tints to the hillsides and summits far on the right, and beneath the purple there is a fringe of green, deep and beautiful, and here and there in the picture is the auburn and the gold, and yonder is the silvery tide of the Coosa over which the train soon passes, and we are plunged into the deep rich foliage of the forest, and then the meadow with its velvet carpet over which the lowing herds wend their way, like us, homeward bound. . . . Homeward bound but not quite through.

JUHL

GEORGIA PRESS EXCURSION   17

. . . And so you were not in Atlanta when the excursion returned? Pity! And you were not at the grand dinner at the National Hotel? Greater pity still! Then you didn't see the gallant veterans of the press as they gathered around the festive board with brows laden with (laurels, did you say?) the ponderous stores of information gathered among the mines and kilns, and quarries and mountains and rivers which they had explored, and resolved should be forthwith "developed." Then you didn't hear the toast to "South Carolina," and the calls for the *Courier* representative and the response which was given, and the thanks which were voted to everybody, except the Great Giver of all good and the Preserver of the party in all its perils by land and water.

Well, you missed it and can enjoy the proud satisfaction of indulging in a little quiet resignation which may do you good. But don't abuse the party and denounce the excursion and slander its motives because you were not invited to it or happened not to be recognized as the big man of the occasion, or because some people went whose politics and persons you didn't like. For certainly it was a grand—as it must be memorable—excursion and furnished an excellent opportunity to examine and explore a section of country rich in its scenery, deeply interesting in its historical associations, and abounding in mineral wealth—and all this in a company which, take it all in all, was intelligent, sociable, good-humored, and pleasant throughout. Many of these comrades on this long and wearisome jaunt we shall remember with affection and respect for many a long day, and to all the gentlemen of the party it is a pleasure to tender our grateful acknowledgements for the uniform courtesy and numberless attentions received at their hands. Long may they wave!

And now adieu to Atlanta—proud, expansive capital of a great commonwealth, growing and destined to grow until its magnitude and wealth shall fill the measure even of its vaulting ambition. And we are once more in the tide of regular travel; and here note what in various ways was impressed on others during this trip, that for expedition, comfort, and economy, the travel north will take the line via Augusta by the South Carolina Railroad to Kingville, and thence by the Wilmington and Manchester Road to Wilmington, North Carolina, by which route the passenger makes no change of cars from West Point, Georgia, to Wilmington, and is in no danger of missing a connection, as the same train runs through.

Or, to those not adverse to a sea voyage on magnificent steamships, they will pass through Augusta and on the South Carolina Railroad, reach Charleston, and thence by the powerful side-wheel steamships of the Adger line to New York. Think of a through ticket by this route from Augusta to New York for twenty-two dollars, omnibus fare, and splendid stateroom and table accommodations included, and from points south and west of Augusta through tickets at proportionally low rates. These are the popular and bound to be generally traveled routes by land or sea, as the traveler may elect; and so we found our fellow passengers on the train from Atlanta to Augusta, some were for New York via Wilmington—preferring the rail, others for the same commercial metropolis via Charleston and the steamer—preferring the sea route.

The attention of the whole section traveled is being also drawn to Charleston as a city inviting and deserving the return of a trade so largely enjoyed in former years. With many of the up-country editors particularly, this subject was discussed, and a liberal course of advertising in such papers as circulate in that country, setting forth what Charleston merchants can offer and what they are prepared to do, would not be without substantial results.

Augusta is an attractive city, rejoicing in suburbs as beautiful as the gardens of the East, and in its public buildings and business marts, solid, substantial, and abreast of the age. Its manufacturing interests are assuming the grandest proportions and huge six-story piles of new masonry to be devoted to cotton manufactures and other kindred enterprises are as grateful to the anxious eye of the Southerner as the fairest scenery in the mountain land. And, crossing over to Carolina, the same indications are presented in the paper mills and cotton factories between Hamburg and Aiken of a people recovering from past disaster, rebuilding their waste places, and stretching forth their hands to be great and prosperous and free once more. A good hope and a healthy energy and a determined will and Carolina comes out all right, the equal of any and surpassed by none. And this is the conclusion from all our travels: Georgia and Alabama and Tennessee are good enough in their way, but South Carolina is better than them all, and it would be a losing exchange for her true children to give the one for the three.

JUHL

Of planting and politics, the one is the hope of the country and the other the curse of it. Both are under full headway—both go in to win, but a man who knows the times and the people will bet on politics against the field.

WHEN JUHL WROTE these words in June of 1870 little did he realize that in October he himself would be running for political office. Late in the campaign he and three other men, two of them Negroes, were nominated as an "independent" slate to oppose the Radical-Republican ticket for the lower house of the South Carolina legislature. With white voters outnumbered 3.5 to 1, the outcome was inevitable. The "independents" were soundly trounced. Juhl was so incensed at the manner in which the election was staged that he suggested the governor should merely fill all offices by appointment. This would save expense, excitement, and the trouble of "counting" votes.

The year ended with "a very bad state of feeling" in the Sumter area. Incendiary fires and thefts were common. Bands of both black and white men were patrolling the highways and frequently taking the law into their own hands. The turmoil created by a rough political campaign refused to subside.

Sumter, S. C., April 21

The celebrated African lecturer, M. Paul du Chaillu, lectured here last night to a crowded audience. Being on a visit to his old friend, Rev. Dr. J. Leighton Wilson, who resides near Mayesville in this county and who was for a long term of years a devoted and successful missionary to Africa, he was induced by an influential invitation from this place to favor our community with some of his experience in equatorial Africa. He was introduced to the audience by Dr. Wilson (whom he regards with filial affection and even addresses affectionately as "father") in a brief address, sparkling with humorous and spicy allusions and for some two hours charmed and entertained his crowded and brilliant auditory with the story of his travels, his language being racy and idiomatic, his English generally excellent and always intelligible, with just enough Gallicism about it to indicate the French descent of the speaker. The applause which attended the lecturer throughout attested the hearty appreciation and delight of his hearers, and the generous and gifted traveler consented to deliver another lecture today for the benefit of the boys and girls of Sumter, of whom there is a legion. It is understood that by the lecturer's imperative stipulation the lectures were free. M. Chaillu and Dr. Wilson are the guests of J. S. Richardson, Esq.

This morning, at half-past eight o'clock, the immense "old hotel" building on Main Street next to the courthouse was discovered to be on fire, and in a short time the flames shot out along the comb of the roof. From the location and surroundings, the burning would have been attended with the ruin of a large part of the town. By admirable management and desperate effort and decided valor on the part of the fire department, the fire was extinguished. Messrs. Schwerin (clothing), Loring (hardware), and Anderson & Co. (drugs) occupied stores on first floor or next door and sustained some trifling damage by removal of stock. The fire was incendiary, as the blazing lightwood was found upstairs where it originated.

JUHL

SUMTER, S. C., June 11

Of planting and politics, the one is the hope of this country and the other the curse of it. Both are under full headway—both go in to win, but a man who knows the times and the people will bet on politics against the field. If he loses his bet, he would still be the gainer and the country would be the gainer, too. Good money taken from honest people will be freely used to secure a new lease of power and plunder. Bad whiskey will also do its work, but such work is on the side of politics, and the planter will be the victim. The experience of this year may justify the conclusion that a wise man will only undertake a crop in this country every alternate year and will allow his lands to lie fallow, except so much as he can cultivate with his own or other reliable hands during the seasons when he may reasonably expect the mass of the laborers to run wild with politics.

Necessity, not choice, may force this issue, for the agricultural interest is of all others the least able to stand the continued and harassing agitation of a political canvass during the crop season, the very part of the year when in this state such agitation comes. And the agricultural interest is that on which all others here depend, and which must really furnish the means to pay the enormous taxes now imposed on the people. As the machine runs, there seems very little prospect of a reduction in the taxes; but there are some indications that the money with which to pay them, after expenses are deducted, will not be made. The current year may be noted for an unusually heavy outlay in fertilizers, an unusually large area in cotton, and an embarrassing disturbance of labor, which has already commenced and will certainly know no cessation until the October elections are over. And superadded to all this is the militia movement—a movement, which it is well understood is intended to marshal the black and to convert peaceful laborers into armed auxiliaries for party purposes—a movement which might be considered questionable if made even in winter, but made as it is during the crop season, betrays the character of those now ruling the country. Such men may be good suckers, but they have not the first element of statesmanship. They may acquire riches, never mind at whose or what sacrifice; but there is a proverb which seldom fails to attend the possessor of ill-gotten gains.

The local news of the week includes a fire on Liberty Street destroying the carriage workshop of Mr. [James T.] Flowers, with a number of valuable vehicles, and a small dwelling house adjoining, occupied by Mrs. E. A. White, and endangering St. Joseph's Academy and other buildings, which however, were saved without damage. The fire was incendiary, and there was no insurance on the property destroyed. There has also been some disorder in the way of street fights, but not on account of political differences.[1] The white population seems to take absolutely no interest whatever in politics, other than the quiet expression of disgust at the kind and character of the men whom the party in power has made its leaders. In that sentiment there is a degree of unanimity as unmistakable as it is intense, and in this particular they are fully endorsed by the leading Republican papers at the North. When the Republican party will itself repudiate the unscrupulous men who are its worst leaders and will show by its own acts a determination to give the state a wise and economical

1. The *Sumter News* (May 26, 1870) reported a "KKK scare" which occurred near the depot at Emmanuel Church on May 20. A large crowd gathered to hear speeches, hold a picnic and a general Sunday School celebration. "In the midst of the proceedings, a shot was suddenly heard, and a ball came flying through the window, and passed near the head of a 'schoolmarm' present, who is said to have leaped over three benches in one jump, in her excitement." It turned out that Tiller, a Negro man who tended the pump outside of the church, had accidently discharged a pistol.

administration, it will show itself a better and truer friend to the black man himself than it is today. When two races are so nearly equal in numbers and an election is made a question of race, neither peace nor prosperity can be relied on for the future. What then shall be said of those who know this well and yet drive an ignorant mass on to ruin?

JUHL

SUMTER, S. C., July 21

The mailbag containing the Charleston papers and letters has, on several occasions recently, been received at this place as per schedule at six o'clock P.M., but has not been opened until two o'clock P.M. on the following day. For twenty hours after arrival here all this mail matter has been no more accessible than if it had never left the city. The reason assigned is that the mail agent secures the bag with a lock for which the postmaster here has no key, and on this account there is no reliance on the evening mail even when the bag comes through. As an evidence of the extent of the annoyance to the public, at noon on Tuesday last we were without news from Charleston later than Saturday morning—nearly four days. A fact very complimentary to the department in this fast age and certainly throwing in the shade the performances of the old time stage which made the distance easily in a day and a half.[2]

The white population in this section are richly entitled to the repose in which they seem inclined to indulge under their present considerate and beneficent rulers. If they were required in this hot weather to turn out in a militia muster, they might grumble and hence the powers that be, considerate of this, have humanely arranged the whole military programme to dispense with their services by making the state militia strictly and exclusively a *corps d'Afrique*. Therefore, we have in this country four Negro companies with improved arms and

2. Juhl is objecting here to the administration of a Radical postmaster, Capt. T. B. Johnston.

ball cartridges who drill and parade often enough to insure skill and efficiency and to impart a feeling of security to the country in case of an invasion by the Prussians or the French. And this seems but fair that the rulers who require the white men of the country to make the crops which are to pay the taxes on which the said rulers depend for their little luxuries should require the black men of the country to do the voting and to carry the arms which the white men have paid for. Some persons might indeed suppose that in a politico-economical sense the Negro would be more useful to himself and the country by practicing his acknowledged skill with the plough and the hoe than he can be in such piping times of peace by any proficiency he may acquire in the manual of arms, and that the whole costly machinery is uncalled for and offensive. But this is a matter of taste in which men will differ.

In another matter, also, some persons may take a jaundiced (?) view of the situation. Some money goes into the militia, and other money derivable from the same source goes into banking schemes. For are not "the people" vulgarly believed to be the source of everything in the state, and does not all money come from them *ver fas et ne fas*? Is there not a new bank started in Columbia of which the present honored and most trustworthy state officials are the directors? And is there not an agency offered to Sumter and sundry citizens very reasonably and kindly invited to subscribe to the stock—not so much, as they are told, for the money subscription, as to have the benefit of their names to give character and respectability to the concern? This surely is clever and considerate and flattering, so to speak. And yet there are found some men who, strange to say, object to going into any partnership with those state officials, lest by so doing they become partners of their fame. To what will not captious men object in an age like this? . . .

JUHL

Sudden wealth excites suspicion. When acquired by inheritance or any other known and lawful means, its possessor is congratulated. When, however, men who two years ago could not pay their washing bills and who, since they have had access to the public treasury, have grown wondrously rich, purchasing lands and houses and furniture and finery and horses and equipages, and actually proposing to become the bankers for the county (thus aiming craftily to secure their victims with money-rivets to their chains), there is *prima facie* evidence of wholesale corruption. Some are cunning enough to make no outward show of their filchings, but others have not been able to restrain their ambition to shine even in borrowed or stolen plumes—perhaps drawn into such displays under the impression that they could astonish the natives and purchase some recognition from those weak souls who are ever ready to do homage to wealth, never mind how acquired. Such incautious exhibitions have excited comments, and even the ignorant classes, who must be the first to waste away under such depletion, have uttered murmurs, not loud but deep. Well-paid agents, white and black, may quiet these murmurs for a while, but it is noted that since the Reform candidates have taken the field, there is a sensible diminution of display in certain quarters. And, wherever sundry relays of fine horses . . . are hid away in stables or retired to pastures until after the election, the temporary self-denial of their owners may be ascribed to a well-grounded apprehension of Carpenter's coming.[3]

There never was a time when public office paid so well in Carolina, and there never was a time when such a number and variety of offices were united in one man. One would suppose that where there are such

3. Judge R. B. Carpenter was the Union Reform (Democratic) candidate for governor against Robert K. Scott, an Ohio carpetbagger, who was governor from 1868 to 1872.

fat pickings promiscuously allowed that any one man would be content with the emoluments of one office. But not so, my brethren. Sumter has three county commissioners entrusted with the powers and duties of all the old boards combined—three northern men who also hold other important and lucrative trusts, including the post office at this place, the census taking for this county, the post office at Camden (in another county), etc. Our county auditor [J. N. Corbett] is also school commissioner, commissioner of elections, etc.

With the liberal margin now allowed by custom (and if custom makes law, what kind of law will this regime establish?) no state pays its public servants better or gives them a more extravagant *carte blanche*. The instances adduced are named only in illustration and are by no means the most signal or notorious. You have still more emphatic examples in Charleston, and they abound in Columbia and all over the state. The party in this, one of its many luminous points, is entitled to the subservient homage of its beneficiaries, if not to the admiration of the rest of mankind. It draws a practical lesson from nature; for, as nature employs a number of colors to make the rainbow, so does "the party" require a number of positions to constitute and fill the measure of the Radical official. And, as the rainbow is wondrously beautiful, so are these—if you can only see it. Alas! that both should be doomed to the same evanescence, and melt into nothingness when the heavens clear.

Sumter has had the misfortune to be the local habitation of certain malign, crafty, and unscrupulous influences, which have actively worked "evil, and only evil, and that continually," and by every appliance known to desperate demagogues and midnight conspirators managed to discourage and paralyze the well-wishers of the county, while consolidating all who could be seduced, bribed, or intimidated into their support. But the champions of reform in the campaign against a corrupt and ruinous administration are waking up the state, and Sumter begins to show signs of returning life.

Whatever may be the result, there never was a party better entitled to success than this which invites all, without reference to race or political peculiarities or old issues of any kind, to unite "in a long pull, and a strong pull, and a pull altogether" for the rescue of the state from misrule and ruin. The other side may hold some who are after money. But a man may pay too much for money. Judas was after thirty pieces of silver—the money did him no good and cost him life and salvation. Arnold secured a British commission and British gold and his country's curse and undying infamy. "From all such," (reverently be it said and speedily be it answered) "good Lord, deliver us."

JUHL

SUMTER, S. C., August 12

The majority of voters in this state are unable to read—a fact in itself full of peril to the commonweal. They must depend for information, in a great measure, on what they hear, and many of them are so controlled and intimidated that they hear but one side, hence the absolute necessity of a thorough canvassing of the county in order to reach the masses. The press is potential with the reading population. The stump is potential with all who have ears to hear. A corrupt administration depends on the blind infatuation of the ignorant masses, whom it confidently expects to hold well in hand and to vote solid under the league manipulations and the party lash.

A few well-paid leaders and tools in each neighborhood find their meat and bread in this service, and the colored voter, who perhaps wishes to do right, is sadly misled by these men, who, to accomplish their ends, respect neither honor nor truth. Men who some time since were honorably and usefully employed as mechanics or farmers now roam the country as agents and emissaries of those who secure their devotion by a present of land or a stipulated salary, all of which, it is well understood, comes out of the people's pockets.

And yet these very people are expected to be gullible enough to do homage to such unscrupulous demagogues and to aid in fastening their rule upon the country by opposing reform. It is possible, however, that even an old fox, however crafty, may be deceived in his expectations, and we read of one instance at least in which Reynard having lost his tail (honor) tried in vain to introduce the fashion among his comrades of bob-tailed foxes. But they were foxes (not geese) and could not or would not "see it."

The old contests between Whig and Democrat and later between Democrat and Republican were often made to depend upon the discussion of the political doctrines of the rival parties respectively and did not necessarily involve a discussion of the moral character of the contestants. But the issue in this state really involves no rivalry between opposing creeds and amounts to nothing more than a combined effort of all well-wishers of the commonwealth to secure a better and more economical administration of our affairs. Hence, every good citizen, however indifferent to politics generally, is vitally interested in this contest in which all he has is at stake. Hence, too, the necessity of discussing the acts and characters of the men who are the rulers complained of and who seek to continue to rule and ruin.

If they are proper men for such a trust, it is strange that their own party at the North repudiates them—that honorable Republicans everywhere condemn them—that the *Tribune* and other leading Republican papers pronounce them "a disgrace to the civilization of the age." And, when they are thus held up to public scorn and disapproval by those who are the outside and distant lookers-on, how can it be expected that any honest native or adopted citizen, living right where he not only sees and hears, but is also obliged to feel in his every interest the monstrous wrong of such a government, will be suicidal enough to give them his support, even possibly by stickling at trifles when urged to unite for their overthrow? And their overthrow will come. They may already read the handwriting on the wall. Our sister states have moved up successfully and may be considered fairly emancipated. And South Carolina is not without hope. Even in this part of the state, where so many adverse influences exist and where the people appeared so long indifferent, a spontaneous expression of accord with the reform movement and a determination to work for it comes up now from every quarter. And this without county leaders and where, as yet, not a meeting has been held nor a speech made here on the subject.

That Judge Carpenter should be abused by the Ring is to be expected, for they fear him more than they would any native Carolinian at whom they might make their stereotyped fling of "rebel." But for any Carolinian to abuse him—a man who gives up office and encounters all which his position in this canvass involves—the fiercest detraction and threats of assassination, and exhausting toil—in order to give the struggling people of this state the advantage of his antecedent political and war record in working out a reformation of existing abuses—seems unnatural and indicative of a loose screw in the mental or moral organism of the man so finding fault. And for such men as [General Matthew C.] Butler and [General Joseph B.] Kershaw, of such revolutionary ancestry and unsullied record, to be abused by anything pretending to speak for Sumter is enough to insure for those gallant leaders a still more general and popular endorsement from the good and true men who know what Sumter feels and what Sumter needs.

The season is propitious—the crops are excellent and the health of the country good. All we want is a government—state and local—which will harmonize the races, promote peace and good will between them, and be honestly and economically administered. Such a government—call it by what name you will—would at once revive the drooping energies of the people and give a new and substantial impulse to every honest enterprise. And good men of every name and everywhere should bid "God speed" to those who are earnestly endeavoring to secure for us and our children this priceless boon.

JUHL

SUMTER, S. C., August 29

. . . There is reason to fear that the records of the courts and the future criminal statistics of the country will exhibit an alarming moral retrogression of the colored population. The Sabbath and the sanctuary are great humanizers and form the real basis of a true civilization, and formerly these hallowed monitors brought both races in this country under the same intelligent ministry. But since emancipation the blacks have been withdrawn to themselves and their own preachers. They are separated most effectually from any of the healthful influences which a higher order of intelligence and virtue could exert upon them; and, while some of their preachers may form exceptions to the remark, as a general thing politics pushes piety out of the pulpit, and the preacher stands before his congregation, not only as a candidate for office or a well-paid canvasser for some other demagogue, but as the very embodiment and teacher of hatred to the white race. The message of "peace on earth and good will among men," which makes indeed a gospel of glad tidings and brings sunshine into the homes of the poor and the rich alike, is neither heard nor felt amidst this ministry of wrath.

The effect of such teachings must be fatal to the moral improvement of the people and, instead of advancing them in virtue and piety, will push them steadily downward in ignorance, degradation, and crime. Nor is such demoralization altogether confined to the colored race. While the two races preserve those distinctions which are of right, which no human law has created and no human law can annul, the best interests of both demand that they should live in peace. And reciprocal feelings of kindness and good will can hurt neither. This one feature alone in the Union Reform movement should commend it to every well-wisher of the country. Justice and fair play to both races and harmony and prosperity in the land.

A meeting may be held in the course of a fortnight to consider the propriety of a Union Reform nomination for Congress from the first district. It is believed to be more than questionable whether any such nomination should be made, as many regard it as a matter of small moment at present who goes to Congress from this district. And, while they repudiate [J. H.] Rainey as a Scott Radical and would protest against any endorsement of the Radical nomination, they believe it best to let him walk over the track rather than do any reformer the injustice of nomination so late in the day.

There are many men now supporting the Union Reform movement as the only available route for an improvement of our state and county governments and who are willing with this view to vote a mixed Republican and Democratic ticket, but who would at once be alienated if an attempt was made to commit them to the support of a Ring Radical for Congress. As far as Congress is concerned, it is palpably the wisest course not to endanger the support which the Union Reform state and county candidates may receive by even an expression of opinion in favor of any candidate who is not known to be conservative and safe.

JUHL

SUMTER, S. C., October 29

The tricks of gamblers in stacking the cards and managing the deal so as to always secure for themselves a winning hand; the sportive license sometimes indulged in by ladies who engage in bowling to pass off the idle hours at summer watering places when running down the alley they only let go the ball within a few feet of the pins and secure a ten strike and win the game by sweeping down with their flowing skirts any of the pins which the ball has spared; the nice little arrangement illustrated in the "heads I win, tails you lose—" all these must give in and cry "dead beat" in view of the recent so-called elections in this state. Universal suffrage, universal contempt, universal anarchy, these three may not be so far removed but what they may be found running together.[4]

The greatest farce connected with the late election is the trouble taken and time consumed in "counting the votes." For, outside of Charleston, and where the boxes have been in the sole and undisturbed possession of the Ring and entirely lost to public view as here and elsewhere, it is very clear the public would have been just as well satisfied with the fairness and correctness of the result if dogmatically announced without a "count" as with it. Under such an election law and such men to manage it, the state might be canvassed fifty times over, and no other or better result would follow. And it will be a clear gain to the white people of the state hereafter to invite and request the Ring to dispense with elections and allow the governor—with or without an advisory board—to appoint the legislature and all the county officers. This will save the expense, excitement, and trouble of a biennial canvass.

JUHL

4. Fleming is especially bitter because he himself was defeated in this election for a seat in the state House of Representatives. According to the *Sumter Watchman* (November 2, 1870), this independent ticket appeared only a few days before balloting took place and "was not generally known." With some 3,556 Negro and 1,088 white voters in the Sumter District, the Scott slate swept to victory. F. J. Moses, Jr. (soon to become governor, 1872–1874) headed the four-man delegation elected to the House. Each House ticket was composed of two white and two Negro hopefuls. The Moses group averaged about 3,550 votes each; the Fleming group, about 700. Fleming himself got 736 votes.

Two gentlemen conversing on Main Street were accosted a few days since by a middle-aged Negro man well and favorably known by one of them who stated that he was in search of his son—a lad of nineteen years of age, who had run away from him and set his parental authority at defiance. He said the boy, although his son, was a great rascal, that he was only nineteen and knew the fact, that he and his wife and the former owners knew the fact, and that he claimed and the boy knew he claimed the son's services for two years more; but the hopeful youth, despite this knowledge and in open contempt of these claims, had voted in the recent election (!) at the town boxes, and had then sent his father word that he (Cuffee, Jr.) was as good a man as he (Cuffee, Sr.) and that he (the said Cuffee, Sr.) might go to ———— some place which has no accessible watering places to relieve the sufferers in an even unusually protracted heated term. The relator, avowing his determination to continue the pursuit until he brought the truant back to his duty, passed on.

But his experience will very probably prove the delinquent to be like the Dutchman's horse: "A capital good horse; but he has two faults. Those faults, however, appear to be serious—he was very hard to catch, and when you catch him he is good for nothing." The incident is mentioned for the moral it conveys—that so general and widespread is the corruption which has demoralized the country and destroyed the integrity of the franchise, that a well-attested instance of a minor voting and perjuring himself once or oftener at the polls in the late so-called election, brought to the attention of conservative citizens by the father of the culprit, excites no surprise and is incontinently dismissed with a jocular remark. It is but a single drop in the desolating shower.

The constitution of this state, framed by a Radical convention, provides for magistrates to be elected by the people. The convention resolved itself into a legislature and, in the latter capacity, coolly snubbed its own organic law and enacted a horde of trial justices to be appointed by the governor. Now, as another move in the same healthy direction, equally permissible and equally constitutional, the incoming legislature, which is but a third and by no means improved edition of the club house assemblage, might respond to a very widespread sentiment and declare the ballot a useless farce, a source of public irritation, an occasion for immeasurable corruption, fraud, and perjury—a thing, in short, altogether repugnant to the advanced opinions and practices of a thorough reconstruction and *ergo*, and therefore, abolish the franchise and authorize and require the governor hereafter to fill all offices in this state, legislative and judicial, as he now fills nearly all others, by appointment; and that when the present incumbent wearies of the executive trust, he shall appoint his own successor from Ohio, Halifax, or—elsewhere—as his tastes may indicate.

Such an enactment would be hailed by many citizens as an honest and therefore unlooked-for "acknowledgement of the corn" and might be accepted as an earnest [sign] of still greater Radical reforms.[5] A memorial to this effect might be prepared and would possibly be numerously signed, but for the unfortunate conviction which has seized the public mind that no important general public measure can be carried successfully through this model legislature without the conciliating influence of a pile of greenbacks, and the work would hardly be worth the money.

The Lynchburg disturbances continue to be a topic of interest. A minister who spent a Sabbath in that village recently states that the usual quiet of that sacred day was broken by a discharge of firearms early in the morning, and that inquiring the cause of his host, he was

5. In the 1890s southern politicians would point to the corruption of the ballot box and use it as an excuse to disfranchise the Negro voter.

informed that it was the Negro guard discharging their guns, that armed bands of colored men guarded the roads every night with orders (from whom received it only conjectured) to fire without challenge upon any parties of three or more persons riding together at night. The advisers of such proceedings can certainly not have the good of the country at heart, and it is a great mistake to suppose that the colored race or the country can be benefited by such disorders. . . .

JUHL

SUMTER, S. C., November 19

There is no doubt of a very bad state of feeling existing in this section. Such actual disturbances as have occurred, however, cannot be truthfully ascribed to any political antagonism. The origin of the whole trouble is the traffic in seed cotton and the plundering to which such traffic leads and the very rough measures adopted in some localities to arrest such traffic and protect the planters. Those who have been visited and ill-treated on this account by disguised regulators have been chiefly white men, and in most cases recognized and avowed Democrats. They have, as far as known, abandoned the trade and resorted to no measures of vindictive retaliation.

But one colored man is known to have been similarly visited and for the same reason, and he lived at Lynchburg. A few nights after this occurrence a valuable barn with its contents was burnt in that neighborhood by an armed band of colored men in retaliation.[6] A

6. This barn, owned by Hosea Wilson, was destroyed on the 15th (*Sumter News*, November 17, 1870). Wilson reported that a band of twenty-five Negroes burned down the building. He was unable to say why this happened, but the *News* blamed Governor Scott and other infamous Radicals. During these same weeks a Negro trader was whipped for buying stolen cotton. And, in Darlington County, fire destroyed W. J. Lockhart's mill at Deep Hole and the mill of H. M. Mims on Bay Branch. The next edition of the *News* (November 24) reported that a public meeting had been held at Lynchburg on the 17th. Maj. H. M. Green presided. Both races deplored the wave of

poor and inoffensive white man was also taken out and whipped by a colored party near Scottsville. A few nights ago another young man (white) in the Montgomery neighborhood, who, it is said, had informed against some Negroes for hog stealing, was taken out and whipped by colored regulators. All this and a great deal more in these "piping times of peace."

These Regulators, white or black, seem now disposed to extend their operations to other matters. A white farmer living in this country has had the liveliest times in his family. The domestic quarrel has been known to all around and has often reached a point and included incidents which would have justified the belligerents matrimonial with a triumphant challenge to the neighborhood of "how is that for high?" Within the past week the Regulators, of what color is not known, paid a nocturnal call to the domicile of this couple, aroused up man, wife, and children, and announced their purpose to take out the man and his wife and whip them both. Some compromise or treaty was, however, made, and the band left without doing other damage than giving the family a most unexpected fright. These jolly night strollers seem to have acted on the principle that, while the constitution implies, the law provides no legal divorce in this state, and therefore where parties, unequally yoked cannot peaceably separate, then, by the fiat of a secret court they shall be required to peaceably live together.

The foregoing outline of the situation is drawn from well-attested facts and presents a picture by no means gratifying to the friends of law and order. The reflecting white men of the country are opposed to the spirit of lawlessness on the part of either race. The colored man who vouchsafes to honor his country by bearing on his shoulders its senatorial responsibilities [W. E. Johnston], has gotten up one or two

unrest and passed resolutions condemning the incendiarism and disorder.

meetings recently at which he has offered resolutions in favor of peace and harmony—presenting the unique and beautiful picture of a Radical senator offering and recommending for adoption *after* the election the very sentiments which made up the gist of the Reform speeches which were so rudely repudiated and hooted during the late canvass. It is a late, but no less important although now idle admission, that the platform which invited both races to work together for good government and to live and labor amicably together as mutually dependent upon each other was the true platform for the best interests of the whole country. We endorsed it then, and the resolutions referred to endorse it now.

Meetings and paper resolutions will accomplish but little while existing sources of irritation are continued. Colored men make a display of their firearms in every direction—sometimes in bands. The colored militia continues to be paraded, armed and accoutred, and drilled from time to time. A difficulty, however, caused between white and black is made at once not (as it should be considered and investigated) as an individual quarrel but as a question of race. Now let the experiment be tried; let the governor direct or advise the leaders here to instruct the colored men to keep their guns at home and not parade them wherever they go (unless while hunting or at night for their protection, if they think it necessary). Let the militia be disarmed, temporarily at least, and the parades discontinued, and the officers and men advised to attend to peaceful industry. And let the people be exhorted to treat every difficulty in the same way, whether the parties are alike or differ in color, not by passion or mob, but by proper legal process.

Such an experiment would doubtless result in reciprocal action, and quiet and peace would follow—and the sooner such or some better plan is adopted, the better for all. The cotton being now out of the fields, the prime *casus belli* is for this season removed. And there is no other cause for a continuance of disorder likely to prejudice the peace of the country, unless a long-persisted-in display of armed preparations on one side, acting as an irritating menace, should lead in some unguarded moment to a strife which every good man must devoutly deprecate.

JUHL

1871

ONLY A HANDFUL of Juhl letters appear in the *Charleston Courier* during 1871, the last being printed on August 9. There are several possible explanations for the end of this correspondence. Fleming's legal practice was demanding more and more of his attention, and he was becoming involved in a number of small business ventures in the Sumter area. At the same time, the old *Courier* was in deep trouble. In fact, it was fighting for its very life against an upstart press which had only appeared at the end of the war, the *News*. Manoeuvring to keep their heads above water, the editors of the *Courier* undoubtedly thought Juhl a luxury they might well jettison. In 1873 the *Courier* gave up the fight and was purchased by its youthful rival, thus forming the *News and Courier*.

During 1871 Fleming made another brief visit to Florida, continued to fight countless courtroom battles, and scanned the horizon for signs of economic and social stability. And in his last letter he was able to point hopefully to an omen of better times. The United States Army, which had been withdrawn from Sumter on several occasions, was once more about to leave the community to its own devices. He noted cheerfully,

Whatever ills we have, the people are bearing patiently, and the recent triumph of conservatism in Charleston induces the hope that, by similar efforts, the rest of the state may be, in time, delivered from the rotten mushroom, political organism, which has brought blight and mildew upon this once fair commonwealth.

SUMTER, S. C. January 26

... The late term of the Sumter court presented in the composition of its juries the usual picture of the times. The grand jury with two or three exceptions is composed of Negroes, and this body constitutes the high inquest of the county for the current year. There were three white men on petit jury number one, and two whites on jury number two. Nearly all the criminals were of the colored persuasion and certainly had fair trials. In this court they can complain of no injustice, and yet in purely criminal cases they gain no advantage in being tried by juries of their own color. In fact, when charged with aggravated offences in which they have the right of challenge, it is noticed that their counsel gives the preference to intelligent and conscientious white jurors. And to just such white juries have many of them been indebted for narrow escapes in which the evidence made out a *prima facie* or presumptive case of guilt, which with an ignorant jury would have been fatal to the prisoners. The small influence of the white element which is still allowed in the jury box exercises in almost all cases a controlling influence in shaping the verdicts, and hence the general run of these judicial findings is, thus far, not much or injuriously affected by the complexion of the panel.

The Manning court, which follows immediately after Sumter, was held under very unfavorable circumstances, and it was a general relief to the bar and doubtless to all concerned that its session was restricted to some two days. The judge was by no means in a state of health to stand the exposure; the solicitor, our genial friend, Major [S. T.] Atkinson of Georgetown, was also in a condition which he expressively described as that of "a walking volcano." Influenza was in full blast among lawyers and litigants; and, to crown the picture, the court was accommodated (?) in a room over a store with a ceiling so low as to necessitate "hats off" without a constable's reminder, and the ceiling and walls newly daubed over with mortar still wet, the dampness from which struck a chill into the system unrelieved by either stove or fireplace. And the building was considered so unsafe that carpenters were employed to prop it, and even then it was regarded, like some of the prisoners who escaped conviction, as still highly suspected.

The new schedule which General [Daniel] Tyler of the South Carolina Railroad has inaugurated is an admirable improvement on the old arrangement. Passengers (and the mails) now leave here at 12 P.M. and reach Charleston for supper and leave Charleston at 8:20 A.M. and arrive here at 4 P.M. This will insure your city a large increase of travel and trade from this section. The morning *Courier* is now read here the same afternoon.

JUHL

SUMTER, S. C., March 1

The excitement of collecting by telegraph, barometrical and thermometrical reports from all important points in the United States at the signal office of the War Department at Washington and by a scientific deduction from such collated reports making accurate and reliable predictions of the weather in time to be of practical service to the country is being fairly tried. The storm centre is defined, and atmospheric changes are carefully noted, and then the scientific watchers at the national capital send their daily dispatches over the wires, predicting at least twenty-four hours in advance the prevailing direction and force of the winds and the character of the weather in the different sections of the Union. On Saturday last, 25 ult., at 4:35 P.M., they announced among the "probabilities" "thick winds on Sunday night" along the Atlantic coast. On the afternoon and night of Sunday, this probability was realized as a certainty by the dwellers in the coast and middle counties of South Carolina. How far the gust or succession of "thick winds" extended cannot here be exactly stated. But there are at least three points in the route of the storm line which can be reliably reported. The storm, passing almost parallel with the coast, reached the vicinity of Ridgeville on the South Carolina Railroad where it prostrated trees and fencing and occasioned the smashing of Dr. Murray's carriage, injuring himself and others of his family and killing one of the children. Crossing the Santee, it came upon the Methodist congregation who had been attending a quarterly meeting at a church three miles below Summerton and were wending their homeward way in their carriages. At this point it was equally severe and several imminent and almost miraculous escapes occurred, the horses being reined up just in time to allow the monster falling tree to reach the ground in advance of them. Thence it came to this town, where towards the close of a balmy day it broke upon the scene with all the characteristics of a tempest, the rain not falling but flying with the wind in lines almost parallel with the surface and making what might be very appropriately designated as "thick winds." The storm, which before reaching Sumter was from south to north as its general course, had here fairly commenced its circular whirl and was from southwest to northeast. No serious damage is reported in this vicinity. The Washington office publishes its bulletins, but can only ascertain how far its predictions are verified by subsequent reports of the actual state of the elements at the times and places predicted. And in this point of view, the foregoing may not be without interest.

JUHL

SUMTER, S. C., April 6

. . . The action recently taken by the Charleston Chamber of Commerce and Board of Trade reflects the sentiment of the taxpayers through all this section.[1] And the people will unquestionably sustain

1. At a meeting held on March 31, the Board of Trade passed resolutions censuring the state government for high taxes, high cost of government, and illegally issuing bonds.

this movement. If the present assessment is to stand for five years, as determined and announced, it is very evident that the result will be ruin, and that such wholesale robbery must be checked some time or other, and the sooner the better. White men who last year were able to assist industrious colored men with advances while working through their crops are no longer able to do so, as the taxes absorb the means. And many white and colored farmers are embarrassed for the want of horse power and provisions, while Radical leaders keep up in their stables numbers of well-groomed and idle horses bought with the people's money.

The May convention is looked forward to with interest and may realize the hopes of the state, especially if the counties will send up as delegates solid, practical men from the county who represent most largely the taxable interest and who will contribute more in the way of wise counsels and determined action than of buncombe speeches. Politicians and speechmakers are palpably not the men for the occasion, however ambitious such may be to participate. The substantial judicious citizen, who has really no political aspirations and no ambition to gratify, is the very man to give weight to the action of such convention, both at home and—what is more important—at the North.

The season has been very favorable for gardens, farms, and fruit. No killing frosts have nipped the cheering promises of spring.

JUHL

OVER THE WAVE TO THE LAND OF FLOWERS[2]

After floating for six days over the calm summer seas and beautiful inland waters which lie between Charleston and the tropics, the steamer *Dictator*, Capt. L. M. Coxetter, returned and safely landed the last of her passengers at her Charleston wharf yesterday afternoon.

2. This letter appeared in the *Courier* on May 22.

The excursion party numbered one hundred or more, taken on at Charleston and Savannah principally, exclusive of a colony of fifty Swedes, who were landed at Palatka, Florida, en route to Melonville, Florida. Ample opportunities were afforded the excursion party to visit and inspect the many points of interest along the route, including Bonaventure, Thunderbolt, and the park at Savannah, the shell road, magnificent beach, and lighthouse at Fernandina, Jacksonville, Palatka, Green Cove Springs, Hibernia, Mandarin (Mrs. Stowe's place), Picolata, and Tacoa, and other points on the St. John's River. Passengers, representing almost every state and clime, were alike impressed by this noble river and freely expressed their admiration, surpassing (as it was unanimously agreed) their largest anticipations. Times may change and centuries roll away, but there the noble river remains in all its silent grandeur and passive beauty, exacting from every visitor the tribute of involuntary homage. . . .

The party also enjoyed a delightful day at St. Augustine in the midst of the orange groves, banana, date palm, *recubans sub tegmine fagi*, with the sea breeze richly laden with the fragrance of a thousand flowers waving ceaselessly the glorious summer foliage, and a sky as pure and soft as a maiden's prayer. The quaint old fortress, with its ancient adjuncts of moat and drawbridge and watchtower and chapel and hall of justice and dungeons, was visited, and many an incident connected with the long ago was related and discussed. In full view from its ramparts and within easy range for modern artillery are the mounds on a cochina island opposite where Oglethorpe planted his batteries several hundred years ago and vainly tried to dislodge the Spanish, and one of the old time cannon then used by the brave old Englishman has been recovered and planted in the plaza of St. Augustine. In the same plaza is a massive monument, suitably inscribed, erected by the Spaniards to commemorate their constitution. Facing the plaza and opposite each other are the Episopal and Catholic Churches. The former is a very elegant, modern structure with an interior invested with an impressive halo by its altar adornments and memorial windows, and the latter is the old Spanish cathedral, grand in area and height, magnificent in its numerous altars and confessionals all richly furnished and quaint as antiquity itself in its structure. Its bells are suspended in openings cut in its cochino front and are arrayed in the form of a cross.

There is also a large convent not far from the cathedral, and the nuns and a considerable Catholic population make up the congregation to which a tall, but delicate-looking priest ministers. There are other churches in the place presenting, however, no unusual features of interest. Near the barracks at the lower end of the town are several mounds of masonry covering the remains of the victims of the Dade massacre, a command of over one hundred regulars under Major Dade, who were decoyed by the Seminoles into an ambush where they became panic-stricken and were shot down like sheep.

The whole waterfront of St. Augustine is protected by a substantial sea wall, and the city presents a very attractive appearance as seen from the decks of an approaching steamer. The people of the place are very attentive to strangers; and, while the men are generally swarthy, the ladies are lively and some of them very attractive. There are several large and handsome yachts in almost constant use for pleasure parties, picnics, fishing, and visits to the lighthouse, and many of our company enjoyed all the pleasure of successful fishing and a glorious sail with a spanking breeze over the sparkling waves.

The excursion was agreeably varied by a number of incidents and was not marred by a single *contretemps*. The night at Jacksonville was enlivened with a ball on board in which the young—and even some of the old—tripped it on the light fantastic toe until "the wee sma' hours agant the twal," and there was not wanting some few cases in which "soft eyes looked love to eyes which spoke again, and all went merry as a marriage bell." There were artists on board who favored their friends with a glance of their sketches, and such pictures as "Red

Hot," "After Supper," and "The Man who Snored" would, if available, be very pleasant accompaniments to this hastily written report.

When your readers want a genuine relaxation, let them place themselves under Captain Coxetter's care to enjoy a week of luxury like this. The steamers of the Charleston and Florida line run with great regularity, and our captain reports that since 1851 not a life nor a boat has been lost by this line, nor twenty-five dollars damage done to boat or cargo at sea. During the same time the Savannah and Florida line, although inland, has lost seven boats by fire or wreck.

The *Dictator* brought on this trip from St. Augustine a fine quantity of palmetto packed in bales, which is shipped hence to England where it is used for the manufacture of bank note paper, for which it is said to be the best material yet found. In Florida this tree grows to its highest perfection and is seen all along the coast. In places where fires have swept off the undergrowth and killed everything else, the palmetto, although lapped by flames, still survives—hopeful and suggestive of the type of people and principles it has so long represented.

Before the Savannah delegation left us, resolutions of thanks were unanimously passed to Captain Coxetter, Purser Cavedo, and the other officers of the ship for their uniform courtesy and attention—every passenger seeming to feel the sentiment.

> For the heart will beat, while it beats at all,
> With a kindly thought for these.

JUHL

SUMTER, S. C., June 29

To do justice to the very interesting entertainments which have this week been afforded this community by the education institution of

Sumter would require more of your space than could be reasonably asked, and hence a brief report must suffice.

On Tuesday evening there was an exhibition consisting of exercises in declamation by the young gentlemen of Mr. T. P. M'Queen's School. The addresses, original and selected, were in good taste and well delivered and received the applause of a large and intelligent audience. The speakers were T. E. Gilbert, C. M. Hurst, Jr., J. R. Harvin, D. J. Chandler, W. W. Deschamps, W. J. Fleming [Juhl's son], A. C. Walker, W. D. Blanding, H. M. Gilbert, A. M. Fraser, and J. C. M'Queen—sons of citizens representing the different professions here. The teacher is the eldest son of Rev. D. M'Queen, Presbyterian pastor, and to a collegiate training has added the usual law course, having been admitted to the bar several years ago, but seems to prefer the business in which he is now engaged and in which he has had a long experience and very decided success. Rev. William H. Fleming, the Methodist presiding elder, officiated as chaplain on the occasion, and a band of music contributed to the pleasures of the evening.

On Wednesday evening the Sumter Female Institute regaled a very large and refined audience of invited guests with one of the most *recherche* entertainments. The hall was tastefully decorated, and the stage was a picture of beauty, the pupils presenting a charming galaxy of loveliness, and the walls sustaining admirable portraits in beautiful wreaths of those three illustrious dead heroes—[Sir Henry] Havelock, Lee, and Stonewall Jackson. The exercises were, as usual on such occasions, instrumental and vocal music, compositions, diplomas conferred on the graduates, and short addresses. The compositions of the graduates were unusually excellent and worthy of publication, and in themselves give evidence of the thorough efficiency of this school. . . .

On Thursday (this) evening came off the annual distribution of St. Joseph's Academy under the charge of the Sisters of Mercy. In no respect was this occasion less interesting or gratifying than its many predecessors, and nothing but an unwillingness to further tax your columns prevents a more extended report. This school is well established, admirably directed, and commands a patronage which must be gratifying to the devoted and untiring sisters who give it their best energies and tireless vigilance.

JUHL

SUMTER, S. C., August 7

... The inevitable excrescences which mar the comeliness of the body politic everywhere in this state are visible in Sumter. The Negro militia, which has been disarmed at some other points, is here more rampant than ever before and is not only armed with guns and ammunition, but with what is to many a much more offensive weapon—a big drum which is allowed but little repose. A black brass band sometimes attends the muster and plays very often when there is no muster. And, in fact, they play so oft and so loud the few tunes they have learned that if the entire population of the town has not learned them as well, it is certainly not the fault of the band. Many a weary citizen has had cause to exclaim of nights, "Music hath charms to drive all sleep away," while the band keeps up the endless refrain of "Shoo fly! don't bother me." There are also United States Infantry and cavalry stationed here, and some of the cavalry have had difficulties with the colored population in which the latter have been roughly treated. But after the law was invoked, there seemed to be no further trouble between them, and the cavalry are to leave tomorrow for Atlanta to appease, by their removal, the black Nemesis. Whatever ills we have, the people are bearing patiently, and the recent triumph of conservatism in Charleston induces the hope that, by similar efforts, the rest of the state may be, in time, delivered from the rotten mushroom, political organism, which has brought blight and mildew upon this once fair commonwealth.

In the domestic establishments at the South the changes which late years have effected in all our economy are very apparent. Kitchens and yards are no longer crowded with oftentimes useless servants, and housekeeping arrangements are on a basis which would charm even a tidy and thrifty New England *mater-familias*. It was at first said that the refined and accomplished southern matron or maiden never could maintain such independence of sable attendants, but five years of facts have proved the contrary, and in many things they wait upon themselves with more satisfaction than they often felt of yore in being waited upon. It is well known that one skilled hand can do more and better work, with certain labor-saving machinery, than was formerly done by fifty or more operatives without such mechanical appliances. Steam and machinery and the skill to direct and control them can accomplish wonders. And so the many conveniences which modern ingenuity has furnished to render light and easy the duties of the housekeeper go very far towards superseding the necessity for servants. Let kitchen, washroom, ironing-room, etc., be provided with these, and the labor in each of those departments is rendered comparatively light. Cooking, for example, when carried on over large, open fires is what few would like to undertake; but, with the right kind of a cooking stove, it is but a simple process with no annoyance from heat, without fatigue, with hands and dress alike unsoiled. The Western Empire No. 8 is an admirable stove for a family. Numbers of these have been in use here for five or six years past and have given great satisfaction. For durability, elegance of finish, and completeness of outfit, there can be no better. They are furnished at factory prices by Munsell & Thompson, No. 218 Water Street, New York, who will give all information desired by application. These gentlemen are eminently reliable, and all their work in stoves and stove furniture of every kind and size is manufactured at their immense establishment at Manhattanville, New Jersey, and subjected to the highest tests before being offered to the trade.

1871

August 7

A long and, in some places, disastrous spell of dry weather has been succeeded by grateful showers, and the crops—although in some localities a failure—in others are reported fine. It is not improbable that at least an average yield of cotton and provisions will be realized.

Juhl

Index